TURNING POINTS IN BUSINESS CYCLES

TURNING POINTS
IN BUSINESS CYCLES

BY
LEONARD P. AYRES

REPRINTS OF ECONOMIC CLASSICS

Augustus M. Kelley · Publishers
NEW YORK 1969

First Edition 1940

(New York: The Macmillan Company, 1940)

Reprinted 1969 by

AUGUSTUS M. KELLEY · PUBLISHERS

New York   New York   10010

By Arrangement With THE MACMILLAN COMPANY

LIBRARY OF CONGRESS CATALOGUE CARD NUMBER

68-20527

PRINTED IN THE UNITED STATES OF AMERICA
by SENTRY PRESS, NEW YORK, N. Y. 10019

PREFACE

BUSINESS cycles result from the fact that all industrial nations produce their durable goods in waves or surges of output instead of manufacturing them in steady flows varying little in volume from month to month and year to year. By contrast they manufacture their nondurable goods, such as textiles, and foods, and gasoline, paper and printing, soap and tobacco, tires and shoes, in comparatively steady volumes of production. These nondurable goods have to be produced in fairly regular amounts, for we are constantly using them up, or wearing them out, and replacing them. Most of them are necessities of life and so we consume almost as much of them in hard times as we do in prosperity.

Durable goods include all the machinery of production, everything that goes into construction, all plants and power lines of our public utilities, all appliances of business offices, as well as some things used by families, such as automobiles, house furniture and furnishings, refrigerators and radios. These are long-lasting goods, and the ones we have can almost always be made to do service for additional years if that seems desirable. In fact we do postpone replacing them in all the depression periods, and we busily renew and increase them in times of prosperity. We have been alternately speeding up and slowing down our production of durable goods for a great many years, and so have all the other industrial nations, and it is that uneven production that causes the expansions and contractions of business activity which we know as business cycles.

This book is the account of a study undertaken in the attempt to find out why the expanding production of durable goods turns downward at the top of prosperity and begins to contract, and why it stops shrinking at the bottom of depression and turns upward and begins to expand once more. Clearly these turning points result from decisive changes in the amounts of money being spent for the purchase of durable goods. In recovery and prosperity these expenditures grow larger and larger, and then they stop expanding, and during decline and depression they become smaller and smaller. The changes in the volumes of purchasing of durable goods are largely changes made by business enterprises, but why are they made, and are they made from choice or from necessity?

Business enterprises have two chief sources from which they draw the funds that may be used for the purchase of new equipment, and for the financing of additions, betterments, and expansions. These funds may come from their own previous earnings that have not been distributed as dividends, or they may come from the sales of new securities to investors who wish to participate in the undertakings. Corporation managements control the spending of the undistributed profits, but the changes in the volume of the inflows of new funds derived from the sales of securities depend on the willingness of investors to subscribe to the issues of new securities that are offered for sale.

An important part of the present study is the extension backward over many decades of a series of data reflecting changes in the volume of the purchases of new corporate securities by investors. Until now the series commonly available to students of these problems have covered only periods subsequent to the end of the World War. This new series goes back to the period of the Civil War. It consists of a tabulation of the new bonds and stocks of domestic non-financial corporations listed on the New York Stock Exchange and sold to investors for money.

These new data make it possible to show that there has been in this country during the past 75 years a long series of wide, wavelike fluctuations in the volume of new funds going into business enterprises from the subscriptions of investors buying new issues of corporate securities. These waves of new investment have closely corresponded to the successive bull markets and bear markets for bonds and stocks that have accompanied the business cycles. The amounts of these fluctuations of the inflows of new funds have been sufficiently large to account for the changes that have taken place from prosperity to depression and back again in the pay rolls of all the factory workers engaged in producing durable goods.

With almost complete regularity during the long period studied, the downturns of the security prices at the tops of bull markets, and their upturns from the bottoms of bear markets, have followed upturns and downturns in the levels of short-term interest rates. In bull markets for securities advances in short-term interest rates have brought about downturns in bond prices, which have normally been shortly followed by downturns in stock prices. These declines in security prices have created unfavorable market conditions for floating new securities, and so have resulted in downturns in the volumes of new issues.

When the volume of new issues has turned downward the inflow of new funds into productive enterprise has decreased, and a business decline has been started. The process at the bottoms of the business cycles has been a similar one, but with all the turning movements reversed. When interest rates were low at the bottoms of bear markets for securities, new bull markets have begun. These have shortly brought about favorable conditions for the marketing of new issues of investment securities which have resulted in turn in enlarging the inflows of new funds into business enterprises and in bringing about the expanding phases of new business cycles.

The long wavelike upward fluctuations and downward fluctuations in the levels of short-term interest rates have been caused by the operation of our banking laws and regulations which have controlled the expansions and contractions of bank credit by the intricate monetary mechanisms of reserve ratios which are explained in Chapter XIV. The operations of these reserve ratios, and their control over interest rates, have included the timing mechanism which has been responsible for the former relative regularity and periodicity in the recurrence of the business cycles.

Throughout this book the evidence has supported the central thesis that turning points in business cycles normally result from changes in the volumes of inflows of new funds into business enterprises. In most cases these changes are internally generated by the interactions between and among the reserve ratios of banks, the levels of interest rates, the trends of security prices, and the alternating expansions and contractions in the volumes of new security issues. This means that our business cycles have generally been caused by the operations of our banking laws and regulations, our business procedures, and the processes of our security markets.

Sometimes the forces that have brought about the turning points in business cycles have been externally generated by such developments as the outbreaks or the conclusions of wars, or by business developments in other countries. Nevertheless, an analysis of the evidence over the long period under review leads definitely to the conclusion that turning points in business cycles, whether resulting from forces internally generated or from external forces, are brought about in almost all cases by increases or decreases of the inflows of new money into business enterprises.

Data are available in the business cycles of the past 40 years for studies of the changes in the volumes of production of nondurable or consumers goods. They show that in almost all the cases the upturns and downturns of the volumes of new security issues in the business cycles came before those in the production of consumers goods. The finding is important because it shows that the consumer purchasing power theories of business cycles cannot be valid explanations. Those theories underlie the policies of pump-priming, and of bonuses for veterans and for farmers in so far as those payments have been made as parts of the recovery program. The same theories are parts of the philosophies of such schemes as the Townsend Plan.

Unfortunately much of this book has had to be made up of detailed descriptions of the statistical methods by which the conclusions have been reached. It contains numerous arid and tedious accounts of the historical analysis of the 26 successive business cycles which it studies, and detailed descriptions of the statistical materials which it utilizes. Any careful reading of it will require repeated references to most of its many diagrams. These barriers against easy reading are regrettable, but they seem to be unavoidable.

August, 1939.   L. P. A.

CONTENTS

APPENDICES

DIAGRAMS

TABLES

TURNING POINTS IN BUSINESS CYCLES

CHAPTER I

TURNING POINTS IN EARLY CYCLES

THIS BOOK offers an explanation of an economic mechanism which appears to operate in most business cycles to cause the downturns from periods of prosperity, and the upturns from depressions. At present the problems of these turning points constitute the most important, the most puzzling, and the most controversial issues in business cycle theory. If we can gain understanding of the turning points we shall clear the way for more rapid progress toward agreement about the nature and causes of the cycles themselves, and hasten the time when measures can be intelligently designed to avert them, or at least to mitigate their gravity.

In recent years there has developed among students of business cycles a good deal of agreement about the nature and characteristics of the cycles, but not about the causes of their turns. There is general accord among research workers in business economics in holding that the cycles of business activity which carry employment, production, and national income through long swings alternately up to prosperity, and then down to depression, are irregular in size and irregularly spaced. These students all emphasize the gravity of recurring periods of economic depression, and realize that there is developing a world-wide consciousness of the serious nature of their social and economic effects.

All are agreed that business cycles are never repeated. Each new cycle is an economic and historical individual. There is general acceptance of the convincing nature of the evidence showing that the cyclical fluctuations of employment and production in connection with the output of durable goods are much wider than are those related to the making of nondurable goods. There is growing agreement about terminology, and most students now discuss four phases of the cycle. These are the upswing to prosperity, the upper turning point, the downswing to depression, and the lower turning point.

In addition to these general accords most students agree that the processes of expansion and contraction in business cycles are cumulative in nature. They are self-reinforcing, and when they have once gained either upward momentum or downward momentum they tend to continue for some time as though impelled by an internal energy of their own, and without much regard for the forces which originally set them in motion. But despite so much agreement, there is no general consensus about the forces which initiate the downturns and the upturns.

It should be acknowledged at the outset of this discussion that many careful investigators of business cycle phenomena will probably object to the assumption apparently made in the title of this book, and in that of this chapter, that the turning points of cycles can be readily identified and precisely located. There is some validity in such an objection, for the processes of business contraction from prosperity down to depression, and those of expansion from depression back up again to prosperity, do not conveniently begin and end in specific months.

These processes of contraction and expansion are instead complicated series of changes in varied groups of economic phenomena which are dispersed over considerable ranges of months. However, the difficulties involved in locating turning points of business cycles over a long series of years for the specific purpose of studying factors which may cause the downturns and the upturns are rather matters of the inadequacy of the available statistics than of the complexities of the processes of business decline and revival. There is abundant evidence showing that in our highly industrialized economy the cyclical fluctuations in the production of durable goods are much more regular and of far greater amplitude than are the fluctuations in the production of nondurable goods. This condition affords relatively reliable criteria for locating the upper and lower turning points of cycles.

It appears to the present writer that we should never be much misled in locating the point of downturn from a past period of business prosperity if we should take as that turning point the latest month of the period in which there were employed in factories approximately the maximum number of workers engaged in producing durable goods. In similar fashion we could reliably locate the upturns from the bottoms of past depressions if we should take as the upward turning point of the period the latest month in which there were employed in factories approximately the minimum number of workers engaged in producing durable goods.

In order to locate these turning points satisfactorily we should need to have well compiled series of data showing monthly changes in factory employment. These data would have to be classified so as to show employment among workers producing durable goods, and they would have to be adjusted to eliminate seasonal variations. Unfortunately such data are available only for the brief span of years since 1922.

Results of almost equal reliability might be derived from data of factory employment not classified so as to show separately the employment among producers of durable goods, and that among the makers of nondurable goods. We should be well guided if we could always take as the upper turning points in business cycles the latest prosperity months of approximately maximum total factory employment, and as the lower turning points the latest depression months of approximately minimum total factory employment. Unfortunately our reliable data of total factory employment cover only the months since the beginning of 1919.

The safest guides for locating the turning points of business cycles prior to 1919 appear to the writer to be the seasonally corrected series of data showing monthly changes in the physical volume of industrial production. The general rule to be followed in using these series would naturally seem to be that of taking as the upper turning point in each prosperity period the month of greatest production, and as the lower turning point in each depression the month of lowest production, but there are modifications to be made in attempting to apply such a general rule.

Any diagram showing over a long series of years the monthly changes in the volume of industrial production or in so-called general business activity reveals a good many instances of double or multiple tops in periods of prosperity, and of double or multiple bottoms in depressions. In such cases it appears reasonable and desirable to apply with prudent caution the rule that the latest peak, or the last month before a decided decrease in production in the prosperity period should be taken as the downturn, and the latest trough, or the last month before a decided increase in production, should be taken as the month of the upturn of the cycle.

These rules of procedure have been observed throughout this book which presents arguments about the turning points of business cycles which are based in the main on an analysis of diagrams showing monthly changes in business activity or industrial production, and in certain financial series, over a period of more than 100 years. In order to follow the argument it will be necessary for the reader to refer pretty constantly to the diagrams, and while that will probably become irritating, it seems to be unavoidable. At this point the reader would better turn back and read the Preface. It will tell him what to look for, and it may encourage him to keep on going when he finds the book dull reading.

Diagram 1 on page 6 carries at the top a black silhouette which shows for the 20 years from 1831 through 1850 the monthly changes in the index of business activity of the Cleveland Trust Company, which has been carried back by the writer in monthly data to the beginning of 1790. Its components, and the methods by which it was constructed, are described in Appendix C. The bond prices represented by the heavy line lower down in the diagram were compiled as a part of this study. They represent the prices of state bonds of New York, Ohio, and Kentucky. The prices are the simple averages of yields capitalized at 4.14 percent. An account of this series and of the reasons for that rate of capitalization are given in Appendix D.

The light line showing stock prices is based for the first three years of the period on the quoted prices of four canal stocks, and on those of seven bank and insurance stocks. For the next 12 years through 1845 it is based on two groups of stocks that are so combined as to give them equal weights in the final results. One group consists of bank and insurance stocks and the other of railroad stocks. After 1845, and through 1870, the stock prices are those of railroad shares. This series of stock prices is described in Appendix E.

It should be noted that throughout this study the series of bond and stock prices are not the familiar index number series having a base of a year or a series of years in which the average of the quoted prices is equal to 100. The figures used are dollar prices which have been compiled in the attempt to reproduce as nearly as possible the typical average prices at which the securities were actually bought and sold. The attempt has been to make these price lines reflect changes in conditions as they appeared at the time to business men who were watching the quotations of high-grade securities as they were published in the public prints.

There is a smooth dashed line running through the irregular heavy line representing the monthly changes in the bond prices, and a smooth dotted one running through the irregular light line representing the monthly changes in the stock prices. These are 12 months centered moving averages plotted so that the average for each full year appears in July of that year. These lines have been included in the diagram so as to aid in noting the turning points in the cyclical fluctuations of these security price series.

At the bottom of the diagram the smooth line which moves through wide fluctuations is a 12 months centered moving average of the discount rates on commercial paper. The data used through 1860 are those taken from "The Tariff Question," by Erastus B. Bigelow (Boston, 1862). Running through these short-term interest rates is a much flatter series of long-term interest rates. These are the bond yields of the bond price series shown in the upper part of the diagram. These two interest rate series have a different scale from the rest of the diagram, and it is shown by the small figures

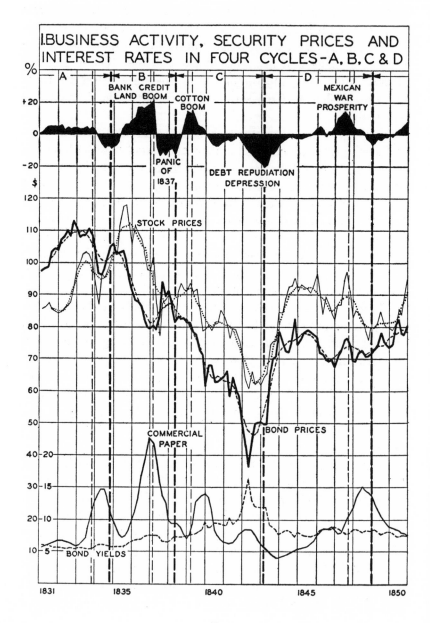

I.BUSINESS ACTIVITY, SECURITY PRICES AND
INTEREST RATES IN FOUR CYCLES-A, B, C & D

6

at the left within the diagram. The short-term interest data are explained in Appendix F.

There appear to have been three complete business cycles, and parts of two others, in the 20-year period covered by the diagram. The downturn from the prosperity period of the first cycle is considered to have been in October of 1833, and a vertical light dashed line is drawn through the diagram at that point. The upturn from the following depression is located one year later in October of 1834, and a vertical heavy dashed line is drawn through the diagram at that point.

In similar fashion vertical light dashed lines are drawn at the points selected as the months of the downturns from the prosperity periods of the subsequent cycles, and vertical heavy lines are drawn at the points selected as the months of the upturns from the depressions. Each cycle is considered to run from one depression turning point to the next, and the cycles are designated for convenience by letters which appear at the top of the diagram just under the title. The cycles shown here are part of A, all of B, C, and D, and part of E.

The main argument of this book, which will be developed in subsequent chapters, is that downturns in business cycles take place when conditions become unfavorable for securing new business capital, or replacing old capital, through the sale of bonds, notes, and stocks, and that upturns occur when market conditions for new capital flotations become favorable once more. In subsequent diagrams data lines will be included showing changes in the sales of new capital securities, but none is available for this early period.

Under this restriction discussion of this first diagram will be devoted to considering the evidence that market conditions did become unfavorable for the sale of new security issues shortly before the important downturns of the business cycles took place, and that favorable conditions for selling new issues did develop shortly before the business upturns got under way. Before this discussion is begun the reader should be warned that all the data on which this first diagram is based fall short of being satisfactory in quality.

The fluctuations of business activity are measured by such unsatisfactory series as those of government receipts and expenditures, exports and imports, ship construction, coal production, and iron exports. The original figures were annual data, and the monthly variations which were fitted to them were derived from price changes of commodities and of stocks. These are unsatisfactory materials from which to construct an index of business activity, but this is the only business index available for these early years.

The series of bond prices is based on insufficient data, and in some instances monthly figures were interpolated where no quotations could be found. The series of stock prices is similarly based on unsatisfactory data, although the original material is more ample than that of the bonds. Finally the commercial paper rates are of somewhat doubtful antecedents. They are described as being discount rates prevailing in New York and Boston, but they are probably rates which prevailed in Boston. The series is described in Appendix F.

If the statistics used in constructing the first diagram, and most of the second one, could be given ratings for quality like those used by the agencies which rate issues of bonds, they would not be classified as of AAA quality, or AA, or even A. They might receive ratings of B, and in spots of only C. The business activity index is much improved beginning with 1855. The bond price series becomes quite good in 1857, as does the stock series, and the data of commercial paper are greatly improved after 1865.

Some writers who have discussed the economic developments of the period covered by Diagram 1 have called these years "The Turbulent Thirties," and "The Depressed Forties." Moderate prosperity prevailed in Cycle A in 1831 and the two following years, and that was followed by a brief depression in 1834. Shortly before that depression developed, short-term interest rates increased sharply, bond prices turned downward, and stock prices followed in decline. The upturn of business activity at the beginning of Cycle B in 1835 was preceded by a decline in short-term interest rates, and by rapid recoveries in bond and in stock prices.

It seems wholly probable that the sharp advance in short-term interest rates, and the downswings of bond and stock prices in 1833 must have operated to discourage and decrease the flow of investment funds into business enterprises, and that the relaxation of interest rates, and the upswings of bond and stock prices in 1834, must have encouraged a resumption of the flow of new capital into business. It will be shown in later chapters that just such sequences of developments did take place in a long series of business cycles.

In 1835 and 1836 there developed in this country a period of extraordinary speculation in farm lands and real estate. It may well be that the land speculation of the 1830's was comparable to the stock speculation of the 1920's in its intensity, and in the widespread participation in its ventures on the part of people throughout the country and in all walks of life. The culmination came in the panic of 1837 which was to usher in a long period of hard times.

While the speculative prosperity of the land boom was increasing, there had developed an exceptional advance in short-term interest rates, and downward movements of bond and stock prices. After the panic these movements were reversed for a short period, and there was a brief resumption of speculative activity in 1838 which was unusually violent in the cotton markets. This did not, however, bring about a real and lasting change in the trend of business, for the long depression of the 1840's was getting under way. It was preceded by another stiffening in short-term interest rates, and by new downswings in bond prices and stock prices.

The long depression of the 1840's is designated on the black silhouette representing the business activity index as being a debt repudiation depression, and probably that is an appropriate term for it. The country was burdened by a huge volume of indebtedness that had been incurred for all sorts of private ventures and for a great many public ones. Many states had floated bond issues for the construction of highways, canals, and railroads, and for the establishment of state banks. As the depression became serious there got under way a decline in commodity prices that greatly increased the weight of indebtedness and made people hopeless about ever being able to pay off their obligations.

It may well be that the depression of the 1840's inflicted more general hardship upon the people than any other of our periods of hard times. Wholesale prices declined 39 percent as compared with the drop of 38 percent in the Great Depression of the 1930's. The Bank of the United States failed. It was reported that some 33,000 merchants failed with liabilities of 440 million dollars. A long list of states repudiated their debts. The worst offenders were Mississippi, Louisiana, Maryland, Pennsylvania, Indiana, Illinois, and Michigan. Later on, all of them except Mississippi paid in whole or in part.

In 1842 there were widespread demands that the Federal Government should assume all state debts, but legislation providing for this failed to pass. Laws were enacted in the western states to prevent property from being sold for debt. Many states passed what were known as extension laws by which the payment of debts was postponed. In 1841 the Congress passed the Bankrupt Act by which any person could become free from debt by assigning his property. Many thousands took advantage of its provisions, but it was found that doing so ruined a business man's credit, and the act was repealed after two years.

It is most difficult to construct a satisfactory index of bond prices covering that period. As repudiation became popular the people lost confidence in bonds, and some business periodicals of the time almost stopped publishing bond sale quotations. The diagram shows that the prices of the leading state bonds dropped to far lower levels than did those of high-grade common stocks, and that seems to have been quite literally the case. The lowest prices for both classes of securities were reached in 1842, and about 10 months after their recovery began, general business improvement got under way.

In Cycle D, which runs from early 1843 to the end of 1848, there was a curious minor dip and recovery of security prices before the downturn from prosperity took place in the autumn of 1847. Both bond and stock prices turned downward in 1844 and 1845, and interest rates stiffened. There followed a minor dip in business in 1846, but no real depression. It may well be that conditions were then developing which might have initiated a real depression, but that renewed business activity was temporarily stimulated by the government expenditures of the Mexican War. The prosperity of 1847 was brief, and in that year interest rates moved sharply upward and bond and stock prices turned downward again, and these developments were followed by the mild depression of 1848 and 1849.

Throughout the 18 years that have been reviewed each downturn of business from prosperity toward depression has been preceded by an increase in short-term interest rates and by downturns of bond prices and stock prices. Each upturn from depression toward recovery has been preceded by declining interest rates and by rising bond and stock prices. On each occasion when business activity turned downward in a major swing, financial conditions had developed which were unfavorable to a sustained flow of new capital into business enterprise. Each time when business activity turned upward in a major recovery swing it did so after financial conditions had become favorable for a resumption of a flow of new capital into business.

In the entire period there was no instance in which the unfavorable financial conditions of rising interest rates and of declining bond and stock prices developed that this combination was not followed by a decline of business activity to below the computed normal level. In the one case in which the appearance of financial conditions unfavorable to the flow of investment capital into business enterprise was not followed by a real depression, there was a sudden flow of government war expenditures which may have checked and briefly reversed the downward trend of business that had been under way.

All the historical review which has been set forth in this chapter and which will be continued in the next one is presented in support of the central thesis of this book. That thesis is that there exists a large mass of evidence indicating that the controlling factor in bringing about upturns from depression toward prosperity, and downturns from prosperity toward depression, in business cycles consists of important changes in the rates of the flow of capital investment into business enterprise. The further argument is that these rates of capital flow decrease in periods of prosperity when financial conditions become unfavorable for attracting new capital, and that in depressions the rates of capital flow increase again when financial conditions once more become favorable for attracting new capital.

CHAPTER II

GOLD INFLATION AND THE CIVIL WAR PERIOD

DIAGRAM 2 on page 14 covers the 20-year period from 1847 through 1866. The data shown are the index of business activity, bond prices, stock prices, and interest rates, just as in the first diagram. The first four years of this diagram are repetitions of the last four years of the former diagram, and they are repeated in order to facilitate the study of the curves. The diagram covers the four cycles designated as E, F, G, and H, and part of the following one.

Business recovery began at the end of 1848, and except for a dip in 1851 the advance continued to the spring of 1854, or for a period of more than five years. During most of that time both bond and stock prices were advancing. In the previous chapter the argument was made that such periods of advancing security prices must have created market conditions that were favorable for attracting increased flows of new capital into business enterprises. We have no direct data with which to measure the increases in such flows in those early years, but nevertheless there are some figures which indicate that they must have taken place.

Federal reports show that in the year 1848, just before the recovery began, there were 398 miles of new railroads put into operation. Railroad construction required new capital, and the advancing security markets created conditions which were favorable for attracting it. The new capital must have flowed in abundantly, for the miles of new railroad increased steadily until in 1853 there were 2,452 miles put into operation, or more than six times as much as in 1848. During 1853 security prices were moving downward again and creating unfavorable conditions for attracting new capital, and railroad construction dropped from 2,452 miles in 1853 to only

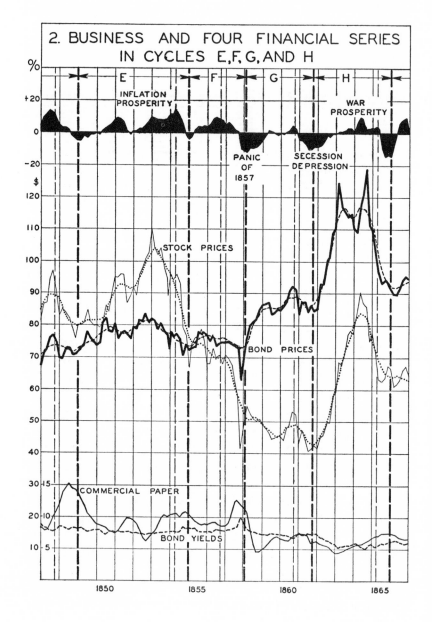

2. BUSINESS AND FOUR FINANCIAL SERIES IN CYCLES E, F, G, AND H

1,360 miles in 1854. In the autumn of that year there was a rather serious stock market panic.

Interest rates were declining, and bond and stock prices advancing, when business recovery got under way again in 1855 at the beginning of Cycle F. The advances in security prices did not long continue, despite the fact that business activity had regained high prosperity levels by the summer of 1856. During all that year the general trend of stock and bond prices was downward and interest rates remained relatively high. Business turned definitely downward late in 1856, and continued to decline through the severe panic of 1857 which was at its worst in October of that year.

The years from 1849 through 1857, included in Cycles E and F, were a period of gold inflation. Hunt's Merchants' Magazine (vol. 45, p. 67) notes that in the famous year of 1849 California gold production amounted to only eight million dollars, but by 1850 it was 33 millions; in 1851 it rose to 55 millions, and by 1857 it had risen to 70 millions. It became the basis for rapidly expanded bank credit, which fostered much competitive railroad construction, and the speculative expansion of building and of many sorts of enterprises. From the end of 1851 to the spring of 1857 there was an increase of 40 percent in wholesale commodity prices.

The upturn of business after the panic of 1857 came in January of 1858. It was preceded by a decline in interest rates and by advances in the security prices. That upturn initiated Cycle G which was to continue until after the outbreak of the Civil War in the spring of 1861. Business activity recovered to the computed normal level in 1859, and there was a short period of mildly prosperous business in 1860. During those years bond prices continued to advance, while stock prices declined a little and then recovered their losses. Interest rates remained relatively low. In those years the growing threat of war between the states was apparently already becoming a powerful force in shaping the course of business.

When Lincoln was elected to the presidency in 1860 a decline of business activity and of security prices began which developed into a real depression in 1861. The outbreak of war in the spring of that year completely disrupted the business of industrial firms in the north which manufactured goods for southern consumption, and that of trading concerns which dealt in such goods. The liabilities of commercial failures in 1861 were far higher in relation to national wealth than they have ever been subsequently, although they were not as large as those caused by the panic of 1857.

Full recovery was regained by the end of 1862, and war prosperity prevailed in 1863 and 1864. The black silhouette representing business activity probably reflects inadequately the degree of war prosperity that existed in Cycle H, because the data from which it is computed during the war years have not been adjusted to allow for the reductions due to the fact that the southern states were not then contributing to the totals of national production.

Inflation prevailed during the war, and both bond and stock prices, as quoted in terms of greenback currency, rose to extremely high levels. Both of them were moving downward in 1864, and continued to do so in 1865 during the short but sharp depression which followed the return of peace. The eight years from 1858 through 1865, which are included in Cycles G and H, constitute an abnormal period in so far as the study of business cycles is concerned, for they were dominated by the prospects of war and the events of war. Even so the characteristic sequences in the movements of interest rates, security prices, and business activity prevailing in prior cycles were continued with rather astonishing fidelity to form during those two cycles.

It is to be noted that the quality of the data on which the diagrams are based becomes much improved just before the Civil War period. Beginning with 1855 the data constituting the index of business become predominantly records of industrial production, and after 1860 their monthly variations are more reliable than they are before that year. Beginning with 1857 the bond price data and the bond yields are derived from the carefully compiled series worked out by Dr. Frederick R. Macaulay of the National Bureau of Economic Research, and the series of stock prices from 1857 through

1870 is also derived from his work. Beginning with 1866 the commercial paper rates are those compiled by Professor W. L. Crum and published in the Review of Economic Statistics of January 1923.

It seems not unlikely that if our statistical records of the business and financial developments during the years from 1831 through 1865 were a good deal more ample and reliable than they are, we should still have much difficulty in reaching satisfactory conclusions about the business cycles of the period. In those years American trade and industry were being developed with great rapidity through the unrestrained initiative and enterprise of a people who were still largely engaged in promoting pioneer projects, and who depended heavily on foreign loans for financing them.

At the beginning of the period there were neither railroads nor telegraphs, but by the close of the Civil War both of them were undergoing vigorous exploitation, and quite largely as highly speculative undertakings. Except for the last few years it was a period during which most business was transacted with money of fluctuating value that was issued in excessive quantities by banks which were often lacking in both responsibility and adequate resources.

The delays and difficulties of communication were so great in the earlier years of the period under review that different sections of the country must have conducted their affairs at times under quite diverse influences of the business cycle, as indeed they do to some degree even today. The railroad and the telegraph began about 1850 to exert important influences in the rapid dissemination of information and the closer coordination of business enterprises. Some idea of earlier business handicaps may be gained from the statement in McMaster's history (vol. 2, pp. 39-41) that on August 11, 1791, the stock of the new Bank of the United States was being traded in at New York at 205, while on the same day it was selling at Philadelphia for 320.

Both commerce and industrial enterprise were largely dependent on foreign credits, and as a result changes in financial conditions abroad exerted large influence on business developments here. Moreover in the absence of cable communication these foreign influences often resulted in violent and unexpected repercussions in this country. Any thorough analysis of our business cycles during the years under review would involve extensive consideration of the business cycles of the leading European nations, and especially of those of England.

No attempt is being made to formulate in this book a complete theory of the business cycle. Such an undertaking would clearly involve among other grave tasks some adequate explanation of the reasons why some depressions are relatively brief while others are of long duration and attended by most serious consequences. That problem is involved in any discussion of business cycles which brings into consideration both the panic of 1837 and the panic of 1857.

The panic of 1837 was followed by a brief and speculative recovery which shortly gave way to one of the longest and most severe depressions that this country has ever experienced. The panic of 1857 was followed by a recovery that lasted long enough to make it seem reasonable to believe that it might have attained considerable magnitude and duration if the Civil War had not intervened. Both panics followed periods of widespread speculation, much unsound banking, general over-trading, and the promotion of numerous large and costly undertakings such as new canals and railroads.

Perhaps part of the explanation of the marked difference between their after-results may be found in the fact that the speculation that characterized the period just prior to the panic of 1837 was predominantly in land, while that of the period just before 1857 was much more largely in securities and in participations in new enterprises. It may be a trustworthy rule that depressions are of long duration if they come when there exists an exceptionally large volume of recently incurred real estate debt. That was the case in this country in 1929.

When security prices fall drastically at the beginning of a depression, holdings of stocks and bonds can be liquidated rapidly even if the losses incurred are severe. The exchanges supply the machinery that facilitates liquidation. There are no real estate exchanges, and no quotations of going values are available. Warren and Pearson have pointed out in their book on "Prices" that under these conditions neither borrowers nor lenders realize what the situation really is and as a result they both try to hold on. Ultimately the creditors foreclose, but even then they do not really want to hold the properties they have just taken over and so the depression in real estate values continues until they become willing to sell at prices low enough so that the properties will pass into the possession of people who do want them.

A rapid review of eight business cycles has been made in Chapter I and in this chapter. Table 1 on this page gives data showing the dates of their upturns and downturns, the months of duration of their upswings and downswings, and the numbers of months by which the turns in short-term interest rates and in security prices preceded the turns in business activity.

TABLE 1

Dates of upturns of business cycles A through H, durations of upswings and downswings of business, and months by which turns in short-term interest rates and in security prices preceded business turns.

Cycle	Date of Upturn	Months of Up-swing	Months by which turns preceded business upturn			Date of Downturn	Months of Down-swing	Months by which turns preceded business downturn		
			Top of Interest	Bottom of Bonds	Bottom of Stocks			Bottom of Interest	Top of Bonds	Top of Stocks
A	Sep. 1829	49	—	—	—	Oct. 1833	12	36	12	4
B	Oct. 1834	28	5	6	8	Feb. 1837	14	19	29	18
C	Apr. 1838	11	16	11	10	Mar. 1839	47	3	19	6
D	Feb. 1843	55	39	10	10	Sep. 1847	15	46	35	1
E	Dec. 1848	63	6	10	1	Mar. 1854	9	19	19	15
F	Dec. 1854	21	2	3	0	Sep. 1856	16	14	16	14
G	Jan. 1858	32	6	3	3	Sep. 1860	12	24	1	0
H	Sep. 1861	42	8	4	3	Mar. 1865	9	28	8	11

The table shows that during these eight business cycles the major swings of short-term interest rates and of security prices preceded those of business activity with notable consistency, but with wide variations in the numbers of months by which they did so. One item in the table calls for special comment. That is the entry of 14 in the third line of figures from the bottom and the third column from the right. That entry indicates that in Cycle F the bottom of short-term interest rates was reached 14 months prior to the downturn of business.

That was actually the case, for the records show that in June and July of 1855 the rate on commercial paper was 6.5 percent and no other rate as low as that was recorded until the spring of 1858. Nevertheless the 12 months moving centered average shows a slightly lower figure in the autumn of 1856 than those of the summer of 1855. Despite that fact the lowest month of the original data has been used in this case because it appears to represent most truly the upward turning point of the short-term interest rates in that cycle.

The use of some sort of moving average to represent the changes in short-term interest rates is almost unavoidable, for the original data are so irregular that a line representing them swings through such wide fluctuations as to make the record most difficult to interpret, and if used it would introduce confusing crossings and recrossings of the other lines. The 12 months moving centered average has been used in these diagrams because it is the most simple available statistical device for largely eliminating the erratic variations and seasonal fluctuations of the original data.

One feature of Table 1 which deserves special mention is the evidence it affords indicating that the characteristic cyclical turns of interest rates, bond prices, and stock prices not only normally take place before the cyclical turns in business activity, but they tend to take place in the order in which they are listed in the columns of the table. In most of the cases the downturns of the short-term interest rates occur before the upturns of the bond prices, and those upturns generally precede the upturns of the stock prices. Similarly the bottoms of the swings of interest rates tend to come earlier than the tops of the swings of bond prices, and those are usually followed by the tops of stock prices.

Chapter III

A NEW RECORD OF CAPITAL ISSUES

Cycle I, which covers the five years immediately following the Civil War, is most unsatisfactory as a subject for business cycle analysis. When the war came to an end in the spring of 1865, the return of peace was immediately followed by an abrupt and severe depression which was of exceptionally short duration. Cycle I begins in that depression in December of 1865. The depression was followed by a short period of prosperity which had run its course by the end of 1866, and which does not appear to have included the downturn of the cycle as had most previous definite prosperity periods.

The prosperity of 1866 was followed by four years during which the fluctuations of business activity above and below the computed normal level appear to have been of smaller amplitude than during any other four consecutive years in our business history. During those years from 1866 through 1870 the changes in bond prices, in stock prices, and in interest rates were small. The unusually vigorous prosperity which preceded the long depression of the 1870's did not get under way until 1871.

These exceptional conditions are shown in Diagram 3 on page 22 which covers the 21 years from the beginning of 1864 to the end of 1884. The first three years of this period were shown in the previous diagram, and are repeated in this one. This diagram differs from the two preceding ones in that the section at the bottom showing changes in interest rates and bond yields is really an added diagram with the heavy line just above it serving as the base line of the main diagram.

After careful consideration of the usual characteristics of the post-war Cycle I, decision was reached to consider its downturn as

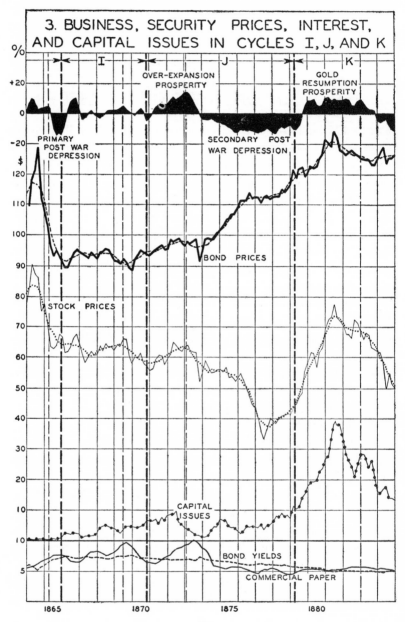

3. BUSINESS, SECURITY PRICES, INTEREST, AND CAPITAL ISSUES IN CYCLES I, J, AND K

being located in June of 1869 at the top of the mild prosperity period of that year. The end of the cycle was considered as located in October of 1870 at the bottom of the mild depression dip of that year. If we accept these dates as being the most probably valid ones, the lowest prices for bonds at the beginning of the cycle came three months after the upturn of business, and those for stocks 16 months after the business upturn, instead of preceding it. The highest point of short-term interest rates came three months before the business upturn, but the change in interest was only a minor one.

Bond prices finally turned downward 11 months before the downturn of the cycle in June of 1869, and interest rates reached their lowest point 32 months before that date. Stock prices turned downward in the same month that business activity did. Commercial paper rates were higher in 1869 than they had been at any previous time since the panic of 1857, and that fact contributes important evidence to indicate that there was a genuine, even if rather indecisive, business cycle which had its downturn in that year. It should be noted here that after 1870 the stock price line is based on the index of the Cowles Commission for Research in Economics which covers the prices of all stocks and not solely those of railroad stocks.

In Diagram 3 there is a ball-and-chain data line just above the heavy base line which shows the changes in a newly compiled record of capital issues listed on the New York Stock Exchange. It is a 12 months moving centered total of domestic corporate issues listed on the Exchange and sold for cash. The data of this new series do not include federal, state, or foreign issues, or those of banks, financial corporations, or holding companies. They omit all securities issued in exchange for properties or for other securities, and include only the domestic corporate issues shown by the listing statements to have been sold for money. Where sales were made at prices differing from par values, the actual sales prices were used.

The dates at which issues were entered in the tabulations were the issue dates of new flotations unless other dates of actual sale were noted in the applications for listing. In the cases of additional issues of securities already listed, the dates of the applications were used in making the tabulations. The unit used in plotting the series in the diagrams is 10 million dollars, so that when the data line almost touches the level of 10 in this diagram, as it does in the summer of 1872, it indicates that the total of the issues tabulated for that year was approximately 100 million dollars and that this total was plotted as of July of that year.

There are four readily available statistical series of new capital flotations. The longest one is that of the New York Journal of Commerce which begins in 1906. The tabulations of the Commercial and Financial Chronicle start in 1919. Those of the Standard Statistics Company begin in 1924. The new series of the Securities and Exchange Commission begins in 1933. The new series of listings, compiled as a part of this study, has been carried back to the beginning of 1863 and continued to 1924.

The data of the new series from the beginning of 1863 up to the middle of 1884 have been transcribed from the records of the New York Stock Exchange which were made available through the cooperation of the economist of the Exchange, Mr. Bradford B. Smith. Beginning with June of 1884 the data are available in the Listing Statements of the New York Stock Exchange published by Francis E. Fitch. These listing statements from 1884 through 1923 fill 27 volumes, and include some 6,200 separate listings.

This new series does not afford a good measure of the changes in the flows of new capital into business enterprises. It comprises only corporate issues of non-financial American companies newly listed on the New York Stock Exchange. Of course it cannot include bank credits. It omits nearly all equipment issues of railroads. In the early decades it reflects almost entirely issues of bonds, for in those years new stock issues were seldom listed until long after their original issue dates. The data of this new series reflect changes in the flow of a combination of new capital and the replacement of old capital being refinanced.

In a subsequent chapter consideration will be given to the degree of agreement between the cyclical fluctuations of this new series and those of the Journal of Commerce and the Commercial and Financial Chronicle. There will be discussion also of the cyclical importance of refinancing as distinguished from changes in the flow of strictly new capital. For the present such important matters will be deferred, and the only claim made for the new series will be that it does furnish an indicator extending over the years of many decades which tells us when important changes took place in public offerings of new corporate securities that were sold for money.

Cycle J is one of the long cycles. It covers more than eight years from late in 1870 to the spring of 1879. It is one of the most important of the cycles, for it includes the long and severe depression of the 1870's. The upswing of the cycle began in October of 1870 some 10 months after bond prices had turned upward, and 14 months after the downturn of interest rates. Stock prices did not turn upward until three months after business activity did. The trends of both bond prices and stock prices were slowly advancing in 1871 and 1872 during the exceptional prosperity which preceded the panic of 1873.

The dates of the turning points of the financial series prior to the downturn of business in 1873 form a fairly conventional pattern. Bond prices turned downward six months before the downturn of business, stock prices nine months before, and security listings seven months before. The bottom of interest rates was reached 21 months before the business downturn. This conventional pattern is interesting and significant, but it seems to fall short of being convincingly satisfying when we are seeking an explanation to account for the cause of the business downturn of 1873.

Let us assume for the sake of the argument—as this book does assume—that in typical business cycles the downturns of business activity take place because of important shrinkages in the flow of new capital funds into business enterprises. Our immediate question would then be one which asks what are the causes of the shrinkages in the flow of new capital. The normal and natural answer to that question is that the flow of capital issues decreases when conditions develop in financial markets that are unfavorable to new financing. The ordinary symptoms of the development of such unfavorable conditions are advancing short-term interest rates, falling bond prices, falling stock prices, or some one or two of these three factors.

Those who have long participated on the issuing side in the planning of new corporate financing will vividly recall the change of sentiment which takes place in the policy-planning groups of large corporations when the underwriters who were to take a new security issue send word that they cannot make the favorable bid that had been previously discussed, and that they cannot do so because interest rates have risen, or bond prices, or stock prices, or both, have turned downward. When such information comes from the underwriters telling of the development of unfavorable market conditions, the policy-forming group in the corporation begins at once to modify its plans.

If the underwriters think that the new financing can still be done, but at a higher coupon and a greater discount than at first proposed, the corporation management may approve of going ahead, and perhaps of reducing the size of the proposed issue. Then the legal staff sets to work to modify the indenture, alter the terms of the sinking fund, and introduce such other changes as may be necessary. Meanwhile all the plans for spending the new funds are hurriedly revised. Construction firms and suppliers of materials and equipment are notified to suspend or reduce the estimates on which they have been working, and in general a whole series of contractions of planning is put into effect.

Sometimes several successive reductions of plans are worked out on paper as market conditions continue to grow still more unfavorable, and each reduction causes a far-reaching series of contracted estimates of activity by other organizations. If interest rates continue to rise and security prices keep falling, the proposed new issue is likely either to be entirely abandoned or to be reduced to the smallest amount that will suffice to meet the pressing needs of the corporation.

Somewhat similar results often take place when the problem is one of refunding an old issue rather than that of floating a new one. If the plan is to call an existing issue and replace it by a new one carrying a lower rate of coupon, the development of unfavorable market conditions will usually cause the project to be given up. In that case the corporation at once contracts its plans because now it must forego the savings it had expected to effect through the refinancing.

The case is much more serious when the contemplated new financing was planned for the purpose of replacing an existing bond issue that is maturing. When a maturing issue cannot be replaced by a new one because market conditions have become unfavorable, recourse must be had to bank loans or note issues, and those credits must be secured despite unfavorable conditions for getting them. Probably the most drastic economies suddenly imposed by corporation managements are those resulting from inability to refinance maturing issues of long-term obligations.

The flow of new security listings turned downward sharply after June of 1872 and their decline continued until it was reduced to almost nothing by the end of 1873. The downturn came after market conditions had been rendered unfavorable for floating new securities by a persistent advance in interest rates and by a decline in stock prices. It was accompanied by a decrease in bond prices. Despite the consistency of these developments, it seems a little hard to believe that they were adequate to explain the abrupt downturn of business at the beginning of 1873, which preceded the famous panic of that year, and initiated the long depression of the 1870's.

Before the downturn of 1873 both bond and stock prices had fluctuated within a narrow range of a few points for a period of seven years. They had developed a stability that has never been even approached during a similar period of years either before or since. Their minor declines in the late months of 1872 can hardly have been regarded at the time as being very serious.

The decline in security listings was of considerable importance. In the middle of 1872 they were running at the rate of about 100 millions a year, and by the end of 1873 they had declined almost to nothing. They did not all represent new capital, and some part of the new capital they did represent had already been spent and was represented by new issues which capitalized previous expenditures, as has always been a frequently followed practice in railroad financing. Nevertheless their shrinkage of nearly 100 millions a year within a short time was a decrease equal to about one-third of the annual payroll of all factory workers then engaged in producing durable goods, so it was large enough to be important.

What seems to have happened is that the flow of new capital from Europe was sharply curtailed in 1872. Railroad construction especially was then heavily dependent on foreign funds. The curtailment of foreign lending prior to the downturn of 1873 is mentioned by Otto C. Lightner in his "History of Business Depressions" (p. 160), by Harold G. Moulton of the Brookings Institution in his "Formation of Capital" (p. 59), and it is discussed in numerous passages in the second volume of E. P. Oberholtzer's biography of "Jay Cooke, Financier of the Civil War." These views have support from the fact that new railroads put into operation amounted to 7,379 miles in 1871, and to only 5,870 miles in 1872.

If the downturn of Cycle J in 1873 was caused by a decrease in the flow of capital into enterprise, the unfavorable conditions responsible for that decrease may well be considered to have been initiated both here and abroad with the factors of foreign origin exercising a large, and perhaps a preponderating, influence. The chief reasons for the long duration of the depression may also have been largely of foreign origin, for the depression of the 1870's was a world-wide depression up to 1880, and especially severe in England, France, Germany, and Austria.

The upturn to Cycle K came in March of 1879. It was preceded by an advance in stock prices which began 21 months earlier, and by an increase in security listings which also gained momentum 21 months earlier. Bond prices continued to advance during almost the entire duration of the preceding depression and their upturn took place 64 months before that of business. Interest rates were relatively low during the same years, and their downturn came 69 months before the upturn of business.

Cycle K lasted for 45 months and came to an end in September of 1885. The downturn was in December of 1882. It was preceded by downturns of bond prices and stock prices 18 months earlier. Interest rates turned upward 50 months before the downturn of business. In 1881, when business activity was at the high tide of full prosperity, security listings were running at the rate of nearly 400 million dollars a year. In midsummer bond and stock prices turned downward and then security listings turned downward.

The listings continued to fall so rapidly that by the summer of the next year they were running at scarcely more than the rate of 200 millions a year. In 1882, just after new listings reached their top, there were put into operation in this country 11,569 miles of new railroads, but in 1883, after new listings had declined, the construction of new railroads was only 6,745 miles, or a shrinkage of about 44 percent. It seems highly probable that the flow of new security issues decreased because market conditions had become unfavorable for their continued increase, and that their decrease was largely responsible for initiating a continuing shrinkage in railroad construction which continued until only 2,975 miles were built in the depression year of 1885.

CHAPTER IV

TWO DECADES OF DOUBTS ABOUT MONEY

The business and financial records of the 20 years beginning with 1883 and continuing through 1902 are shown in Diagram 4 on page 31. The first two years are repeated from Diagram 3. The 20 years included in the diagram cover all of the five cycles from L through P, and most of Cycle Q. The downturn of business which preceded the depression of 1884 has already been reviewed in the last chapter. The upturn from the depression came in September of 1885. It was preceded by a downturn of interest rates, followed successively by upturns in bond prices, in stock prices, and in security listings.

Cycle L got under way in September of 1885. It had a double top and its decisive downturn came in November of 1887. Its downturn was preceded in conventional fashion by an advance in interest rates followed in succession by declines in bond prices, in stock prices, and in security listings.

In the following upturn, which came in July of 1888, and introduced Cycle M, the conventional pattern was not complete. The upturn of business was preceded by a downturn of interest rates, and by upturns of bond and of stock prices, but not by an advance in security listings, which instead of increasing kept on declining for eight months after business had turned upward. It is interesting to note that business did not continue to advance. It moved upward for six months and then turned and declined for five more until it had dropped to just below the computed normal level.

By that time security listings had been moving upward for three months. It would be illuminating and valuable to have a better insight into the reasons why the pattern of business recovery in 1888 and 1889 makes it appear as though business had made a

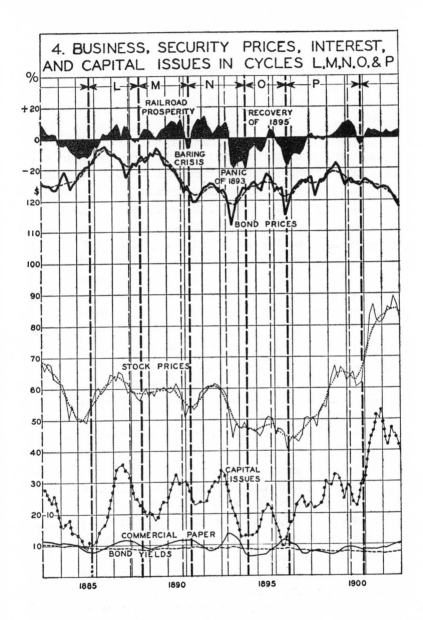

4. BUSINESS, SECURITY PRICES, INTEREST, AND CAPITAL ISSUES IN CYCLES L, M, N, O, & P

false start, and then had sunk back again to just below the normal line and made a new recovery start after the volume of security listings had finally turned upward. It may be that the records are distorted by some inadequacy of the statistical data, or perhaps there was some additional factor not included among the series shown here which was responsible for the upturn of business late in 1888.

Cycle M came to a sudden end in the Baring Crisis of 1890 and 1891. It seems probable that but for the intervention of that foreign crisis the cycle would have been somewhat longer than it actually was. The prominent London banking firm of Baring Brothers became heavily involved in speculative holdings of Argentine securities, and in November of 1890 decided to default on $105,000,000 of liabilities. This did not actually happen, for the important English banks combined to guarantee the creditors of the firm against loss, and announced their decision on November 14.

The action of the banks probably averted a serious English panic, and their plan was so successful that the creditors of Baring Brothers did not suffer loss, and the firm was reincorporated some years later and was able to continue in business. Nevertheless the crisis caused a serious degree of financial strain all over the world, and resulted in a sudden downturn of business in this country in October of 1890. The downturn was preceded by the familiar sequence of an upturn of interest rates, followed by downturns of bond prices, stock prices, and security listings in that order.

The upturn came only six months later and the pattern of the accompanying financial movements was unusual. Interest rates had turned downward only one month before, and stock prices had turned upward four months earlier. However, the lowest prices of bonds were not reached until five months after the upturn of business, and the security listings turned upward five months after business. It seems reasonable to believe that the foreign origin of the crisis produced changes in the financial series which were different from what they would have been if the cycle had come to an end as a result of developments predominantly of domestic origin.

Cycle N came to an end with the famous panic of 1893. The

downturn of business was in April of that year. The pattern of movements of the financial series was conventional enough, for interest rates had turned upward 10 months earlier, and that was followed by downturns of bond prices, stock prices, and security listings in that order. All these changes took place before the downturn of business.

Despite the normal character of these movements one cannot help wondering, as in the case of developments before the panic of 1873, whether the advance in interest rates, and the declines in security prices in the opening months of 1893, had been sufficiently drastic to cause a sharp curtailment in the flow of new capital into enterprise. There is much evidence to indicate that additional financial developments were creating conditions that were unfavorable to a continuation of the flow of capital investment into business.

In the years just before 1893 there was strong political agitation against the gold standard and in favor of bimetallism. There was much hoarding of currency. In 1890 and 1891 we lost large amounts of gold through exports. The Federal Treasury held 190 millions of gold in June of 1890, only 118 millions a year later, and only 95 millions in June of 1893. Our people were very much worried about their money, and increasingly inclined to hide it away instead of investing it. Under those circumstances it is fairly apparent that at the beginning of 1893 conditions were even more unfavorable for attracting a continued flow of new investment into enterprises than was revealed by the movement of security prices.

Cycle O was a brief period of recovery and even of business activity which may be said to have interrupted the long depression of the 1890's. It is sometimes referred to as the submerged business cycle of 1895. The upturn of business activity came in June of 1894 after interest rates had turned downward and bond prices had turned upward. Stock prices turned upward also in the same month as bond prices, but for many months before and after the business upturn stock prices fluctuated within a narrow range, and without any decided upward or downward trend. The 12 months total of security listings turned upward five months before the upturn of business, and then moved sideways for some nine months before making any important advance.

The following downturn of business came in October of 1895 after interest rates had turned upward and the three financial series had turned downward. The cycle came to an end in September of 1896, and Cycle P began in substantially the normal way. Bond prices and stock prices made their characteristic upward turns after interest rates had turned downward and one month before business activity turned upward. Security listings turned upward in September, which was the month of the business upturn, although the first considerable advance in business activity was not recorded until one month later. The upturn to Cycle P is another case in which the flow of new capital was increased after conditions in the security markets had become favorable for the initiation of new financing.

Cycle P finally brought an end to the long depression period of the 1890's. A vigorous recovery continued for more than three years from the upturn in the autumn of 1896 to February of 1900. In 1898 the war with Spain was in progress. The downturn of business in 1900 was preceded in approximately conventional fashion by an upturn in interest rates, and by downturns in bond prices, stock prices, and security listings. In this case the stock prices turned downward first, and then the security listings and the bond prices.

The downswing of Cycle P was brief, lasting only nine months, and the depression period was short and mild. The recovery from it was preceded by a decline in interest rates and by upturns in bond prices, stock prices, and security listings. In this instance the upturn of security listings came some months earlier than that of stock prices, but after the upturn of bond prices.

It should be noted that beginning with 1901 the index of business activity is in reality an index of the physical volume of industrial production. From 1901 to 1919 the annual totals are those of the Thomas index of manufacturing production with mining production added, while from 1919 to date the index is the Federal Reserve (Thomas) index of industrial production.

A summary of the records of the turning points of the first eight cycles (A through H) was given in Table 1 on page 19. Tables 2 and 3 give similar data for the next eight cycles which have been considered in this chapter and in the preceding one. These are Cycles I through P, and they cover the years from 1865 through 1900. The data of the upswings are summarized in Table 2, while those of the downswings are given in Table 3.

TABLE 2

Dates of upturns of business cycles I through P, durations of upswings, and months by which turns in short-term interest rates, security prices, and security listings preceded business upturns.

Cycle	Date of Upturn	Months of Upswing	Months by which turns preceded business upturn			
			Top of Interest	Bottom of Bonds	Bottom of Stocks	Bottom of Listings
I	Dec. 1865	42	3	−3	−16	—
J	Oct. 1870	27	14	10	−3	—
K	Mar. 1879	45	69	64	21	63
L	Sep. 1885	26	30	24	8	3
M	July 1888	27	14	9	1	−9
N	Apr. 1891	24	1	−5	4	−5
O	June 1894	16	13	10	10	5
P	Sep. 1896	41	3	1	1	0

TABLE 3

Dates of downturns of business cycles I through P, durations of downswings, and months by which turns in short-term interest rates, security prices, and security listings preceded business downturns.

Cycle	Date of Downturn	Months of Downswing	Months by which turns preceded business downturn			
			Bottom of Interest	Top of Bonds	Top of Stocks	Top of Listings
I	June 1869	16	32	31	32	—
J	Jan. 1873	74	21	6	9	7
K	Dec. 1882	33	50	18	18	17
L	Nov. 1887	8	25	16	6	4
M	Oct. 1890	6	21	16	5	4
N	Apr. 1893	14	11	9	8	3
O	Oct. 1895	11	14	2	1	1
P	Feb. 1900	9	30	8	10	9

It is noteworthy that there is distinctly more consistency in the patterns of the movements of the four financial series in the downturns, summarized in Table 3, than there is in their changes when they are related to the upturns as tabulated in the first of these two tables. In Table 2, which deals with the upturns, there are shown two instances in which the bottom of bond prices came after the business upturn, instead of before it. This is not astonishing since both came in abnormal periods, one at the close of the Civil War, and the other following the Baring Crisis.

There are two instances in which stock prices turned upward after business activity instead of before it. One of these was just after the Civil War, and the other was during the very mild depression of 1870. There are also two cases in which the security listings turned upward after the business upturn instead of before it. One of these was in 1889, and it has already been discussed on page 30. The second instance occurred just after the Baring Crisis. That is the doubtful case that has already been considered at some length.

No such discrepancies are shown in Table 3 which deals with the downturns. In that table there are shown no instances in which any of the financial series turned downward after the downturns of business. It is noteworthy also that there was a strong tendency for the business downturn to be preceded by the upturn of interest rates and by downturns of bond prices, stock prices, and security listings in that order. The sequence appears fully in three of the cycles, and small changes would have produced it in the four other cycles.

CHAPTER V

THE NEW CENTURY THROUGH THE WORLD WAR

CYCLE Q began in November of 1900, and was preceded by a decline in interest rates, and by advances in security listings, stock prices, and bond prices. For two years there was a great advance in the prices of railroad stocks. The volume of business in many lines was of record-breaking proportions. The panic of 1903, known as the Rich Man's Panic, was impending and its approach was indicated far in advance by financial developments which were in reality warning signals, but which were not at the time recognized for what they were.

The downturn came in April of 1903. For 29 months previously interest rates had been advancing, and during 26 months bond prices had been falling. Security listings turned downward 17 months before the downturn of business, and stock prices began to decline seven months before. The depression was not very long, and the reductions in production and employment were not particularly serious. It was reported that Mr. J. P. Morgan said in reply to a question that the cause of the panic was undigested securities.

He meant that the volume of new capital issues floated had been so great that the market for them had become saturated. Banks had lent heavily against bonds and stocks as collateral, and both banks and insurance companies had invested in large totals of the new securities. The upturn to Cycle R came in August of 1904, and was preceded by a decline in interest rates, and by advances in security listings, stock prices and bond prices.

The prices of bonds did not advance far or long. They entered upon a prolonged decline shortly after industrial production

37

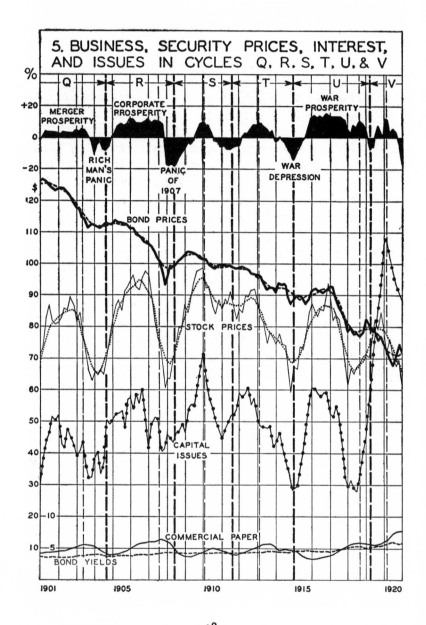

5. BUSINESS, SECURITY PRICES, INTEREST, AND ISSUES IN CYCLES Q, R, S, T, U, & V

reached prosperity levels, but stock prices and security listings advanced vigorously until late in 1906. The panic of 1907 was approaching. Industrial production turned downward in July of 1907. Interest rates had been advancing for 32 months, and bond prices had been declining for 29 months. Both stock prices and security listings had been moving downward for 10 months before the downturn of business.

The panic was sudden and severe. It was at its worst in October and November of 1907. In two months from October to December the volume of industrial production fell from nearly eight percent above the computed normal level to more than 17 percent below it. New railroad construction, which had amounted to nearly 6,200 miles in the year ended in June, 1907, fell to only 3,900 miles in 1908. Declines in security prices were most severe. The panic may be credited with bringing about the organization of the Federal Reserve System six years later, for it demonstrated that both our banking system and our money system had to be reformed.

Beginning in 1906 there becomes available another statistical series of monthly data of the volume of new security issues. This is the series compiled by the New York Journal of Commerce and it covers new security issues of domestic corporations. The issues include bonds, stocks, and notes, and cover both those issued for new capital and those floated for refunding old issues. This new series has been combined with the old series representing corporate issues listed on the New York Stock Exchange and sold for cash, and the two series have been so combined as to give them equal weight in the numbers represented by the ball-and-chain line in the diagrams. That line continues to represent a 12 months moving centered total.

The recovery introducing Cycle S began after a brief decline in interest rates, and after advances in bond prices, stock prices, and new issues. The upturn of the moving total of new issues came two months before bond and stock prices turned upward, but the month when the total of new issues was smallest came three months later than the upturns of bond and stock prices.

The downturn of the cycle came in January of 1910 after an advance in interest rates and a decline in bond prices, and only one month after downturns in stock prices and new issues. The decline of industrial production introduced a period of dull business in 1911 that was hardly serious enough to be considered a real depression.

The poor business of 1911 seems to have been largely caused by a sudden curtailment of railroad purchases, which resulted in greatly decreased demand for iron and steel products. In 1910 there were general advances in the wages paid to railroad workers. Some of the increases were granted in settlement of successful strikes, and others were ordered by the newly created Federal Arbitration Board. The railroad managements believed at the time that their operating costs would be increased as a result of the wage advances by as much as 150 million dollars a year, although the actual increases proved to be only about 100 millions a year.

In order to offset the unexpectedly increased operating costs they curtailed purchases, and in 1911 the production of rails fell about 23 percent below that of 1910. The managements planned to make up for the higher wages by instituting increased traffic rates but early in 1911 the Interstate Commerce Commission used its recently increased powers to decline to sanction higher tariffs for carrying freight and passengers. Probably these railroad developments largely account for the poorer business of 1911.

Technically the recovery came in the conventional way, for interest rates declined, and stock and bond prices and new issues advanced before industrial production turned upward. The advances of security prices were only moderate, and perhaps the most important influence in bringing about business improvement was the rather prompt adjustment that the railroads made in their operating practices in order to meet the new conditions.

Cycle T began in the summer of 1911 and reached its top in January of 1913. The downturn was preceded by advances in interest rates, and by declines in bond prices, new issues, and stock prices. The decline of industrial production which followed was to continue until after the outbreak of the World War. It was a severe decline which developed into a depression that was serious, but which proved to be brief because of the inflow of war orders in 1915.

The stock market was closed in 1914 during August, September, October and most of November, but an index has been constructed for those months by using the bid prices of 20 leading stocks quoted in the over-the-counter markets that were then in operation. That index clearly shows that the lowest stock prices of the period were recorded in October of 1914. It has been possible to find similar quotations for only six bonds, and that index also reached its lowest levels in October. These two short indexes have been used to close the gaps in the regular bond and stock indexes during the weeks that the Stock Exchange was closed.

The conditions attending the upturn of business after the outbreak of the World War were in many respects similar to those accompanying business recovery after the beginning of the Civil War. In both cases recovery was postponed until five months after hostilities had begun. In both periods stock and bond prices failed to register important advances until vigorous business recovery was well on its way. In the first two years of both wars interest rates declined sharply, and they remained low until business activity had risen to prosperity levels. It seems clear that in both cases business recovery was initially started off by war orders, and without much dependence on the flow of new capital into enterprise.

The downturn of Cycle U has been located in August of 1918. It was preceded by an advance in interest rates, and by declines in new issues, stock prices, and bond prices, but it cannot be supposed that those developments had much to do with causing the downturn to come when it did. The timing of the downturn of that cycle was surely destined to be decided by war developments and the prospects for peace, and not by ordinary operations of normal economic forces.

One unusual feature of the downturn from Cycle U is that the flow of security issues turned downward before the downturns of stock prices and bond prices. The amount of its decline was not large until after the declines of stock and bond prices were well under way, but it is noteworthy because there has been no previous case in which the flow of security issues began to decline before the downturn of bonds or stocks or both. The sharp decline in the flow of issues after we entered the war in the spring of 1917 was no doubt largely caused by the rulings of the Capital Issues Committee, which rigorously restricted new flotations during the war and sanctioned only those considered necessary.

The minor depression immediately following the war was brief. Its bottom was reached in March of 1919, and it was preceded by declining interest rates, and by advances of stock prices, new issues, and bond prices. Cycle V was exceptionally short. Its downturn came in February of 1920, and it was preceded by advancing interest rates, and by declines of bond prices, stock prices, and new issues. The most striking feature of Cycle V was an additional and post-war inflationary advance of wholesale commodity prices which reached its top in the spring of 1920.

Beginning in 1919 there becomes available another series of data covering the flotations of capital issues. This is the series compiled by the Commercial and Financial Chronicle. It constitutes an exceptionally complete and workmanlike piece of statistical reporting, and its classifications are so numerous that a running table of its data comprises 42 columns of figures. Data from it have been assembled so as to give each month the total in millions of dollars of the domestic corporate issues for refunding and for new capital minus those of investment trusts, trading companies, and holding companies after 1924.

The new series includes bonds, notes, common shares, and preferred shares. The data have been assembled into 12 months moving centered totals and combined with the two previous series in such a way as to give all three of them equal weights in the data represented by the ball-and-chain lines in the diagrams. This new combination is continued from 1919 to 1924 when still more data become available and further changes are made.

CHAPTER VI

THE NEW ERA AND THE GREAT DEPRESSION

THE final diagram of this series is Diagram 6 on page 44. It covers the 20 years from 1920 through 1939, and Cycles W, X, Y, and part of Z. The year 1920 is repeated from the preceding diagram. The downswing of business in Cycle V, from the peak of prosperity in February of 1920 to the upturn from the following depression in July of 1921, was greater in amount than any previous downswing. The peak of prosperity was over 12 percent above the computed normal level, and the trough of the depression was 27 percent below the normal level.

The total downswing to the Primary Post War Depression was over 39 points. The longest previous downswings, measured in the same way, were those of 33 points each in Cycles B and C, not far from 100 years before. The upturn from the depression was preceded by declining interest rates, advancing bond prices and an increasing volume of security issues. Stock prices did not turn upward until one month after the business upturn.

In following these movements on Diagram 6 it should be noted that the scale at the left for stock and bond prices and security issues is quite different from those used in the preceding diagrams of the series. This has been necessitated by the fact that no more than 140 units have been previously needed to show the extreme top ranges of the financial series. Conditions were so entirely different in the great speculative era which came to an end in 1929 that in this diagram the financial scale has a range of 240 units.

Interest rates rose and bond prices declined for seven months before the top of Cycle W was reached in April of 1923. Security issues also declined for six months and stock prices for one month

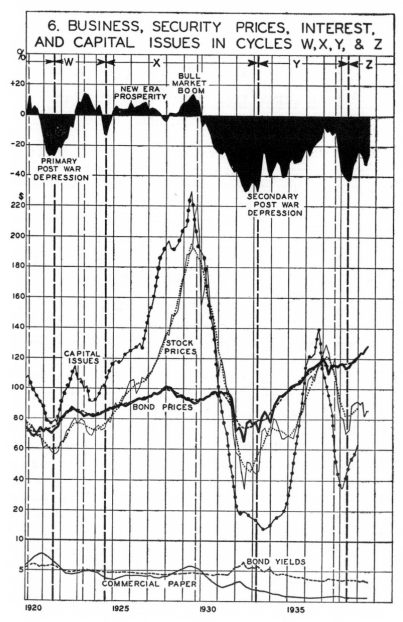

6. BUSINESS, SECURITY PRICES, INTEREST, AND CAPITAL ISSUES IN CYCLES W, X, Y, & Z

44

before the downturn of business. The following depression in 1924 was relatively deep but it lasted for so brief a period that its business and financial consequences were not very serious. Industrial production fell almost as far as it did in 1914 or in 1885, but recovery came so promptly that the depression has been almost forgotten except by students of business cycles.

Interest rates declined, and bond and stock prices and security issues advanced before the upturn in July of 1924. The upturn which introduced Cycle X was the beginning of a period of five years of nearly unbroken prosperity. It was a period of enormous speculative activity in stocks and in real estate. When it began in 1924 we had about 17 million automobiles, and five years later in 1929 we had not far from 27 millions. We doubled our mileage of hard-surfaced highways. We largely rebuilt the business sections of our cities, and created far-spreading suburbs, and we experienced the greatest building boom of our history.

Prosperity lasted so long, and permeated so many kinds of business activity, that it came to be rather generally believed that we had entered upon a genuine new era in which the problems of abundant production had been largely solved, while those of equitable distribution were well on their way toward solution. There was a minor business downturn in 1927 which was not sufficiently important to be considered as marking the end of a cycle. There was a coal strike in that year, and disastrous floods in the Mississippi Valley, but the real explanation of the brief downturn seems to be that the great Ford automobile plants were closed down for some months while a change of model was being made.

Another compilation of data reporting the flotations of security issues is introduced in 1924 into the series of new issues represented by the ball-and-chain line in the diagrams. The new series is that of the Standard Statistics Company. It is another competent and valuable record of statistical reporting. The figures used here represent the data of domestic corporate issues floated for operating and producing purposes. Canadian issues and those of Newfoundland are included with domestic issues, but other foreign issues are excluded. The issues of banks, investment trusts, insurance companies, and holding companies are excluded.

When this new series of the Standard Statistics Company is introduced into the record of security issues in 1924, it replaces the tabulation of stock exchange listings. From 1924 to 1933 the ball-and-chain line in the diagram represents a combination of the three series taken from the tabulations of the New York Journal of Commerce, the Commercial and Financial Chronicle, and the Standard Statistics Company. The three series are given equal weights in the combination, and the ball-and-chain line continues to represent a 12 months moving centered total.

The flotations of security issues mounted to such high levels during the boom years of the New Era period that one cannot help wondering why the inflow of such enormous sums into the treasuries of corporations did not result in lifting the volumes of industrial production to even higher levels than those that are recorded in the years from 1925 through 1929. Most of the explanation is to be found in the evidence of the production records of former years which clearly indicate that after the volume of industrial production has been lifted in times of prosperity to levels about 10 percent above the computed normal level, it becomes extremely difficult and expensive to lift them much further.

Perhaps the validity of this generalization is best exemplified by the records of production during the years of the World War. It is true that in those years industrial output was lifted to high levels by the insatiable demands of war and by the eager spendings by governments which were untrammeled by any necessity for making profits out of their transactions. Even so, a person not versed in the detailed statistics of the production records might hesitate to pick out the war period on a diagram showing the course of industrial output during the first three decades of this century, if the diagram did not carry dates and was not subdivided by years.

In the black silhouettes showing monthly changes in the volume of industrial production in these diagrams the average level above normal in 1906 was 10.2 percent. In 1916 during the World War it was 13.8 percent. In the first year of our participation in the war it was 11.9 percent, and in 1918 when the war came to a close it was only 7.0 percent. In 1923 it was 8.9 percent, and the average for the first nine months of 1929 was 11.1 percent.

Another reason why the immense volume of new financing during the New Era period did not result in lifting the volume of industrial production to even more notably high levels appears to be that a considerable part of the new funds raised by corporations was not expended for the production of goods. The financial reports of all corporations made annually to the Treasury Department indicate that in the five year period from 1925 through 1929 non-financial companies increased their holdings of cash by over a billion and a quarter dollars.

Their investments advanced by nearly five and a half billions, and their miscellaneous assets increased by seven and a quarter billions. A considerable part of the money the corporations received as new capital through the sale of security issues in the five year period was obtained in the first three-quarters of the last year of prosperity just before the stock market crash of 1929. If the companies had obtained that money earlier it is entirely likely that a larger proportion of it would have been used to pay for new plants, extensions, and new equipment than was actually the case.

The downturn from the long period of New Era prosperity has been located in September of 1929 when stock prices started on their great decline. The highest level of industrial production came in June of 1929, but factory employment held up well into September, and nearly every consideration concerning the business conditions which prevailed in 1929 leads to the conclusion that the downturn of that cycle coincided in time with the downturn of its spectacular stock market speculation.

When the downturn of the cycle came, short-term interest rates had been advancing for 56 months. Bond prices had been declining for 21 months, but later on they regained most of the ground lost in that decline, and there seems to be little basis for believing that the decrease in bond prices was of much influence in bringing about the business downturn. The flow of security issues turned downward four months before the downturn of business, and again it is hard to believe that the decrease in new flotations had much to do with the downturn of business in 1929.

In 1929 the volume of new capital raised through the sale of stock issues was more than three times as great as that realized from the marketing of bonds. Until the downturn of stock prices came in September new capital could be raised with the utmost ease for almost any plausible purpose through the sale of common stocks. Because of those circumstances Cycle X is in a class by itself. It is even more exceptional than the cycles of the Civil War and World War periods. We may well be astonished to find that in 1929 the movements of the financial series conformed as closely as they did to normal patterns, but our memories of the period must convince us that the dominating economic factor of the time was the feverish speculation in stocks and its final collapse.

The downswing of Cycle X lasted for 42 months, and came to an end in March of 1933, which was the month of the bank crisis. When the upturn came interest rates had been falling for 45 months and bond and stock prices had been advancing for nine months. The upturn in security issues did not come until six months after the upturn in business, and even then its advance was very slow for another year. It is difficult to reach judgments about the economic significance of the movements of security issues in that period, for they were much influenced by new legislation.

In July of 1933 there was put into effect the federal Securities Act, which required the registration at Washington of new issues of securities except those of railroads and of such public governmental divisions as states and municipalities. The requirements for registration were so rigorous that the flow of new issues that had to be registered sharply decreased in the months following the enactment of the new law, although that of securities not requiring registration increased. In July of 1934 the Securities Exchange Act went into effect, and its requirements were much less rigorous than those of its predecessor. It is impossible to judge what the record of new issues would have been in 1933 in the absence of the new legislation, but it is clear that with respect to security issues that year is not comparable with other years of business upturns.

Beginning in 1934 still another series of data is combined with the three previous series reporting the issues of securities. The new one is that of the Securities and Exchange Commission reporting the cash proceeds of new securities registered. The proceeds used for the purchase of securities of other corporations are omitted, and since railroad securities are not registered with the Commission, those reported by the Commercial and Financial Chronicle are added as though they were registered. The new series is given a weight equal to that given to each of the three other series, and the ball-and-chain line continues to represent a 12 months moving centered total.

The downturn of Cycle Y came in August of 1937. It was preceded by a minute advance of interest rates 11 months earlier, and by declines in security issues, bond prices, and stock prices. The flow of new security issues turned downward after September of 1936, four months before the downturn of bond prices and six months before that of stock prices. This circumstance is worth noting, for among the 16 downturns of business in the cycles since the records of listings and issues became available, there is only one previous case in which the volume of securities began to decline before the downturns of both bonds and stocks.

That instance was in the downturn from the World War prosperity in Cycle U, but that case is not comparable with the others, for during the war much of the expansion of productive capacity needed for filling war orders was financed by grants of bank credit guaranteed by the warring nations that were purchasing the goods. It is to be noted also that the decline in security issues during the war was only of minor proportions until after the declines in stock and bond prices had gained considerable importance.

It is especially difficult to arrive at satisfactory judgments about the causes of the early downturn of the flow of security issues in 1936 because of the many new factors that are involved. By 1936

the Stock Exchange was operating under the new controls, regulations, and prohibitions of the Securities Act of 1933, the Securities
Exchange Act of 1934, the Banking Act of 1935, and the Public
Utility Holding Company Act of 1935. The downturn in the floating
of security issues in 1936 was not caused by a reduction in the totals
of new issues sold by corporations to secure additional capital, but
rather by a sudden contraction in the refunding of old bond issues
of public utilities.

That reduction in the volume of refunding may have resulted
from the cumulative restrictions of the requirements of registrations, but it seems more likely that it was influenced by a ruling of
the Federal Reserve authorities requiring member banks to increase
their reserves by 50 percent beginning in August of 1936. It was
widely believed at the time that this requirement would constitute
a strong restraint against credit expansion, and the large New York
banks began promptly to sell parts of their holdings of federal
securities. Within some 15 months they sold nearly one and a half
billion dollars of them. That liquidation began in July and the flow
of security issues turned downward after September, and the two
declines may be closely related.

The downswing of Cycle Y lasted for only nine months from
August of 1937 to May of 1938. The upturn to Cycle Z was not
preceded by any real change in the levels of short-term interest
rates. Bond prices turned upward 13 months before the upturn of
business and stock prices one month before. The flow of capital
issues turned upward four months before business. It will probably
be generally agreed that the real cause of the business upturn in
May of 1938 was that in that month federal legislation was enacted
appropriating huge sums of public funds for expenditures designed
to stimulate a new business recovery.

Tables 4 and 5 on page 51 summarize the statistical facts about
the durations of the last 10 cycles, and the turning points of production and the financial series, much as Table 1 on page 19 gave the
information for the first eight cycles, and Tables 2 and 3 on page
35 gave the data for the next eight cycles.

TABLE 4

Dates of upturns of Cycles Q through Z, months of upswings, and months by which upturns of industrial production were preceded by the tops of interest rates, and the bottoms of bond prices, stock prices, and security issues.

Cycle	Date of Upturn	Months of Upswing	Months by which turns preceded business upturn			
			Top of Interest	Bottom of Bonds	Bottom of Stocks	Bottom of Security Issues
Q	Nov. 1900	29	9	11	2	5
R	Aug. 1904	35	14	5	10	12
S	May 1908	20	9	6	6	8
T	July 1911	18	13	11	12	7
U	Dec. 1914	44	20	2	2	1
V	Mar. 1919	11	8	6	15	10
W	July 1921	21	8	14	−1	2
X	July 1924	62	10	15	9	9
Y	Mar. 1933	53	45	9	9	−6
Z	May 1938	—	8	13	1	4

TABLE 5

Dates of downturns of Cycles Q through Z, months of downswings, and months by which downturns of industrial production were preceded by the bottoms of interest rates, and the tops of bond prices, stock prices, and security issues.

Cycle	Date of Downturn	Months of Downswing	Months by which turns preceded business downturn			
			Bottom of Interest	Top of Bonds	Top of Stocks	Top of Security Issues
Q	Apr. 1903	16	29	26	7	17
R	July 1907	10	32	29	10	10
S	Jan. 1910	18	11	11	1	1
T	Jan. 1913	23	16	11	4	7
U	Aug. 1918	7	31	19	21	33
V	Feb. 1920	17	8	15	7	1
W	Apr. 1923	15	7	7	1	6
X	Sep. 1929	42	56	21	0	4
Y	Aug. 1937	9	11	7	5	11
Z		—	—	—	—	—

Tables 4 and 5 continue to exhibit the consistency with which the characteristic movements of the financial series precede the upturns and downturns of the business cycles. The only important exception in Table 4 is that in the upturn to Cycle W in 1921 when stocks turned upward a month after the upturn of business. The exception in Cycle Y in 1933 when security issues were late in turning upward has already been discussed.

The data of Table 5 are more consistently regular than are those of Table 4. The pattern of the movements of the financial series is more faithfully followed in relation to the downturns of business cycles than it is in relation to the upturns. There is no case in Table 5 in which one of the turns of a financial series came after the downturn of the business cycle. The rule has been that interest rates have advanced first and that their advance has been followed by declines of bond prices, stock prices, and security issues. This sequence has not been as closely adhered to in the cycles of Table 5 as it was in those of Table 3, but nevertheless the data of both tables show pretty definitely that there has been a strong tendency for the movements to follow that rule.

Chapter VII

THE DATA OF SECURITY ISSUES

The student who wishes to use the statistics of American security issues has available six sources of data, and unfortunately the information of all of them falls short of being fully satisfactory. The source furnishing the earliest material is the listing statements of the New York Stock Exchange. Monthly data from these listing statements have been compiled as a part of this study for the 61 years from 1863 through 1923. The data do not have enough volume to be of much significance until about 1872. The series has been described in Chapter III.

These data cover the listing of securities of domestic, non-financial corporations which were shown by the statements to have been sold for cash. In many instances the statements do not give information clearly showing whether the sales were made for money or in exchange for properties or other securities, and in such cases the issues were omitted from the compilations. These numerous omissions constitute one of the shortcomings of the new series. The data include both the securities sold to obtain new capital and those floated to refund old issues, and the near impossibility of tabulating the two classes separately is another shortcoming.

The data cover the listings on only one exchange, and they omit most railroad equipment issues, and most note issues. In the early years they consist almost entirely of data of bond issues, for in the early decades of the series stocks were seldom listed until long after they had been issued. The new series furnishes us with a probably trustworthy indicator of the major changes in the volume of the public takings of new corporate securities that were sold for money. Its great value is that it covers many decades in which we have no other source of similar information.

Another series becomes available beginning in 1906. This is made up of monthly data of the volume of new security issues as compiled by the New York Journal of Commerce. It covers the capital issues of domestic corporations which were offered in amounts of $100,000 or over. Both new capital issues and refunding issues are included, and the figures cover bonds, notes, and stocks. In 1906 and the next few years the money volume of the Journal of Commerce series is about three times as large as that of the series taken from the Stock Exchange listings.

In Diagram 7 on page 55 the solid line shows the changes from 1907 through 1923 in the volume of the issues compiled from the listing statements. The line is a 12 months moving centered total. The dashed line shows the changes in the volume of capital issues as compiled by the Journal of Commerce. This line is also a 12 months moving centered total and the data have been multiplied by a constant so as to make the totals of the two series equal for the 17 year period.

The agreement between the two series is only fairly good, but they do show the same cyclical advances and declines with a reasonable degree of accord. In the last five years covered by the diagram there is still another line which is dotted. This dotted line represents changes in the data of new capital and refunding issues of domestic corporations as compiled by the Commercial and Financial Chronicle. This line also is a 12 months moving centered total, and the data have been multiplied by a constant to make their total for the five years equal to that of the listings series in the same period. The agreement between this line and the other two is fairly good.

The diagram illustrates some of the difficulties encountered in dealing with the statistics of security issues. Except for the listings series, the data are compilations of material gathered from the most varied sources, and combined by methods which may have changed from time to time over the years. Fortunately they agree fairly well in their major swings, and in their turning points, but clearly they cannot be considered as representing precise records of the economic phenomena which they represent.

The series taken from the compilations of the Commercial and Financial Chronicle has been described in Chapter V. It begins in 1919. In 1924 there becomes available the series of data compiled by the Standard Statistics Company, and this series has been described in Chapter VI. There is not good agreement even in recent times among the figures of the three series which purport to measure the volumes of approximately the same categories of security issues.

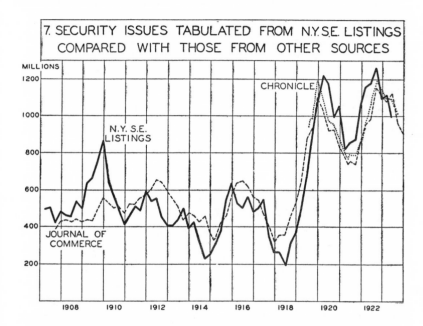

In 1925 the total of the Journal series is 3.64 billions, while the Chronicle total is 4.72 billions, and the Standard Statistics total is 4.18 billions.

These are serious differences, for the Chronicle total is more than a billion dollars greater than that of the Journal of Commerce, while the Standard Statistics total is about halfway between the other two. These differences are not at all constant in nature, for in 1930 the Journal total is 5.22 billions, while that of the Chronicle is almost the same at 5.24 billions, and the Standard Statistics total is 4.53 billions. In 1935 the Journal total is 2.67 billions, while the Chronicle total is 2.26 billions, and that of Standard Statistics is closely similar at 2.15 billions.

The discrepancies between the Chronicle series and that of the Standard Statistics Company are by no means limited to the rather serious differences between their annual totals. There is much disagreement between them as to the proportions by which the monthly totals were divided into issues for new capital and those sold for refunding old issues. Diagram 8 on page 57 shows the monthly changes in the new-capital issues and in the refunding issues of the Chronicle series from 1919 through 1938, and in those of the Standard Statistics series from 1924 through 1938. All these data lines are 12 months moving centered totals. The solid lines represent issues for new capital, while the dashed lines represent the refunding issues. The black silhouette at the top of the diagram represents the index of industrial production.

The lines in the diagram clearly show that during the eight years from 1924 through 1931 the tabulations of the Chronicle allocated a far higher proportion of the securities to the classification of issues for new capital than did those of the Standard Statistics series. In those eight years the total issues tabulated by the Chronicle amounted to 43.62 billions, and 80.5 percent of them were classified as being sold for new capital. The total issues of the Standard Statistics tabulations in the same eight years amounted to 37.11 billions, and the amount classified as being for new capital was only 58.6 percent of the total in contrast to the Chronicle's 80.5 percent.

It is regrettable that the differences are so great, for it is highly important in the study of capital formation to know whether the security issues sold to obtain new capital in a period of eight years amounted to about 81 percent of all new issues, or to only about 59 percent of them. For many years the Commercial and Financial Chronicle published annual totals showing the volume of issues listed on the New York Stock Exchange that were sold for new capital and the totals of those sold for refunding. These data are available beginning in 1885.

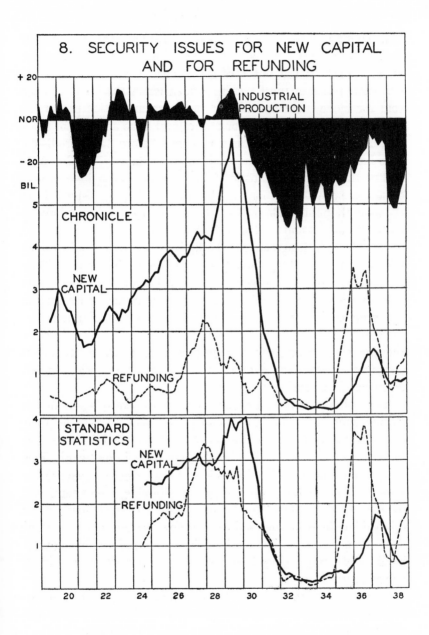

8. SECURITY ISSUES FOR NEW CAPITAL AND FOR REFUNDING

INDUSTRIAL PRODUCTION

CHRONICLE

NEW CAPITAL

REFUNDING

STANDARD STATISTICS

NEW CAPITAL

REFUNDING

In connection with the tabulation of listings compiled for this study, an attempt was made to analyze and verify some of these annual totals. It was unsuccessful because it was found that the Chronicle totals of those years included issues that had not been sold for money, but had instead been exchanged for properties, and they included as issues for new capital large amounts of stock that had been outstanding for many years before they were listed. It is interesting to note that since 1934 the data of the Chronicle and of the Standard Statistics Company have been in relatively close agreement, and it may be that this has in part resulted from the monthly publication of the data of new registrations tabulated by the Securities and Exchange Commission.

Despite their disagreements the lines of Diagram 8 tell us some highly important things about the flows of capital issues. They clearly show that in the period covered the cyclical turns of the refunding issues have come much earlier than have those of the issues for new capital. In 1920 the volume of refunding issues of the Chronicle tabulations turned upward in the summer just after the time when bond prices turned upward in Cycle V. It turned downward in the early autumn of 1922, when bond prices turned downward in Cycle W.

The volume of refunding issues turned upward again in the closing weeks of 1923 when bond prices were starting on their long advance of the New Era period, and it turned downward at the close of 1927 just before bond prices turned downward. This downturn of the refunding issues late in 1927 also took place at the same time in the line representing the refunding issues tabulated by the Standard Statistics Company. Both dashed lines turned upward late in 1933, and both turned downward in the autumn of 1936 when the great New York banks were rapidly reducing their holdings of bonds, as has been noted in Chapter VI. Both turned upward early in 1938.

Probably it is true that the flow of refunding issues of securities typically makes its cyclical turns almost coincidently with the cyclical turns of bond prices. The evidence is not quite as clear with respect to the cyclical turns of the series representing issues sold for new capital, but the rule during the past 20 years has been that these series have made their cyclical turns at approximately the times of the turns of stock prices.

The solid line representing the Chronicle series of issues sold for new capital turned downward at the end of 1919 just after stock prices turned downward. It turned upward with stock prices in the summer of 1921, and downward again late in 1922 before the final downturn of stock prices. It turned upward early in 1923 before the turn of stock prices. In 1929 the Chronicle line turned downward in the middle of the year before the end of the great bull market, but that of Standard Statistics turned early in 1930 after the downturn of stocks. In 1937 the lines of both series turned downward just before the downturn of stock prices.

It appears to be quite reasonable that the flow of refinancing should swell and diminish in close accord with the cyclical advances and declines of bond prices. Refinancing or refunding issues are preponderantly bonds, and include only small amounts of common and preferred stocks. Bonds issued for refinancing are in part issues floated to take the place of previous issues of the same corporations that are maturing. Much of such refinancing is done without great regard for the conditions existing in financial markets when the maturity dates are approaching, for in general the companies that must refund maturing issues have little choice or leeway either as to time or as to terms, although they will of course try to carry through the operations on conditions as favorable to themselves as possible.

The case is quite different with respect to bond issues that are to be called and replaced by new ones carrying lower coupons, and having perhaps other conditions more favorable to the borrower than were those of the old issue. Such refundings must be made when market conditions are favorable for them, and that means when bond prices are rising. If the operation is postponed until the long advance in bond prices has given way to a decline, they will almost surely be first postponed and then abandoned until the next cycle comes along.

The raising of new capital is not so directly related to the movements of bond prices, for it is primarily a concomitant of business expansion, and as such it depends pretty closely on advancing stock markets. This is particularly the case if the raising of new capital is to be done wholly or partly through the sale of stock, for then both the facility with which the sales of shares can be made, and the amounts which can be realized from them, will depend in large degree on the conditions prevailing in the stock market.

There is not good agreement between the different series of available data about security issues in even such a simple distinction as that of the relative proportions of the totals that were made up of stocks. For example in the 11 years from 1919 through 1929 the figures compiled by the Journal of Commerce show that 38 percent of the dollar values of the issues consisted of stocks, while the rest was made up of bonds and notes. For the same years the data of the Commercial and Financial Chronicle give a closely similar grand total, but show that only 34 percent consisted of stocks.

Both series do agree, however, in showing that in years of serious depression nearly all the financing is done by means of the sale of bonds, while in times of prosperity, and particularly in years of strong advancing stock markets, much larger proportions of it are done through the marketing of new stock issues.

Thus in 1919, when there was a strong stock market, only about 45 percent of the value of the issues sold consisted of bonds, but two years later in the depression of 1921 the proportion of bond sales was about 85 percent of all. At the top of the great bull market for stocks in 1929 only about 36 percent of the dollar volume of new issues sold consisted of bonds, but in 1938 about 95 percent of the sales were made up of bond issues.

Probably it is true that one of the important symptoms of a healthy economic condition in this country is to be found in the possibility of marketing a considerable volume of stocks to raise new capital. Nevertheless when that possibility becomes extremely ample, as in 1929, the condition is unwholesome, and when it almost disappears, as it did in 1938, that condition also is unwholesome.

Diagram 9 on page 61 has been drawn to illustrate the fact that even since the appearance of the new official data covering the registration of security issues there is little month-to-month agreement among the available series of statistical information on these matters. The three lines in the diagram represent the monthly data during 1936 and 1937 of the reports on issues for new capital made by the Commercial and Financial Chronicle, The Standard Statistics Company, and the Securities and Exchange Commission. This last set of data has been increased by adding to the figures of

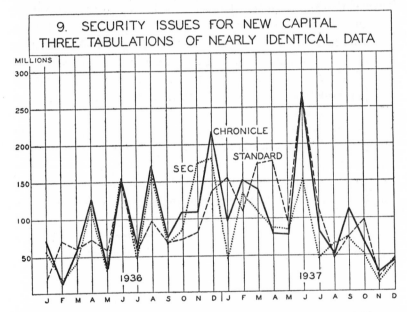

9. SECURITY ISSUES FOR NEW CAPITAL
THREE TABULATIONS OF NEARLY IDENTICAL DATA

the Commission those of the Chronicle reporting railroad issues, for these are not registered by the Commission.

There can be no doubt that the volume of these issues sold for new capital was rising during most of 1936, and that it was falling during much of 1937, but it would be difficult to be sure that the data tell much more than that. The totals of the three series for the two years are close together, but their month-to-month disagreements are numerous and serious. It is because of such conditions that the practice has been adopted in this study of using 12 months moving centered totals of the data, instead of the monthly figures, and of combining all the available series in the belief that the resulting combination would yield results more trustworthy than those of any single series by itself.

There is still another series of data relating to security issues, but it has not been utilized in this study. It is a series compiled by Moody's Investors Service from the data compiled by the Commercial and Financial Chronicle. The Moody organization have believed that the Chronicle data have included under the classification of securities sold for new capital many issues that were primarily financial in nature, and that did not genuinely constitute new capital. Mr. Adam Gortomski of the Moody organization has accordingly reworked the Chronicle data so as to segregate the clearly productive capital issues of corporations and municipalities monthly back to 1921.

This Moody series should clearly receive careful attention by anyone who is primarily interested in separating for recent years the issues sold for new capital from the refunding issues. The reclassification of the data has been done with great care, but it may have been carried out somewhat too rigorously, for the corporate totals of new productive capital since 1934 seem too small when they are compared with the figures for the same years compiled by the Securities and Exchange Commission.

CHAPTER VIII

THE TYPICAL CYCLE

IN an earlier chapter it was noted that business cycles never repeat. Each one is an historical individual. Business cycles are irregular in size and irregularly spaced, and they have widely varying characteristics. Because all business cycles are highly individualistic, and each is different from all the others, a typical cycle is of necessity a kind of mathematical abstraction. It is not closely similar to any actual cycle, but in each feature and characteristic it represents as nearly as may be the central tendencies of many of them.

It is worth while to attempt to construct a typical cycle because the result is a simplified and conventionalized picture of a series of changes that are so beset by irregularities in their original historical forms that they are difficult to study because of their complications. The conventionalized picture presented by a typical cycle facilitates study. It promotes understanding of the changing relationships that are always going forward between and among the major financial series that participate in the successive phases as the cycle expands from depression to prosperity, and then contracts from prosperity back down again to depression.

The material reviewed in this study covers the records of the changes which took place in five series of data during the histories of 24 complete business cycles, and in parts of two others, making 26 in all. These five series are those of business activity, short-term interest rates, bond prices, stock prices, and security issues. This last series is not present until the Civil War period. The data of interest rates are 12 place moving centered averages, and those of security issues are 12 place moving centered totals.

The records of these series were followed through from the initial trough of each cycle up to its peak, and then down to the concluding trough. A count was made of the number of months that elapsed from the upturn of business with which each cycle began to the low of interest rates which normally comes a little later than the business upturn. Then the months were counted from the low of interest rates to the high of bond prices, from the high of bond prices to the high of stock prices, and from the high of stock prices to the peak of business activity.

These successive turning points normally occur in that order during the business upswing of each cycle. After the peak of business was reached, the count was continued on the downswing of each cycle from the top of business to the top of interest rates, from that point to the low of bond prices, and from that low to the low of stock prices. Where there were two or more months of unchanged interest rates or bond or stock prices at the top or bottom of any swing, the latest one was taken as being the turning point.

The results of these counts for the 25 cycles lettered A through Y are given in Table 6 on page 65. Minus signs are used in the table to designate instances in which turns of series preceded those of other series which they would normally have followed. For example in the first line of the table the sixth entry is —1. This means that in Cycle A the low of bond prices occurred one month before the top of interest rates instead of following it as it usually does. Zeros appearing in the table mean that the turning points of the two series came together in the same month without either lag or lead. The first four columns of figures apply to the upswings of the cycles and the second four to the downswings. The eight numbers in the first line of the table really tell in outline the history of Cycle A; those in the second line tell the history of Cycle B, and so on.

The figures in each of the eight columns of the table were arranged in ascending order from the largest negative number to the largest positive one, and their medians were found. Then arithmetic means were found of the nine numbers in each column comprising the median, the four numbers next above the median, and the four numbers next below the median. Finally somewhat arbitrary decisions were made as to the numbers of months which

TABLE 6

Months by which turning points followed one another in 25 business cycles,
A through Y.

Cycle	Low of Business to Low of Interest	Low of Interest to Top of Bonds	Top of Bonds to Top of Stocks	Top of Stocks to Top of Business	Top of Business to Top of Interest	Top of Interest to Low of Bonds	Low of Bonds to Low of Stocks	Low of Stocks to Low of Business
A	13	24	8	4	7	−1	−2	8
B	9	−10	11	18	−2	5	1	10
C	8	−16	13	6	8	29	0	10
D	9	11	34	1	9	−4	9	1
E	44	0	4	15	7	−1	3	0
F	7	−2	2	14	10	3	0	3
G	8	23	1	0	4	4	1	3
H	14	20	−3	11	6	6	13	−16
I	10	1	−1	32	2	4	13	−3
J	6	15	−3	9	5	5	43	21
K	−5	32	0	18	3	6	16	8
L	1	9	10	6	−6	5	8	1
M	6	5	11	5	5	6	−9	4
N	13	2	1	8	1	3	0	10
O	2	12	1	1	8	2	0	1
P	11	22	−2	10	0	−2	9	2
Q	0	3	19	7	2	9	−5	10
R	3	3	19	10	1	3	0	6
S	9	0	10	1	5	2	−1	12
T	2	5	7	4	3	18	0	2
U	13	12	−2	21	−1	2	−9	15
V	3	−7	8	7	9	−6	15	−1
W	14	0	6	1	5	−5	6	9
X	6	35	21	0	−3	36	0	9
Y	42	4	2	5	1	−5	12	1

would be considered to constitute the typical spacings from turning
point to turning point within the typical cycle. These medians,
means of median groups, and typical spacings were as follows:

	Medians	Means of Median Groups	Typical Spacings
Upswings			
Low of business to low of interest............	8	8.0	8
Low of interest to top of bond prices.........	5	6.0	6
Top of bond prices to top of stock prices.....	6	5.3	6
Top of stock prices to top of business........	7	7.0	7
Downswings			
Top of business to top of interest............	4	3.8	4
Top of interest to low of bond prices.........	3	3.4	3
Low of bond prices to low of stock prices.....	1	2.1	1
Low of stock prices to low of business........	4	5.0	5
	38	40.6	40

If the primary purpose of this part of the study were that of attempting to determine the length of the business cycle, this statistical procedure could not be well defended, for it produces a typical cycle that is shorter than the median of all the cycles considered. The 25 cycles included in Table 6 have a median length of 45 months, and the median of their upswings plus the median of their downswings is 43 months. Nevertheless there is a good deal to be said in favor of selecting 40 months as the length of the typical cycle.

One good reason for doing so is that 40 months is approximately the sum of the means of the median groups of monthly measures from turning point to turning point of all the American business cycles of the past 100 years. Moreover several careful earlier studies of this matter have reached the conclusion that 40 months is the best typical measurement of cycle length. In the Review of Economic Statistics for January 1923, both Professor W. L. Crum and Mr. Joseph Kitchin report studies which reach that conclusion.

Professor Wesley C. Mitchell in his book, "Business Cycles, The Problem and Its Setting," concludes that 40 months is the median value of observations on the duration of American cycles from 1878 through 1923. This finding is based on an analysis of the data of 101 cycles taken from five indexes of business conditions. Bulletin 69 of the National Bureau of Economic Research, published in May of 1938, presents data on the duration in months of the expansions and contractions of 20 business cycles from 1855 through 1933. The sum of the median of the expansions, and the median of the contractions is 40 months, although the median full duration of the 20 cycles is 41.5 months.

After it had been decided to consider the length of the typical cycle as being 40 months, attention was given to the 16 cycles which include records of the swings of capital issues. It was found that the median of months elapsed from the high of stock prices to the high of issues was zero, but that there were three cycles in which it was one month, and no other measurement occurred as many as three times. It was also found that the median of months from the low of stock prices to the low of issues was 1.5, and that the mean of the six measures nearest the median was 1.8.

The evidence indicates rather indecisively that both of these measures should be considered as being one month, although almost as good an argument could be made for considering them as being zero and two. The trouble is, of course, that we do not have data for enough cycles to enable us to reach firm conclusions about central tendencies. To do that with confidence we should need data for several times as many cycles as are available. Since we do not have them we must make the best use we can of those we have. The decisions about the spacing of the turning points of security issues leave us with a final time-table of the months from turning point to turning point in the typical cycle as follows:

Upswings	Months
Low of business to low of interest............................	8
Low of interest to top of bond prices.........................	6
Top of bond prices to top of stock prices.....................	6
Top of stock prices to top of issues..........................	1
Top of issues to top of business..............................	6
Downswings	
Top of business to top of interest............................	4
Top of interest to low of bond prices.........................	3
Low of bond prices to low of stock prices.....................	1
Low of stock prices to low of issues..........................	1
Low of issues to low of business..............................	4
	40

The next step in the construction of the typical cycle was that of finding the contours of the patterns followed by the five series for which the sequences of turning points had been found. For this purpose only cycles including the security issues were used, and the highly exceptional cycles were eliminated from that list. The cycle of the long depression of the 1870's and the long cycle following it were omitted, as was the submerged cycle of 1895. The World War cycle and the brief one following it were eliminated, as were the cycles of the New Era period and the Great Depression. Those used were the cycles lettered L, M, N, Q, R, S, T, and W.

The monthly data of business activity in these cycles were tabulated by placing under one another the eight numbers representing business in the peak month of each cycle, and then at the left the figures for business one month before the peak, two months before, and so on out to those 26 months before the peaks. In similar fashion figures were tabulated to the right of the peak figures showing business one month after the peak, two months after, and so on out to 13 months after. Then the eight rows of numbers were added and their averages were found.

When the work of combining the monthly figures of business activity of the eight cycles for the 26 months preceding their peaks, and for the 13 months following them was completed, the process was carried through again by putting the eight numbers for business activity at the troughs of the cycles under one another and tabulating the data for the months preceding and following the troughs. This gave new and different sets of averages for the upswings and the downswings, and the new sets were then combined with the first sets, and then slight adjustments were made to bring the two sets of figures together at the peaks and at the troughs. The resulting combined data were slightly smoothed by a three place centered moving average which was not carried over the peak or across the trough.

Similar computations were carried through with the data of each of the four financial series. In each case the monthly data of the eight cycles were tabulated with the peaks brought together, and the averages of the eight sets were found. Then the process was repeated with the troughs brought together, and another set of averages was found, and then after small adjustments the two sets of averages were combined and the resulting data were smoothed by a three place moving centered average which was not carried over the peak or across the trough. The final figures resulting from these tabulations are shown in Table 7 on page 70, and the diagram representing them appears on the page facing this one. The black silhouette at the top of the diagram is the conventionalized representation of cycles of business activity.

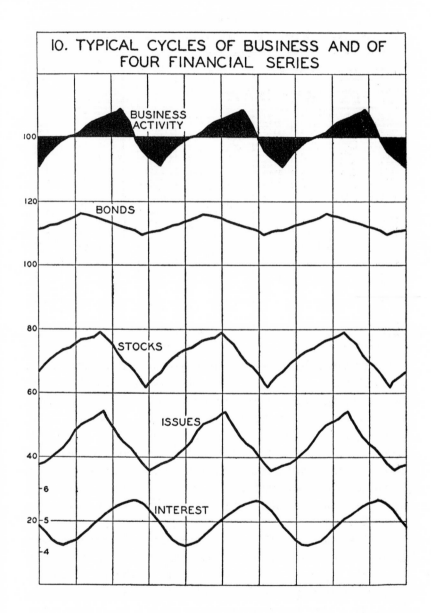

10. TYPICAL CYCLES OF BUSINESS AND OF FOUR FINANCIAL SERIES

TABLE 7

Data of the contours of cyclical movements of five series in the typical business cycle.

Business Activity		Bond Prices		Stock Prices		Security Issues		Interest Rates	
27 Mos. Up	13 Mos. Down	20 Mos. Up	20 Mos. Down	25 Mos. Up	15 Mos. Down	25 Mos. Up	15 Mos. Down	17 Mos. Down	23 Mos. Up
90.9	108.7	109.5	116.1	61.9	79.1	35.9	54.4	5.64	4.25
92.3	107.4	110.0	115.9	63.1	78.2	36.4	52.5	5.63	4.28
93.8	105.9	110.4	115.7	64.3	77.2	36.9	50.8	5.60	4.31
94.9	103.8	110.7	115.6	65.2	76.3	37.3	49.2	5.54	4.35
95.9	101.3	110.9	115.3	65.8	75.2	37.7	47.9	5.46	4.40
96.7	99.1	111.0	115.0	66.5	73.9	38.0	46.3	5.36	4.47
97.6	97.3	111.1	114.6	67.9	72.1	38.3	45.1	5.24	4.55
98.5	95.9	111.4	114.3	69.1	70.8	38.7	44.1	5.11	4.64
99.1	94.8	111.7	113.9	70.2	69.6	39.5	43.5	4.98	4.74
99.7	94.0	112.1	113.5	70.9	68.9	40.4	42.7	4.85	4.84
100.0	93.4	112.5	113.2	71.7	68.0	41.3	41.6	4.73	4.93
100.2	92.8	112.7	113.0	72.3	67.1	42.2	40.2	4.61	5.02
100.5	91.9	113.0	112.7	72.8	65.8	43.0	39.7	4.50	5.09
101.0	90.9	113.2	112.4	73.5	64.3	44.1	37.9	4.41	5.17
101.7		113.6	112.1	73.8	63.0	45.3	36.8	4.34	5.22
102.5		114.1	111.8	74.1	61.9	47.0	35.9	4.29	5.30
103.5		114.4	111.5	74.7		48.4		4.26	5.36
104.4		114.7	111.1	75.5		49.6		4.25	5.43
104.9		115.1	110.9	76.3		50.2			5.48
105.4		115.6	110.2	76.8		50.8			5.52
105.6		116.1	109.5	77.1		51.3			5.56
106.1				77.3		51.8			5.59
106.4				77.4		52.3			5.62
106.9				77.8		53.0			5.64
107.3				78.4		53.8			
107.7				79.1		54.4			
108.1									
108.7									

The data of Table 7 are shown in graphic form in Diagram 10 on page 69. Forty months are three and one-third years, and the 40 months cycle of business activity is repeated from trough to peak and back to the trough again until three full cycles cover just 10 years. The four other series are entered in the diagram in the same arrangement of order that they had in the previous historical diagrams, that is with the bond prices next below business activity, the stock prices below the bond prices, the security issues below the stock prices, and the interest rates with a different scale at the foot of the diagram.

The lags and leads of the five series are those that have been discussed earlier in this chapter. Except for those of the security issues they are based on the medians of the numbers of months by which the turning points of the series followed one another in 25 full cycles. The turning points of the security issues were deter-

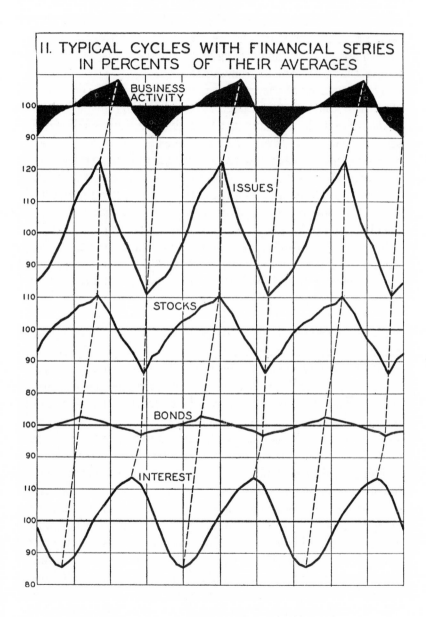

II. TYPICAL CYCLES WITH FINANCIAL SERIES IN PERCENTS OF THEIR AVERAGES

BUSINESS ACTIVITY

ISSUES

STOCKS

BONDS

INTEREST

mined by an analysis of 16 cycles. In all the series except that of bond prices the upswing is longer than the downswing. In the case of business activity the upswing of 27 months is just over twice as long as the downswing of 13 months.

The sequences of the turning points can be more conveniently studied in Diagram 11 on page 71. In that diagram the locations of the series in the diagram have been changed, and each line represents the data of its series after they have been recomputed so as to represent them in each case as percentages of their averages. The low point of interest rates as shown in Table 7 is 4.25 and the high point is 5.64. The average of all 40 entries in the interest rate series is 4.967. The low point of 4.25 is 85.6 percent of that average and the high point of 5.64 is 113.5 percent of it. In Diagram 11 the low point of interest rates is entered at 85.6, and the high point at 113.5, and all the data of all the series are treated similarly. In each case the average is 100, and the data are plotted as deviations above and below that average level.

A dashed line runs from the bottom of interest rates to the top of bond prices six months later. It continues to the top of stock prices another six months later on, and to the top of capital issues one month later, and finally to the top of business activity six more months later. Another dashed line runs from the top of interest rates to the bottom of bond prices three months later, then to the bottom of stock prices one month later, and to the bottom of security issues still another month later, and finally to the bottom of business activity four more months later.

The dashed lines emphasize the sequences of the turning points, but it must be noted again that these typical cycles shown in the diagram present an over-simplified picture of the changes that actually take place as the business cycles go through their phases of expansion and contraction. In a good many instances turning points which should normally follow other turning points actually precede them, and this is noticeably true with respect to those related to the troughs of the cycles. Table 6, which does not include data for security issues, shows a total of 10 minus signs in the first four columns dealing with 100 turning points related to the peaks of cycles, and 19 in the four remaining columns dealing with 100 turning points related to the troughs.

The amplitudes of fluctuation of the five series differ widely. Business activity has a total swing of 17.7 points from trough to peak. That of security issues is the greatest of all, being 41.6 points, for the trough of security issues is 19.1 percent below its average, while the peak is 22.5 percent above it. The swing of stock prices from trough to peak is 24 points, while that of bond prices is only 5.8 points. The swing of interest rates is 27.9 points.

The data and the diagrams of the typical cycles furnish a tentative explanation of the economic mechanism which appears to operate to produce the downturns and the upturns of actual business cycles. It is an explanation which must be submitted to many different challenges, but it is supported by so much consistent evidence that it deserves careful consideration. Its steps can be most readily followed through by considering them with reference to Diagram 11.

That diagram begins with business activity at the trough of depression, just as the expansion phase of the cycle is about to get under way. Interest rates are falling and in a few months, and while business activity is still in the depression area, the interest rates reach their lowest point and then begin to move upward. A little later bond prices, which have been rising, reach their peak and turn downward, and a little later on stock prices also turn downward. During all this time the volume of security issues has continued to rise, and the funds derived from their sale have been flowing into business activity which has kept on expanding.

With the downturn in bond prices, market conditions have become less favorable than they had previously been for the continued sale to the public of new issues of corporate securities, and with the downturn of stock prices those market conditions have become definitely unfavorable. When stock prices turn downward, or very shortly thereafter, the sale of new issues of securities turns downward, and falls rapidly and far. That decline sharply curtails the flow of new money into productive industry, and a few months later on business activity turns downward.

All these processes are reversed in the next phase of the cycle. While business activity is still expanding the interest rates continue to advance, and they reach their top shortly after business turns downward from its peak. Then interest rates move downward and soon bond prices begin to rise, closely followed by an upturn in stock prices. This easing of interest rates, combined with upward trends for bond and stock prices, creates a favorable market for new issues and shortly they begin a sharp advance. That advance in the volume of corporate financing results in an increased flow of new money into productive enterprise, and a little later business activity begins to expand.

In the actual business cycles these sequences are not nearly as regularly spaced as they are in the synthetic typical cycles. Even if they were, we should still need to consider whether or not the available evidence indicates that the cyclical increases and decreases in the dollar volume of corporate financing through the sale of new security issues have been sufficiently large to account for the subsequent upturns and downturns in the volume of industrial production.

Moreover we need to consider the cases in which the records indicate that the upturns and downturns in the volume of security issues appear to have taken place after the upturns and downturns in business activity instead of before them. Again the explanation of the economic mechanism which has been discussed in connection with the typical cycles, and referred to as appearing to account for the upturns and downturns of the actual cycles, includes the assumption that the turns of bond prices or stock prices, or both of them, have preceded the turns of security issues, and created favorable or unfavorable markets for new securities. The validity of these assumptions needs also to be checked. All these matters will be considered in the next chapter.

CHAPTER IX

CAPITAL ISSUES AND BUSINESS ACTIVITY

A FAIRLY close comparison can be made between monthly changes over the past 40 years in the flow of the dollar value of new financing and the changes in the volume of industrial production. A still more helpful comparison can be made between the changes in the volume of security issues and those in the pay rolls of factory workers producing durable goods. This comparison is of special importance because the great and serious fluctuations which the business cycle produces in our industrial activities are those in the employment and pay of the factory workers normally engaged in the production of durable goods.

The index of the physical volume of industrial production compiled by the Federal Reserve System gives monthly figures for the outputs of durable goods and nondurable goods back to the beginning of 1919. Moreover the Thomas index of the Federal Reserve System gives annual data of factory production back to 1899. This index has been recomputed so as to give monthly data for the production of durable goods and nondurable goods back to the beginning of 1899. The resulting series are based on the data, the weightings, and the methods used by the Census and the Federal Reserve System in the construction of their indexes of production. It is believed that the totals for each year are relatively reliable throughout, but due to the inadequacy of data the monthly figures prior to 1910 are no better than good approximations.

A close estimate of the annual totals of wages and salaries paid by manufacturing establishments from 1899 through 1937 is found in Table 25 of a volume by Robert F. Martin published in 1939 by the National Industrial Conference Board and entitled, "National Income in the United States, 1799-1938." There have been 14

Census reports on manufacturing production since the beginning of 1899, and those data together with the Martin data of earnings, and the series showing the monthly changes in the production of durable and nondurable goods, have been used in the construction of a monthly series showing from 1899 through 1938 the dollar earnings of all factory workers engaged in producing durable goods.

The Martin data were used as representing the total annual earnings of all factory workers. The Census figures were used for computing the division of those earnings between producers of durable goods and makers of nondurable goods. The monthly data of production were used to estimate the monthly fluctuations in the earnings of the durable goods workers. After the data were worked out on a monthly basis they were multiplied by 12 so as to convert them into a monthly series representing annual rates of pay for the entire working group making durable goods in factories.

Diagram 12 on page 77 covers the 40 years from 1899 through 1938 with the records for the first 20 years of that period represented by the two lines in the upper portion of the diagram, and those of the second 20 years by the lines in the lower portion. The solid line represents the monthly changes in the wage and salary payments received by the workers in the durable goods industries. The dashed line represents the dollar totals of the combined series of security issues used in this study. It will be remembered that this series has been throughout a 12 months centered moving total, so both the pay roll series and the security issue series in Diagram 12 are monthly series on an annual basis. The scale is in billions of dollars.

In order to facilitate the study of the diagram the dashed line representing security issues has been further smoothed by a five place moving centered average for the 11 years from 1899 through 1909. Pay rolls of producers of durable goods reached a high point in the middle of 1900, and then moved downward to the end of Cycle P near the close of that year. The flow of capital issues had been decreasing from the middle of 1899 to the middle of 1900, and then it turned upward four months before the pay rolls had their upturn.

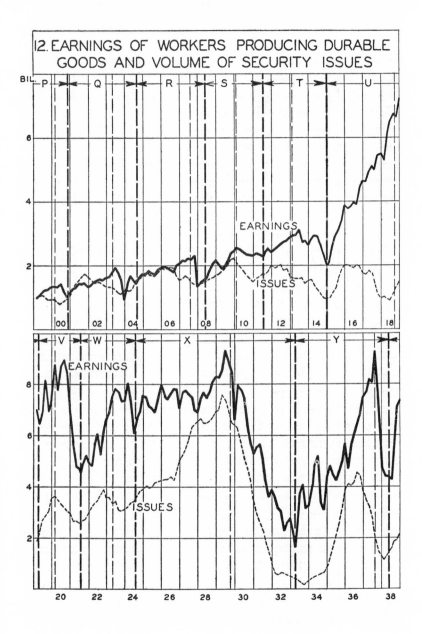

12. EARNINGS OF WORKERS PRODUCING DURABLE GOODS AND VOLUME OF SECURITY ISSUES

In similar fashion one may follow the changes of the two series through to the spring of 1933 and find a high degree of consistency in the action of their swings from upturn to downturn and back again. The downturns of the capital issues precede those of the pay rolls by consistently longer intervals than do the upturns. The two series are closely similar in magnitude, and the total upswings and downswings of both are fairly alike in size, although the upward trend of the pay rolls is somewhat steeper than that of the security issues. Until 1933 the turning points of the capital issues are all earlier than those of the pay rolls, although in 1914 the upturn of the issues came only one month before that of the pay rolls, and in 1929 the downturn of the issues came only one month before the downturn of the pay rolls.

The diagram, and the related facts explaining it, afford clear evidence that during the entire 40 year period, with the single exception of the upturn in 1933, the cyclical turns of the capital issues all preceded those in the pay rolls of the workers in the durable goods industries. Moreover, except during the war and the years immediately following it, the upswings and the downswings in the volume of money for which the new issues were sold were similar in magnitude to the upswings and downswings in the amounts of money paid to the factory workers making durable goods. Of course it would not have been possible for all the money paid over by investors for the purchase of the new securities to have been spent a little later on for durable goods, for some of the new issues were floated to refund previously existing issues.

We do not know what proportions of the money spent by investors for the new issues represented new capital and what parts of it went for refunding issues, but it is clear that expansions and contractions in the flow of new money were sufficiently great to account for alternating increases and decreases in the employment and earnings of the workers in the durable goods industries. We know, moreover, that the influence of the changes in the flow of refunding must have operated in the same directions as did the influence of the changes in the flow of new capital, for the firm that has just refunded a bond issue normally becomes a more eager customer for materials and equipment, while one which has been unsuccessful in attempting such a refunding becomes a more reluctant customer.

The records of these same 40 years afford evidence indicating that the cyclical upturns and downturns in the flow of security issues resulted when market conditions had become favorable or unfavorable for the floating of new issues. The downturn of security issues in 1899 came after the downturn in stock prices in that cycle. The upturn of issues in 1900 came after that of bond prices. The downturn of issues in 1901 followed the downturn of bond prices. In the Rich Man's Panic of 1903-04 business activity, bond prices, stock prices, and security issues, all had double bottoms at the trough of the depression, and while the first slight upturn of issues came before the first upturns of bond and stock prices, the second and real recovery in issues came after the upturns of both bond prices and stock prices.

The downturn of security issues in 1906 came after the downturn in bond prices. In the Panic of 1907 both bond and stock prices reached their lowest levels in November and the real upturn in security issues followed in December and January, although the moving totals of issues used in this study show the bottom of issues as having come in September. The downturn of issues at the end of 1909 came after the downturn of bond prices. The next upturn a year later came after the upturns of both bond and stock prices.

In the last prewar cycle the downturn of issues in 1912 came after the downturn of bond prices, and in 1914 the upturn of issues followed the upturns of bond and stock prices. The whole record of those five cyclical downturns and five upturns shows consistently that the upturns of issues came after market conditions had turned favorable for floating new issues, and the record of the downturns shows that they took place after market conditions had turned unfavorable for the further originating of new issues.

The outbreak of the World War introduced a new era in finance, as it did into almost all other forms of organized human activities.

Diagram 12 shows clearly enough that the great increases in the pay rolls of workers making durable goods in that period were not mainly financed by increases in the volume of corporate financing. The upturn of issues late in 1914 came before the upturn of pay rolls, but its downturn a year later was not accompanied by any downturn of pay rolls. After the war the old sequences continued and the downturn of issues in 1920 came before the downturn of pay rolls, and it was preceded by downturns of bond and stock prices.

The upturn of issues in 1921, the downturn in 1922, and the upturn in 1923, all came before the corresponding turns in pay rolls, and all of them were preceded by upturns or downturns of security prices. In 1929 the downturn of issues came before the downturn of pay rolls and after the downturn of bond prices, but it seems quite improbable that the downturn of those pay rolls in the middle of 1929 was caused by a contraction in the flow of new capital coming from the sale of new issues. It seems more likely that it resulted from the increasing apprehensions of a minority of business men who feared that an important break was coming in the stock market, although perhaps none of them anticipated anything like the collapse of prices that actually began in September.

It should be noted at this point that there has recently been published an index compiled by the Federal Reserve authorities which shows monthly changes in the pay rolls of factory workers making durable goods, and covers the period since the beginning of 1923. That index indicates that the high point of wages of those workers in 1929 was reached in May rather than in June, which would bring the downturns of both wage payments and capital issues in the same month. The new figures have not been used in the index shown in Diagram 12 because they are available for only the latter part of the 40 year period, and because they are closely similar to those that have been used.

Moreover, the Federal Reserve data do not include salary payments as the other figures do, and it appears that the reason why they show the downturn in May of 1929 instead of in June is merely

that there happened to be an abnormally large pay roll in automobile plants in the earlier of those two months. Automobiles are
classified as durable goods, but they are for the most part durable
consumers goods, and only small numbers of them can be considered
as being capital goods, or producers goods.

Pay rolls turned upward sharply in 1933 after the bank crisis and
when fears of inflation were widely prevalent. It is noteworthy that
the sudden upturn was not financed either by proceeds from the sale
of new securities, or from increases in borrowings from banks. It
appears to have been financed in the main by the use of the working
capital of corporations, and by inter-corporate credits. The flow of
security issues did not turn upward until late in that year. It turned
downward late in 1936, and it did so before the downturn in the
pay rolls. It seems probable that the pay rolls of the workers in the
durable goods industries were sustained by the demand for automobiles and household equipment resulting from the flow of federal
expenditures and especially from the payment of the bonus to the
veterans.

Capital issues turned upward early in 1938 before the upturn in
pay rolls. The upturn in the security issues was preceded by an
upturn in bond prices. In general the characteristic sequences of
the series have been maintained with remarkable fidelity in both
the prewar years and in those since the end of the war. The pattern
of their movements since 1933 has undoubtedly been greatly influenced by the huge expenditures of public funds, and perhaps
that period should not be too seriously considered in an analysis
which seeks to throw light on the ordinary causes of the turning
points of business cycles.

There remain to be considered the earlier cycles in which the
series for security issues is available. That series turned downward
in 1872 shortly prior to the beginning of the long depression of the
1870's. The downturn of issues came after that of stock prices and
one month before that of bond prices. It seems probable that while
the downturn of issues marked a large decrease in the flow of
domestic capital into industry, a much more important decrease in

the flow of foreign capital into American enterprise was already under way. The record year of railroad construction up to that time had been 1871, and the important declines in railroad building in 1872 and 1873 appear to have largely resulted from decreased lending by foreign investors.

Security issues turned upward again with bond prices in 1873, but they did not make any important advance in volume until stock prices turned upward four years later in 1877. They turned downward in Cycle K well before business declined, and after the downturns of bond and stock prices, and the same normal sequences were followed in the upturns at the beginning of Cycle L and in the downturns from its peak. There was a departure from this familiar pattern in 1889, early in Cycle M, as may be noted by referring to Diagram 4 on page 31.

Business activity declined at the end of Cycle L to just below the normal level, but there was no real depression. Bond prices turned upward, and stock prices moved sideways, but security issues continued to decline. Business activity had a small recovery, and then declined again to just below the normal level in the middle of 1889. Meanwhile stock prices made a small advance and then security issues moved strongly upward, and business activity had a real recovery. In that cycle security issues were late in turning upward, but they did so after favorable market conditions had developed, and business activity did not have a sustained recovery until the advance in security issues was well under way.

The prosperity of Cycle M was interrupted late in 1890 by the Baring Crisis which originated in London. The crisis was severe but brief, and full business recovery followed within a few months. The upturn of business took place after that of stock prices, but before the upturn of bond prices and before that of security issues. It was an exceptional period and probably we are warranted in assuming that the failure of bond prices and security issues to conform to their normal patterns of movement was due to the fact that the brief financial crisis which brought the cycle to an end was of foreign origin.

The downturns of Cycle N followed the normal pattern and introduced the long depression period of the 1890's, which was interrupted by the curious submerged Cycle O of 1895. In the beginning of that cycle the movements of business activity and of security issues were somewhat similar to those at the beginning of Cycle M. Business activity started upward before the upturn of security issues, but it did not continue in a steady recovery. After a few months of advance it had a relapse and then moved upward again while security issues were rising. Even so the pattern of movement of the financial series was a normal one, for security issues turned upward after bond and stock prices, and before the final upturn of business activity.

The downturn of issues in 1895 came in the normal way, after the downturn in bond prices, and before that of business activity. The following upturn of issues was a normal one. It came simultaneously with the upturn in business activity, and one month before its first important increase. In Cycle P the downturn of issues in 1899 came after the downturn in stock prices and before that in business activity.

The review of the movements of security issues which has been carried through in some detail in this chapter has covered the 67 years from 1872 through 1938, during which there have been 16 complete business cycles. The evidence that has been discussed shows that throughout this long period the volume of new security issues has consistently moved upward and downward in the business cycles, normally making its upturns and its downturns shortly before those of business activity.

The three cases in which the turning points of the security issues followed those of business activity, instead of preceding them, were attended by other exceptional circumstances. In Cycle M in 1889 business activity started upward before the upturn of security issues, but suffered a relapse, and then resumed recovery attended by advances in the security issues. The business recovery from the Baring Crisis in 1891 preceded the upturn in security issues, and that crisis was foreign in origin. Finally security issues turned upward after business activity at the bottom of the Great Depression in 1933.

Among the 16 upturns and 16 downturns which have been discussed there are three cases of upturns in which security issues moved upward after business activity instead of before it. One of these three cases appears to be only a partial exception to the general rule, since in that instance in 1889 business activity suffered a relapse after the initial upturn, and then resumed recovery accompanied by an advance in security issues. The other two cases were those of the exceptional economic conditions of the Baring Crisis, and the bottom of the Great Depression.

In 30 of the 32 cases of cyclical upturns and downturns in the 67 year period under review the security issues began their characteristic expansions and contractions after market conditions had become favorable or unfavorable for the floating of new issues because bond prices, or stock prices, or both of them, had turned upward or downward. One of the two exceptions is found in the downturn of issues in 1916 during the World War. The other case is that of the downturn of 1936 and 1937 when security issues turned downward before bond and stock prices. That downturn took place just after the Federal Reserve authorities announced that they were about to increase the reserve requirements of member banks, and since the announcement was followed by heavy selling of security holdings by the great New York banks, it may well be that it constrained underwriters to look unfavorably on the floating of new security issues.

The evidence that has been reviewed shows that during most of the past 40 years the fluctuations of the upswings and downswings in the dollar totals of new security issues have been about equal to the upswings and downswings in the dollar totals of the pay rolls of all factory workers engaged in producing durable goods. This should not be interpreted as being evidence that nearly all of the proceeds from the sales of new security issues have been shortly spent for durable goods. It does, however, show that the fluctuations in the flow of new money into corporate enterprise as a result of the sales of new security issues have been amply large enough to account for cyclical upturns and downturns in the pay rolls and employment of workers in the durable goods industries.

The chief conclusions of this chapter are that there is an economic mechanism which normally operates shortly before the cyclical upturn of each business cycle to increase the flow of new money into corporate enterprise, and that the same mechanism regularly operates shortly before the cyclical downturn of each business cycle to decrease the flow of new money into corporate enterprise. It is an automatic mechanism which operates because the prices of bonds and stocks move upward and downward in bull and bear markets, and thereby create alternately favorable and unfavorable market conditions for the sale of new securities.

CHAPTER X

CONSUMER PURCHASING POWER

PROBABLY the theories relating to depressions which are most widely accepted in this country are the ones that hold that hard times are caused by a lack of purchasing power on the part of consumers. The wide acceptance of these theories is of special importance because they underlie the policies with respect to wages and hours that were formerly embodied in the provisions of the NRA codes, and those that are now incorporated in the terms of the Wages and Hours Act.

The theory that prosperity can be engendered, and depressions avoided, by supplying consumers with increased purchasing power is the basis of the Townsend Plan. It was adopted as the most powerful argument of the advocates of the bonus payments to the veterans, and it is the fundamental doctrine of the whole program for spending our way out of depressions by priming the business pump through huge governmental expenditures financed by continued budget deficits. It is heavily relied upon by the advocates of our many and varied sorts of bonus payments to farmers.

It was noted in the last chapter that we now have index numbers based on the production data of the Federal Reserve System which show monthly changes since the beginning of 1899 in the physical volume of manufacturing production. These series show separately the output of durable goods and that of nondurable goods, and this latter compilation may be made to throw much light on the theories of the business cycle which place responsibility for depressions on shortages of consumer purchasing power.

Durable goods are the long-lasting goods. They include such things as iron and steel, building materials, machinery, automobiles, furniture, bridges, ships, locomotives, cars, and a long list of articles made of the lasting materials such as the metals, lumber, clay, stone, glass, and cement. One of the most important characteristics of durable goods from an economic point of view is that at any given time the demand for them is mainly optional.

Individuals and corporations alike are quite free to postpone the buying of durable goods if they think it is to their advantage to do so. Most existing buildings can be made to serve for many years longer if it does not seem advisable to their owners to replace them. The same is true of locomotives, and cars, and ships, and bridges, and most machinery, and office and household equipment. It is true to a considerable degree even of trucks and automobiles.

Depressions are periods during which the purchasing of goods is being postponed, and that means mainly the purchasing of durable goods. The unemployment among workers normally producing such goods is the central problem of depressions. It is important not only because of its magnitude, but also because it is the unemployment among producers of goods that causes most of the unemployment among providers of services.

During depressions it is because there has been a great reduction in the output of goods, and especially of durable goods, that fewer workers are needed in transportation, in communication, in the professions, in wholesale and retail trade, in banking, in office work, and consequently that there are fewer opportunities for workers in personal and domestic service. It is a significant fact that nearly one-half of depression unemployment is mostly caused by the other half of it.

Nondurable goods are in the main consumers goods. They are made of the short-lasting materials. They consist mostly of things that we use up or wear out and replace relatively quickly, such as food, clothing, gasoline, soap, tires, tobacco, and the like. For the most part the demand for consumers goods is almost obligatory even during hard times, instead of being largely optional as is the demand for durable goods. We cannot avoid or long postpone most of our purchases of such things as food, clothing, tires, gasoline, and the rest, and so it is because such purchases are almost obligatory that there is not even in times of depression any very great volume of unemployment among producers of consumers goods.

There is another important difference between the economic characteristics of durable goods and those of consumers goods which we should note before proceeding to a consideration of the theories of consumer purchasing power. It is a difference in the methods by which the production of the two classes of goods is financed. The production of consumers goods, which are short-time goods, is largely done by short-term credits, and it presents relatively little difficulty even in times of serious depression. These goods are mainly bought in stores at retail by the ultimate consumers, and paid for out of wages. Since the purchasing of them is largely obligatory, the demand for them is relatively steady, and so the financing of their production is comparatively simple.

The problems of financing the production of durable goods are entirely different, and far harder. These are long-time goods, and in the main their output is financed by long-term credits. They are largely purchased from the producers, and paid for either out of borrowed funds, or out of depreciation reserves taken from corporation treasuries. New bridges and ships, factories and industrial equipment, are often paid for by funds raised through bond issues. Locomotives and railroad cars are purchased through the sale of equipment trusts. Most residences and many other buildings are constructed with the help of money secured through mortgages. Automobiles, furniture, and such household equipment as ranges and refrigerators, are largely paid for over periods of many months by the use of finance company notes.

In Diagram 13 on page 89 the solid line represents the monthly changes in the physical volume of manufacturing production of nondurable goods during the 40 years from 1899 through 1938. The first 20 years of the period are shown in the upper half of the diagram, and the second 20 years in the lower half. In the original Federal Reserve index of total manufacturing production, the average for the years 1923, 1924 and 1925 is taken as being equal to 100. In those three years the average for the production of non-

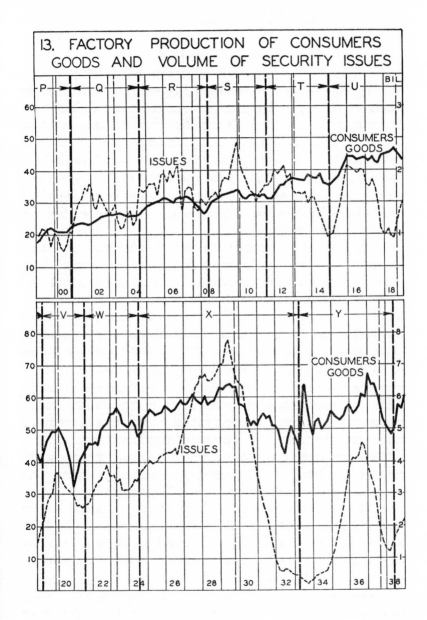

13. FACTORY PRODUCTION OF CONSUMERS
GOODS AND VOLUME OF SECURITY ISSUES

durable goods was a little more than 50, since it was somewhat over half of all manufacturing production. The scale at the left of the diagram is in those units of the original index.

The dashed line represents in billions of dollars the 12 months moving centered total of new capital issues. The scale is on the right, and the dashed line is the same as the corresponding one in Diagram 12 except that it has not been given any additional smoothing in the 11 years from 1899 through 1909. It should be noted that the scale on the right gives twice as much vertical distance to each billion dollars in the upper part of the diagram as it does in the lower part. This is merely to aid in making visual comparisons between the cyclical swings of the issues line and those of the production line.

There are two features of the diagram that call for special comment. The first is that most of the cyclical swings of the production of nondurable goods are made up of small and slow fluctuations. The problems of business cycles would not be very serious or pressing if they had to do only with such fluctuations of production and employment as those relating to the output of nondurable manufactured goods. The second important feature of the diagram is that it shows that throughout these 40 years all except one of the cyclical downturns in the production of nondurable goods have come after the downturns in capital issues, and all the upturns in production have come later than those in the issues except at the bottoms of the depressions in 1921 and in 1933.

There are three principal classes of economic theories which concern themselves with alleged insufficiency of expenditure for consumers goods as constituting the originating cause of depressions. All of them concede that the great cyclical fluctuations of production and employment which characterize the swings of business activity from depression to prosperity and back again are largely concentrated in the industries that are engaged in producing durable goods which are not for the most part consumers goods.

Nevertheless they argue that since in the long run, and in ways that are sometimes direct, and sometimes very indirect, all finished goods are used by, or for the benefit of, individual consumers, variations in the demand for such goods must originate with the consumers themselves. A popular form of statement which attempts to show that fluctuations of industrial production must necessarily be caused by variations in consumer purchasing power is that consumers have no source of income except industry, and industry has no source of income except consumers.

Perhaps the best reasoned of the theories that are included in the general class under discussion is that of the brilliant French economist, Albert Aftalion. His is the "over-production-under-consumption" theory of crises, and he argues that for the purpose of explaining the periodicity of the business cycle we may assume a stable monetary unit, and conclude that the business cycle is caused by the forces of production and consumption alone.

Professor Aftalion rests his theory largely on the principle of acceleration. He points out that relatively small increases or decreases in the volume of production of consumers goods bring about relatively large fluctuations in the volume of production of durable goods in the form of capital equipment. The cycle begins in the depression with a shortage of consumers goods, and to supply the resulting demand there takes place a vigorous increase in the production of capital goods. A long time elapses before these new capital goods are in turn producing consumers goods, and meanwhile business is active, prices are high, profits are large, and prosperity prevails.

Eventually the enlarged factories and the new equipment begin to pour out consumers goods in unprecedented quantities, and then the crisis develops. Consumers will not take all the goods that are offered, and at once producers realize that they have overexpanded their facilities. The demand for producers durable goods drops at the same time that the demand for consumers goods is declining. Then prices fall, output decreases, employment falls off, purchasing power shrinks, and depression is on its way.

The essence of Professor Aftalion's theory is that prosperity breaks down because of insufficiency of demand for consumers goods when there is a rapid increase in the output of those goods well along in the prosperity phase of the business cycle. It is his view that the crisis is caused by the operation of the principle of diminishing utility by which the desires of consumers for additional units of over-plentiful goods become too feeble to induce the prospective buyers to purchase enough of the goods to cover the expenses of producing them.

When this theory was fully developed some 25 years ago, there was not available any long-term monthly index of the production of consumers goods against which the assumptions of the theory could be tested. Now we have such an index for this country and it covers by months the fluctuations in the manufacture of consumers goods during the past 40 years. The components of the index include textiles, foods, tobacco, leather goods, rubber goods, paper, printing, and petroleum refining, although not all of them are available during the whole period.

In Diagram 13 on page 89 the heavy vertical dashed lines are located at the points in the depression periods where the upturns of business activity took place, and the light vertical dashed lines are located at the peaks of prosperity where the downturns occurred. The letters between the horizontal arrows designate the cycles, as they do in Diagrams 1 through 6. According to the theory there should be a vigorous and large and rather sudden increase in the volume of production of consumers goods just before each light dashed line is reached at the peaks of prosperity of the cycles.

In point of fact the diagram shows few such instances in the 10 cycles that are included. There were such sudden increases in Cycles V and W, following the World War, and in Cycle Y there were two notably sudden increases, one at the bottom of the depression, and the other some eight months before the peak of prosperity in the summer of 1937. Most of the fluctuations in the solid line showing the production of consumers goods are very moderate, and the line itself is a poor indicator of the locations of the prosperities and depressions of the successive cycles.

By contrast the movements of the dashed line showing changes in the volume of new corporate capital issues are notably consistent. That line turns decisively downward before the peaks of prosperity, and upward before the bottoms of the depressions. In nearly all the cases its downturns and upturns come well ahead of those of the solid line showing production of consumers goods. The two important exceptions are the upturns at the bottoms of the depressions in 1921 and in 1933 when the issue line turns upward after the production line.

Nevertheless the record is clear that in at least 17 out of the 20 turning points of these 10 cycles the dashed line representing capital issues makes its decisive cyclical changes of direction ahead of those of the solid line representing the production of consumers goods. Since nearly all the cyclical turns in the volume of capital issues came earlier than those of the production of consumers goods, it seems clear that the theory of over-production-under-consumption as formulated by Professor Aftalion and his followers cannot have accounted for the business cycles in the United States during the past 40 years.

According to the theory we have been discussing, the abstention of the consumers from purchasing was voluntary rather than forced upon them. The assumption is that they would not buy the goods at prices high enough to pay for producing them for the reason that there was a great over-supply of the goods offered for sale. There are other variants of under-consumption cycle theories which consider that the abstaining from purchasing on the part of the consumers is involuntary rather than voluntary.

Such under-consumption theories are well over a century old, and various versions of them are to be found in almost all countries. The modern authors who have best re-stated them are Hobson in England, and Foster and Catchings in the United States. In their writings under-consumption involves, and almost means, over-saving. Their argument is that depressions result from the condition that too large a proportion of current income is saved, and too small a part of it is spent for consumers goods.

The arguments go on to the claim that the principal cause of the over-saving is the inequality with which incomes are everywhere distributed in capitalistic economies. A major proportion of the saving is done by those who receive large incomes, and so if there should be a redistribution of wealth and income, and an increase in the proportion of the national income paid out as wages, the purchasing power of consumers could be increased and the dangers of over-saving largely averted.

All such theories of under-consumption assume that there comes a time in the prosperity phase of the business cycle when there develops an insufficiency of spending for consumption goods. Some of them argue that the cause of the insufficient spending is that consumers do not have large enough incomes to buy the consumers goods that are offered, while others contend that they are unwilling to spend enough because they are saving over-large proportions of their incomes, and these savings are either not spent, or they are invested and spent for durable capital goods. Whatever the form of the argument, the theories agree in holding that the purchases of consumers goods are adequate to promote business revival in the early recovery stages of the business cycle, and that they become inadequate when prosperity has developed.

Whichever type of argument is used the two data lines in Diagram 13 afford evidence of the inadequacy of the explanations. In almost all the business cycles of the past 40 years in this country the decrease in the volume of new capital issues in the prosperity phases of the cycles was operating to curtail the flow of money into productive enterprise before there was any real downturn in the production of consumers goods. Similarly in the depression phases of the cycles the advances in the volume of new capital issues increased the flow of funds into productive enterprises before there were upturns in the production of consumers goods. The same priorities of downturns and upturns of issues ahead of production are maintained if we combined the outputs of durable goods and nondurable, or consumers goods, into total industrial production.

There is one cycle among the 10 that are represented in Diagram 13 which would afford supporting evidence for almost all the consumer-purchasing-power theories, and even for some of them that are inconsistent as between one another. That is Cycle V immediately following the World War. In that cycle there was a vigorous increase in the production of consumers goods in the prosperity phase of the cycle, and the downturn of the cycle came simultaneously with the downturn in the production of consumers goods and one month later than that of capital issues. In the depression phase of the cycle there was a sudden increase in the production of consumers goods before the upturn of the cycle and before that of capital issues. There were somewhat similar developments at the bottom of the Great Depression in 1932 and 1933, but the most exceptional conditions then prevailing make that evidence less important.

In Cycle V the price inflation of the war period reached its peak and turned downward. Wholesale prices in May of that year were almost two and a half times as high as they had been just before the outbreak of the war in 1914. They fell away so rapidly after their May peak in 1920 that they were not much more than half as high by the summer of the next year. Retail prices as represented in the cost of living reached their highest point in July of 1920 and then fell with great rapidity.

Apparently these sharp reductions in prices greatly stimulated the demand for consumers goods, and the outputs of processed foods, leather goods, textiles, and tobacco turned upward before the end of 1920, and some months before the production of most kinds of durable goods. The developments of 1920-21 seem to be a special case in which consumer demand was suddenly released when the prices of the necessities of life were greatly reduced. The demand for durable goods responded much more slowly both because of the huge losses in inventories which corporations had to absorb, and because much industrial equipment was nearly new and over-adequate in amount as a result of war-time expansions.

Much of the discussion of business cycles, and particularly discussion based on theories relating to consumer purchasing power, appears to assume implicitly that substantially all purchasing of goods, except that of producers goods, is done by individual ultimate consumers. Such reasoning seems to assume that finished goods, except capital goods, are produced by business enterprises and purchased by individual consumers, and that hence the changes in business activity that bring about business cycles must be caused by alternate increasing and decreasing swings of individual consumer purchasing.

Nevertheless we know that the great alternate expansions and shrinkages in employment, pay rolls, and production which characterize business cycles take place in the industries related to the production of durable goods, which are largely capital goods, rather than in those making nondurable goods, which are mostly consumers goods. The question at issue is really whether the decisions which result in the cyclical upturns and downturns of business activity are normally reached by business enterprises or by individual consumers.

If we can find out in what proportions the purchases of each important class of all finished goods produced are made by business and by individual consumers, we shall gain insight into the nature of the changes that cause depressions and recoveries. It is important that we restrict our classifications of purchases to those of finished goods, or ready-to-use goods, in order to avoid the duplications of purchasing that exist in the records of distribution to business enterprises, and which are absent from the records of retail distribution to individual consumers. Such duplications are, for example, present in the wholesale records of production and distribution in the steps from iron at the blast furnace, to ingots at the steel mill, to sheets at the rolling mill, and finally to the production of the automobile, which then goes to the individual consumer in a single transaction.

Much valuable new information about the distribution of goods has recently been made available by the Census reports on wholesale and retail trade and on the distribution of manufactured products, and by the painstaking compilations contained in a recent volume by Professor W. H. Lough, assisted by Mr. M. R. Gains-brugh, on "High-Level Consumption." The book was published in 1935 by the McGraw-Hill Book Company. The importance of the new information lies in the fact that it shows that the distribution of finished goods to consumers is very different from that which much recent and current economic reasoning about business cycles assumes it to be.

It is true that in the long run all finished goods are used by, or for the benefit of, individual consumers, but it is not true that all important changes in the volume of purchasing of finished goods are those made by individual consumers. Huge volumes of both finished durable goods, and finished consumer goods, are purchased by business enterprises both at wholesale and at retail, in connection with their activities in furnishing goods and services for the benefit of individual consumers.

Hotels make such purchases, but they sell meals and shelter to the individual consumers; theaters make them, but they sell entertainment; public service corporations make them, but they sell gas, and electricity, and telephone service. Innumerable other examples could be cited, and they would all reinforce the conclusion that if we are to examine into the distribution of finished goods to locate the responsibility for the great changes in the volume of purchasing that cause the depressions and recoveries, we must take into account not only all individual buying but all business buying also.

Table 8 on page 98 shows the allocations as between business purchasers and individual consumer purchasers of all finished and ready-to-use goods produced in 1929. It assumes that all the goods produced were sold and that goods exported were in general offset by goods imported. It attempts to exclude all the duplications in business purchasing by restricting the data on industrial goods to finished articles, and its totals of manufactured articles correspond closely with the estimates by the Department of Commerce of the value of all manufactures excluding duplications.

The values used are wholesale and not retail, and most of the

TABLE 8

Finished goods produced in 1929 in billions of dollars at wholesale values.

Products	Total Values	Business Commodities		Individual Consumer Commodities	
		Dollars	Percent	Dollars	Percent
Durable Goods					
Railroad repair shops..........	1.27	1.27	100.0	.....	.....
Construction (labor only)......	2.63	2.45	93.2	.18	6.8
Iron and steel................	2.51	2.21	88.0	.30	12.0
Machinery...................	4.25	3.55	83.5	.70	16.5
Miscellaneous................	.51	.41	80.4	.10	19.6
Cement, stone, clay, glass.....	.75	.55	73.3	.20	26.7
Lumber and products.........	2.44	1.54	63.1	.90	36.9
Non-ferrous metals...........	.65	.25	38.5	.40	61.5
Transportation equipment.....	4.50	1.70	37.8	2.80	62.2
Total durable..............	19.51	13.93	71.4	5.58	28.6
Consumers Goods					
Paper.......................	1.37	1.07	78.1	.30	21.9
Printing....................	2.40	1.70	70.8	.70	29.2
Rubber.....................	1.12	.62	55.4	.50	44.6
Petroleum and coal products...	2.64	1.44	54.5	1.20	45.5
Coal.......................	1.25	.58	46.4	.67	53.6
Miscellaneous................	1.08	.43	39.8	.65	60.2
Chemicals and drugs.........	1.16	.26	22.4	.90	77.6
Textiles....................	6.42	1.32	20.6	5.10	79.4
Foods, processed............	11.03	1.73	15.7	9.30	84.3
Tobacco....................	1.41	.14	9.9	1.27	90.1
Farm prod., not processed.....	4.88	.24	5.0	4.64	95.0
Leather....................	1.24	.04	3.2	1.20	96.8
Total consumers...........	36.00	9.57	26.6	26.43	73.4
Total all finished goods......	55.51	23.50	42.3	32.01	57.7
Total manufactured goods.......	46.75	20.23	43.3	26.52	56.7

figures for purchases by individuals are taken from the book by Professor Lough on "High-Level Consumption," which gives explanations of the methods by which they were derived. The attempt is made to include in this table all the goods turned out in 1929 by all producing workers, who are considered to include not merely the factory workers but also farmers, miners, and those engaged in fishing, forestry, construction, and the workers in electric power plants. Construction is included as though it were a commodity, but only the labor value is used, since the materials of construction are included among the other items.

The most important fact shown by the figures of the table is that the purchases of nearly three-quarters of the finished durable goods are made by businesses instead of by individual consumers. If passenger automobiles were classified as being consumers goods, the altered figures of the upper part of the table would show that the purchases of five-sixths of the finished durable goods are made by businesses instead of by individual consumers. This indicates that the changes in the volume of purchases of durable goods which are chiefly responsible for causing depressions and revivals of trade activity are predominantly the results of business decisions. They are mostly changes in the volume of buying by corporations.

It is believed that the data are adequately reliable guides for the use here made of them. The figures of the table show that the percentage of all manufactured goods going to individual consumers is 56.7. This corresponds closely with the figures published by the Census in its report on wholesale trade in 1929, which showed the proportion of all manufactured goods going to individual consumers in that year to be 55.2. The dollar value of these goods shown in the Census report is too high because duplications were not eliminated, and moreover that study failed to recognize that large amounts of goods are bought by businesses from retail sources.

About one-quarter of the consumers goods are bought by business enterprises, and this proportion is so large as to indicate that declines and recoveries in business activity may be initiated by changes in business purchasing, whether the increases or decreases take place first in the production of durable goods or of consumer goods. This is the chief reason why studies of the priority of such changes at the turning points of business depressions and prosperities do not afford much helpful evidence as to the causes of the turning movements.

The figure for individual consumer purchasing of construction will seem astonishingly low, but probably it is about right. It represents one-half of the estimated value of the construction of one-family houses and private garages as computed from the data on permits and contracts in 1929. The proportion of one-half was used because about one-half of all homes are rented, and were presumably built in the main as business ventures rather than for owner occupancy. Probably many of the remaining single homes were actually built for sale also.

The evidence that has so far been reviewed supports the conclusion that trade cycles are chiefly caused by changes in the volume of purchases of durable goods by business enterprises. An analysis of the data showing monthly changes in the production of durable and nondurable goods since 1899 indicates that in the first 36 years of that period, and without taking into account the remaining depression years, the cyclical fluctuations in the production of durable goods were about three times as great as were those in the production of nondurable goods. The chief reason for this difference is inherent in the very nature of the goods themselves.

As has already been noted the demand for consumers goods is in the main obligatory. We cannot avoid or long postpone most of our purchases of such things as food, clothing, domestic fuel, soap, tires, and gasoline, and so such buying of consumers goods is obligatory. That is why there is not even in times of depression any very great volume of unemployment among the producers of consumers goods.

By contrast our purchases of durable goods are optional, for individuals and corporations alike may put off buying them if they think it is advantageous to do so. When purchases of durable goods are being postponed those who are doing the most important waiting are largely the corporations, for in normal times they are the best customers of the durable goods industries. All manufacturing plants, and their machinery, all equipment of transportation, communication, and the public utilities, and all office appliances are furnished by the durable goods industries.

This chapter offers two chief conclusions. The first is that the evidence of Diagram 13 indicates that theories of business cycles that are based on alleged insufficiency of consumer purchasing cannot account for business cycles in this country during the past 40 years. The chief reason why changes in consumer purchasing, or in purchasing power, cannot account for the downturns and upturns of business cycles is that in nearly all the cases of cyclical turns of business activity, important changes in the volume of investment took place earlier than the turning points in the production of consumers goods or of all manufactured goods.

The other chief conclusion of the chapter is that changes in the degree of business activity are caused primarily by changes in the volume of business spending. Business is the exchange of money and credit for goods and services. There is constantly under way a circuit flow of purchasing by which each business enterprise pays out money to other businesses and to individuals in return for goods and services, and each individual consumer pays out his income for the goods and services he uses.

About half of the gainfully occupied individuals are in normal times engaged in providing services, and the other half in producing goods. The earnings which they receive in return for their efforts are in the main paid to them by business. As long as the businesses for which they work are making profits, and believe they have the prospect of continuing to do so, these individual workers have employment. They are able to exchange what they do for what they want, and when that opportunity is generally available we call the condition prosperity.

There comes a time in each period of prosperity when security prices turn downward, market conditions become unfavorable for selling new capital issues, and there takes place a sharp shrinkage in the flow of funds into productive industry. Then businesses curtail their purchasing, reduce their outputs, and pay out less in wages and salaries. When these restrictions take place businesses buy somewhat smaller volumes of consumers goods, but sharply lowered amounts of durable goods. The purchases of durable goods are cut perhaps three times as much as those of the consumers goods, and the reason for the difference is that the existing durable goods may be made to serve for extended periods of time.

When business slows down, the earnings of individual consumers are reduced, and as a result their purchases are curtailed. The sequence in time and in causation is: first, reduction of flow of money into industry; second, curtailment of business production and purchases; third, reduction of individual incomes and so of individual consumer purchases. This has to be the order in which these influences operate, for if the flow of funds into industry continued unimpaired, business activity and the earned incomes of the individual consumers would be sustained, and their purchasing would continue without diminution. These individual consumers spend most of what they earn. They get their incomes from business, and do not curtail their purchases until their incomes fall. Their incomes fall when business restricts its operations, and that happens after the inflow of new capital decreases.

There is ordinarily no reason why the great mass of individual consumers should decide to buy less as long as their incomes are not reduced. Such mass restrictions of the exercise of individual satisfactions do not spontaneously develop. Something else has to happen first, and that something else is the curtailment of buying from business enterprises by other business enterprises, and the chief reason for this curtailment is the decrease of the inflow of new capital. Similarly the theories which claim that changes in consumer purchasing by individuals account for business cycles fail with few exceptions to offer adequate explanations of recoveries. It is hard to believe that at the lowest point of most depressions large numbers of individuals simultaneously decide to increase their purchasing despite the fact that their incomes, which mostly come from business, have not been raised.

At the bottoms of depressions it is the business enterprises that start the flow of increased purchasing which initiates recovery. They finance these increases by using the funds which are derived from the newly expanding inflows of capital resulting from the sales of capital issues, and they also use their working capital, their accumulated surpluses, their depreciation reserves, and their credit facilities. Under normal conditions businesses have both the power to initiate recoveries, and the incentive for doing it, but consumers cannot ordinarily initiate them unless they are supplied with new purchasing power by the governmental expenditures that we have come to term pump priming expenditures. That subject will be considered in the next chapter.

CHAPTER XI

PUMP PRIMING RECOVERIES

DURING the past seven years from 1933 through 1939 there has been in operation in this country a governmental plan for a managed recovery. The essence of the plan was that the government at Washington should assume responsibility for solving the economic problems of its citizens. The basic assumption on which the whole vast project rests is the theory that recovery from depression can be secured by increasing and spreading individual consumer purchasing power, and that the recovery so engendered will later on develop into a normal self-sustaining recovery.

Among the undertakings which were parts of this new policy were the support of the unemployed, vast programs of public works, mortgage loans for farmers and urban home owners, financial aid for railroads, banks, and other corporations, and the regulation of stock exchanges. There were two other undertakings that were even more sweeping in their purposes and applications. One of them undertook to make farming profitable by taxing the rest of the population to contribute to its support. The other sought to institute a program of higher wages and shorter hours throughout industry, with greatly increased power exercised by labor organizations.

During the first years the lavish spending which the plan entailed was not regarded with widespread apprehension. One of the fundamental assumptions behind the plan, and perhaps its most fundamental assumption, was that we could spend our way out of the depression. The theory was that lavish public spending would supply farmers and urban dwellers with consumer purchasing power which would result in a great demand for all sorts of consumption goods. Then more manufacturing capacity would be required to produce the goods, and industry and transportation would increase their facilities in order to meet the demands. The result would be the restoration of prosperity carried forward by private enterprise.

This plan for a managed recovery has from the beginning been based on the theory that we should spend our way back to prosperity by using public funds, and then that private enterprise would support and continue the prosperity, and furnish jobs for all the workers. This reliance on the ultimate ability and willingness of private enterprise to take over the task of maintaining prosperity was the essential condition of the undertaking. No one has ever supposed that the national government could continue indefinitely to spend enough money to create and then sustain an ever progressive recovery.

Two conditions were necessary in order to have the plan succeed. One of them was an economic condition, and the other a political condition. The necessary economic condition was that the investing public, made up of both individuals and corporations, should continue to have confidence in the prospects for future profits. Our economy is a profit and loss economy, and it can keep going only as long as business men have enough confidence in the prospects for profits to make them take present risks in the hope of being rewarded by future gains.

The political condition that was necessary for the success of the plan was that the public generally should continue to believe that progressive improvements in popular well-being were taking place because they had been planned that way. The success of the plan for a managed recovery has depended all along both on business confidence and on popular support.

Perhaps the ablest debate that we have had on the subject of pump priming in America was one that took place five years ago between two distinguished English economists. In the issue of the magazine Red Book for December, 1934, John Maynard Keynes of Cambridge University and Harold J. Laski of the University of

London contributed articles on the subject, "Can America Spend its Way Into Recovery?"

Professor Keynes began his article with the words, "Why, obviously! ... No one of common sense could doubt it, unless his mind had first been muddled by a sound financier, or by an orthodox economist ... We produce in response to spending ... So, as I have said, the answer is obvious."

He went on to develop the argument that each dollar of government expenditure would bring about the spending of three or four private dollars, and so greatly increase the effectiveness of the federal contribution. He said that, "The object must be to raise the total expenditure to a figure that is high enough to push the vast machine of American industry into renewed motion."

The essence of the Keynes argument was that large emergency expenditures by the government would induce private expenditures that would be several times as great. This huge total of new spending would largely go into consumption goods and residence building. And then follows the most important part of the argument. It is that in order to meet these increased demands for goods, manufacturers would have to enlarge their plants and improve and increase their equipment, and the self-sustaining recovery cycle would get under way.

Professor Laski took the negative side in the debate. He said that the very existence of wide-spread unemployment showed that there was not enough current demand to utilize the productive resources of the community at the going levels of wages and prices. Under those conditions large government expenditures would not operate to cure the existing maladjustment because they would tend to sustain wage rates and to lift prices.

He went on to point out that large-scale intervention by government in the affairs of business must always result in ever-widening ranges of interference, controls, and regulations. This continuously widening interference ultimately becomes dangerous to a capitalistic system, and undermines the business confidence which is essential to a real recovery. He concluded that a prolongation of the dose ultimately means a movement to a planned society in which the control of capital and labor is determined by the state.

We now know that Professor Keynes was right in contending that a business recovery can be induced by government spending that is continued on a large enough scale for a long enough time. It has to be deficit spending of borrowed money, for if the government was taking away in taxes as much as it was spending, there would result no net contribution to the flow of public purchasing power. Huge expenditures of borrowed funds will actually induce for a while a period of synthetic prosperity. That has been pretty well proved in the United States in the past six years.

On the other hand Professor Keynes appears to have been wrong in the most important part of his argument. There was a moderate increase in the demand for consumption goods and residences in the last recovery period, and an enormous increase in the demand for automobiles and iceless refrigerators. The steel makers erected strip mills to meet those demands, but the general rebuilding of manufacturing plants, and their reequipment with improved machinery, never developed. Business supplied the demands created by the pump priming spending, but venturesome enterprise did not come forward with large investments in new undertakings.

Professor Laski was right in pointing out that pump priming would fail to produce lasting recovery because it would not succeed in curing the conditions that characterized the depression. He was right in contending that large-scale governmental intervention in business would inevitably and increasingly become governmental interference. He was especially right in holding that this increasing interference would undermine the business confidence which is essential to a real recovery.

If we were seeking to identify the most influential economic doctrine that ever gained general acceptance in America it seems probable that first place should be given to the Keynes doctrine of the effect of pump priming as a national policy. It is in essence that when pump priming is done on a large scale, manufacturers will have to enlarge their plants and improve and increase their equipment in order to meet the increased demands for goods, and then the self-sustaining recovery cycle will get under way.

There seems to have been a fundamental error in Professor Keynes' theory of pump priming recoveries. He recognized and stated that the huge total of new spending would largely go into consumption goods. And then he stated that in order to meet those increased demands for goods, manufacturers would have to enlarge their plants and improve and increase their equipment, and the self-sustaining recovery would get under way. There is the weak link in the chain of reasoning.

The fact is that manufacturers do not have to increase their plants greatly, or to improve their equipment much, in order to produce volumes of consumers goods that are no greater than those that they were recently producing. It did not require much additional equipment to produce in 1937 as large a volume of consumers goods as had been produced in 1929. It required repairs and replacements and not much more than that. That is the dilemma that confronts a pump priming recovery. It can go as far as it is pushed, but it does not generate its own momentum.

Professor Keynes introduced his doctrine of pump priming with the proposition that we produce in response to spending. Of course the statement by itself is valid, but its implications with regard to pump priming and recovery seem to be not valid. The increased production that causes normal self-sustaining recoveries does not result from current consumer spending. Effective recovery production consists of important increases in the output of goods that we know as producers goods, or capital goods, or producers durable goods.

The Erie canal was not produced in response to spending. It was pushed through by a little group of almost fanatical enthusiasts who were denounced at the time as being wild-eyed visionaries. Most American railroad mileage was not built in response to spending. It was built in the faith that the new railroads would result in creating the communities that would eventually produce the traffic to support them.

The automobile industry was not created in response to spending.

It was brought into existence by groups of daring men who realized that the craving for individual transportation is inherent in human nature, and so they went ahead and built the early automobiles before there were hard-surfaced roads on which to operate them.

Similar comments might be made about the introduction of the telegraph and the telephone, typewriters and electric power, motion pictures and radio, iceless refrigerators and rayon, and so on. Our normal recoveries have not come in response to current spending. They have resulted because bold and enterprising men have had faith that future spending could be stimulated into being, and that profits could be derived from it.

The intermediate recovery which terminated in the United States in 1937 was largely a replacement recovery. It was based on short-term expectations because everyone knew that the rates of federal emergency spending that had been maintained in 1935 and 1936 could not be continued indefinitely. Manufacturers installed new machinery to meet the increased demand for goods, but they did not build many new factories. Merchants enlarged their stocks, but not their stores. Everybody tried to play safe and avoid risks.

Professor Keynes appears to have been wrong in supposing that the mere satisfying of a temporarily increased current demand for consumption goods would suffice to stimulate into being a new self-sustaining recovery cycle. He said that the volume of expenditure must be great enough to push the vast machine of American industry into renewed motion, but increased demands for consumption goods do not have that kind of pushing power.

Our recoveries from former depressions have not come because American industry was engaged in replacing the consumption goods that individual citizens were using up or wearing out. They have come because energetic and enterprising men have believed that they could see profit possibilities in building and rebuilding America. Our recoveries have been great waves of activity in the construction of canals, railroads, manufacturing plants, electric equipment, automobiles and highways. Those were bold projects based on faith in the future.

Our banking figures furnish evidence indicating that it is inadequate business purchasing, rather than inadequate consumer purchasing, that is responsible for protracting this long depression. As a nation we have spent during this depression many billions of dollars of private and public funds to increase and spread individual purchasing power by advancing wages through the codes and through the provisions of the Wages and Hours Act, by making bonus payments to veterans and farmers, by lavish outlays for public works, and through huge spending for relief benefits.

It has now become evident that as these funds are spent by the individual recipients they flow into business channels. They are then used by business men, in part to pay down indebtedness, in part to sustain slow-speed business operations, and in large measure to build up the bank balances of business men and of business corporations. They have not operated actively to stimulate a self-sustaining business revival or to make important reductions in the volume of unemployment.

Diagram 14 on page 111 shows the changes during the past 11 years in the demand deposits and the check transactions of reporting banks that are members of the Federal Reserve System. The demand deposits are mostly made up of the funds of business concerns, and since they can only be used by drawing checks against them, the dashed line showing check transactions reflects changes in business activity. In the diagram the demand deposits and the check transactions in 1929 are both taken as being equal to 100.

Check transactions were abnormally high in 1929, due in great part to stock market activity, and so their subsequent decline has been great. That element has been largely absent from them in recent years, and since 1932 they have fairly reflected changes in real business activity. They are widely considered as being among the best of the indicators of business conditions. They declined from 1929 to 1933, and then made a slow and moderate advance to 1937. Since then they have declined once more.

Meanwhile demand deposits fell from 1929 to 1933, and since

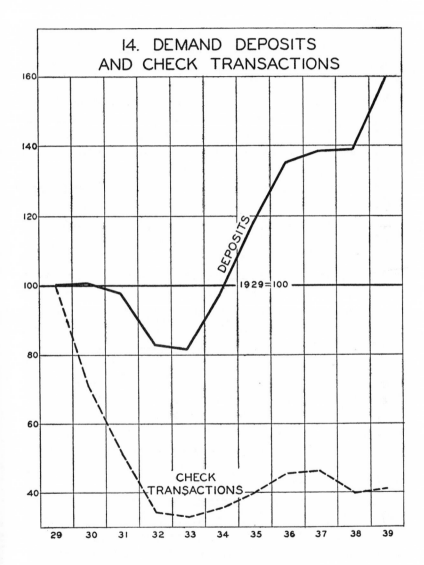

14. DEMAND DEPOSITS
AND CHECK TRANSACTIONS

DEPOSITS

1929=100

CHECK
TRANSACTIONS

III

then they have recovered to levels 60 percent above those of the prosperity period of 1929. The data do not include government deposits. They are mainly business deposits, and they have grown so rapidly since the government began its huge disbursements that they are now very much higher than they have ever been before in our history.

What has happened is that the great federal expenditures, designed to increase consumer purchasing power, have been spent by the consumers, and then passed into the hands of business men, and finally have piled up in the banks as demand deposits without in the main continuing to be productively employed, and without effecting any important sustained increases in business activity. We have tried on a vast scale a great economic experiment based on a consumer purchasing power theory of business cycles, and it has failed because the theory on which it is based is not valid.

Pump priming is a process that was common in the days of the well and the cistern. It consisted of pouring water into the top of a dry pump and then working vigorously at the handle until the pump began to operate in the normal way. It was an artificial expedient put into temporary use, and it never succeeded unless the pump itself had been kept in good working order.

Economic pump priming in our times is the attempt to spend our way back to prosperity by the lavish use of borrowed funds. It goes beyond the necessary relief of unemployment, and aims to revive business by a wide-spread distribution of purchasing power which will create a demand for goods. It assumes that if a renewed flow of the production and distribution of goods can be created, the natural operation of supply and demand will sustain and continue the process, and durable recovery will get under way.

Economic pump priming can never be more than a temporary process. It cannot succeed in restoring prosperity unless the business mechanism of the country is in good working order. There is one condition under which a federal spending program might contribute to bring about a lasting business recovery. That condition is the creation by the Federal Government of cooperative relations between itself and private enterprise that will create confidence in the prospects for future profits.

Further periods of large-scale pump priming not accompanied by a full restoration of business confidence would almost inevitably impair the value of our money. We cannot continue indefinitely to pile up the public debt without decreasing the purchasing power of the dollars which compose that debt. No nation has ever successfully pursued such a course, although many have tried it. The values of all savings, and of all our material well-being, are involved in the policies which we as a nation adopt in our efforts to recover from this depression.

The real issue of recovery that is now before the American people is that of exerting every effort to make sure that measures of temporary relief through federal spending shall be united with measures of permanent relief through the encouragement of private enterprise. Federal spending will not successfully prime the business pump until conditions exist which will permit business to be self-supporting, to make normal profits, and to restore normal employment.

CHAPTER XII

PURELY MONETARY THEORIES OF CYCLES

THE best exposition of a purely monetary theory of business cycles is that of Mr. R. G. Hawtrey, the British authority on banking and finance. It is his view that the upturn of the cycle from depression is caused by an expansion of credit brought about by the banks. They cause this expansion by making it easier and cheaper for bank customers to borrow, and they may do this not only by lending at lower rates than those that have previously been in effect, but by increasing the length of the loans, relaxing the requirements as to the security demanded as collateral, or by scrutinizing less severely the purposes for which the proceeds of the loans are to be used.

When the expansion of business has once been started it becomes a cumulative process and proceeds by its own momentum. It does not require further encouragement from the banks. Merchants have borrowed funds on easy terms, and they use them to increase theirs stocks of goods. They give larger orders to producers, and then increased production results in expansions of the incomes and outlays of consumers. All this brings about a cumulative expansion of productive activity, which is nourished and stimulated by a continuous expansion of credit. No further encouragement by the banks is required to keep it going, but on the contrary once it is well under way they have to be careful not to let it get out of control.

Prosperity comes to an end when expansion of bank credit ceases, and contraction of bank credit begins. Mr. Hawtrey's explanation of the reasons why there must come a curtailment in the expansion of bank credit applies rather to British banking practices while the gold standard was in effect than to American conditions before the advent of the Federal Reserve System. As he explains it the development of prosperity leads to a drain of cash out of the banks as more and more actual currency is needed for pay rolls and ultimately the central bank declines to supply more cash because it must maintain stability of exchange rates between the national money and that of other countries.

The refusal of the central bank to supply more cash leads to difficulties for the commercial banks because the cash holdings of the working population continue to increase for a time, since their expansion lags behind the expansion of credit, and so the drain of cash from the banks continues after credit expansion has been stopped. The result is that the banks must not merely stop expanding credit, but they must begin to contract credit in order to protect their cash positions, and when they begin credit contraction the advance of prosperity comes to an end and the downturn of business activity takes place.

Contraction of business activity is a cumulative process, just as expansion was cumulative. Commodity prices decline, and merchants expect them to fall still further. Because of these expectations they try to reduce their stocks of goods and they give smaller orders to producers. The incomes and outlays of consumers decrease, and so demand falls off. Since production cannot be at once curtailed, stocks of goods increase despite efforts to work them down. Borrowing is further reduced, and all the factors which stimulated the upswing now operate in reverse as if in a conspiracy to push contraction further and to accentuate the depression.

During the depression loans are liquidated, and pay rolls are reduced, and cash gradually flows back into the reserves of the commercial banks. As those processes go forward the reserve ratios of the banks rise to normal levels and even above those levels. Eventually venturesome enterprisers begin to borrow once more. If the reluctance of the business community to resume its use of the credit facilities of the banks continues for an unduly long period, the central bank moves to overcome it by purchasing securities in the open market. That operation pumps more cash into the banks, and increases their liquidity, and shortly a new self-reinforcing process of expansions gets started.

The essence of Mr. Hawtrey's theory lies in the lagging movement of cash, out of the possession of the banks where it served as reserves, into the pay rolls of the workers where it is needed for use in times of prosperity. He explains that if an increase or decrease of credit money promptly brought with it a proportionate increase or decrease in the demand for cash, the banks would no longer either drift into a state of inflation or be led to carry the corresponding process of contraction unnecessarily far. He holds that as long as bank credit is regulated by reserves, and as long as cash movements out of and back into the banks lag behind the corresponding expansions and contractions of credit, the trade cycle is bound to recur and to keep on recurring.

An important feature of the monetary explanation of business cycles as expounded by Mr. Hawtrey is that the relatively periodical and regular movements of business cycles under the automatic workings of the gold standard were dependent on the outflow of cash from the banks to the pay rolls, and its return inflow from the pay rolls back into the banks. The lengths of the cycles depended on the rates of progress of these inflows and outflows. The explanations of Mr. Hawtrey's theory which have been set forth here are largely adapted from the volume on "Prosperity and Depression" by Gottfried Von Haberler published by the League of Nations in 1938.

There is one question which is more important than all the others when we attempt to test the validity of the Hawtrey theory of business cycles, and that of most other related monetary theories of the cyclical swings of business activity. That crucial question is whether or not it has actually been true in the history of past business cycles that bank credit has usually been contracted just before the cyclical downturns of business, and expanded just before their upturns. We might even delimit the question still more narrowly, for unless it can be shown that contractions of bank credit have in fact generally preceded the cyclical downturns of business, it seems clear that the Hawtrey theory, and other similar monetary theories, cannot be adequate to explain the turning points of business cycles.

By far the best statistical records available for making such tests are those of the National Bank System of the United States. The National Banks have made frequent uniform reports on their conditions since the establishment of the System in 1863. During the first few years they made quarterly reports, and then for many decades they reported five times each year at dates fixed by the Comptroller of the Currency without giving previous notice of the call date. No other country has official records of bank reports that are nearly as complete, uniform, and continuous over so long a period.

Statistical material for using the reports of the National Banks is available in admirably complete and accurate data included in four long articles by the late Professor Allyn A. Young of Harvard, entitled, "An Analysis of Bank Statistics for the United States," and published in the Review of Economic Statistics in 1924, 1925, and 1927. The National Bank data used in this book have mainly been taken from that source, but those subsequent to 1914 have been taken from the reports of the Comptroller of the Currency. The deposits of National Banks ranged from being about 77 percent of those of all commercial banks in 1875, to being only about 50 percent of them by 1915, and to being about 56 percent of them by 1938.

Figures are available showing the volume of loans, investments, and discounts of all National Banks at call dates for the 71 years from 1869 to 1939. The data for investments do not include holdings of federal bonds used to cover circulation or to secure government deposits. The records cover the downturns of Cycles I through Y and the upturns at the beginning of Cycles J through Z. In most cases the months of the downturns and upturns of the cycles came between call dates, and the records have been studied to determine whether bank credit was being expanded or contracted when the turns took place.

There are 17 downturns of cycles in the 71 years under review, and the records show that the bank credit of National Banks in this country was being contracted in five of the 17 cases when the business downturn took place, and that it was being expanded in the remaining 12 cases. According to the theory it should have been undergoing contraction in all, or nearly all, of the cases, for the theory is that normally the cause of the business downturns is the contraction of bank credit. Among the 17 upturns of cycles there are six cases in which bank credit was being contracted when the business upturns took place, and 11 in which it was being expanded. According to the theory nearly all the cases should show credit expansion, for that is assumed to be the cause of the business upturns.

Diagram 15 on page 119 shows the changes in business activity from month to month during the 36 years from the beginning of Cycle K in 1879 to the end of Cycle T in 1914. The first 18 years of the period are shown in the upper part of the diagram and the remaining 18 years in the lower part. The loans and investments of all National Banks at call dates are represented by the data line below the silhouette, and that line is kept thin so as to show as visibly as possible the changes in bank credit from call date to call date. The heavy vertical dashed lines are located at the upturns of the cycles, and the light ones indicate the locations of the downturns. The letters at the top of the diagram designate the cycles.

The evidence of the diagram makes it easily apparent that during that period there was no systematic or regular contraction of bank credit by the National Banks just before the downturns of business in the successive cycles. In most of the instances credit was being expanded at the times of the business upturns, although there was an exception at the beginning of Cycle P. There were other exceptions that are not shown in the diagram. They came at the beginnings of Cycles J, U, W, Y, and Z.

It is a rather astonishing fact that under normal conditions there is little cyclical variation in the volume of bank credit. When the general long-term trend of the volume of bank credit is a strongly

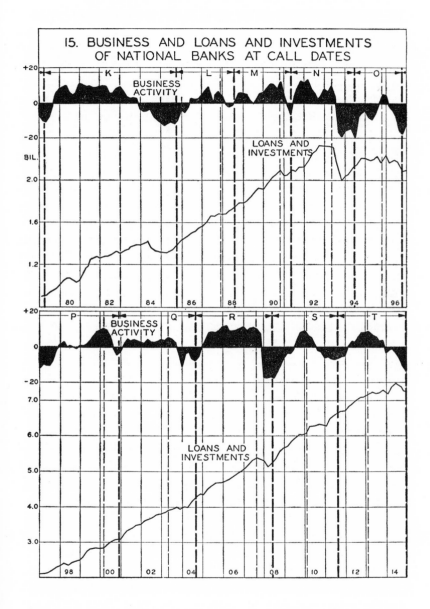

15. BUSINESS AND LOANS AND INVESTMENTS
OF NATIONAL BANKS AT CALL DATES

rising one, as it was during most of the period covered by the diagram, the rate of growth during periods of prosperity is not much greater than it is during times of depression. The general impression entertained by many people that bank loans regularly expand vigorously in times of prosperity, and are contracted rapidly during depressions, is certainly an erroneous one. Bank deposits have much wider cyclical variability than bank credit, and the velocity of circulation has far more amplitude of cyclical fluctuation than either of them.

An attempt was made during this study of bank credit to test the degree of agreement between the fluctuations of the loans and investments of National Banks during successive cycles of depression and prosperity, and those of business activity. Since there were five call dates per year it was decided to construct a trend line for bank credit by using a 17 place moving centered average of the bank credit figures, for 17 call dates should approximately equal the length of a 40 months business cycle. The amounts of credit outstanding at each call date were then computed as percentages of the 17 point moving trend.

It was found that in general the amounts of bank credit outstanding were more than 100 percent of the trend amounts during prosperities, and less than 100 percent during depressions, but the degree of agreement was not great. The computations were carried through for the 67 years from 1869 through 1935, and then coefficients of correlation were computed between the fluctuations of business activity above or below the computed normal level at the call dates and those of bank credit above or below its computed trend level at the same dates. The coefficients of correlation were computed for successive seven-year periods, and finally for the complete period.

The coefficients of correlation were all positive, but they were not high. They ranged from .01 in the seven year period from 1910 through 1916 to .67 in the period from 1903 through 1909. The coefficient of correlation between business activity and bank credit for the whole period of 67 years was only .38. That coefficient indicates that there does exist a tendency for the fluctuations in the volume of bank credit to rise above their long-term trend during prosperity periods when business activity is also above its long-term trend, and that there is a tendency for the fluctuations of bank credit to fall below their long-term trend in periods of depression when business activity falls below its long-term trend.

The tendency toward agreement between these fluctuations of the two series is real and measurable, but it is not strong and consistent. There are great numbers of months in the long period studied when the fluctuations of the two series are in disagreement. Another study of the same data shows that the rate of increase in bank credit during periods of business depression has been astonishingly similar to its rate of increase during times of business prosperity. During the 15 depression periods between 1868 and 1929 the volume of bank credit increased at the average rate of .5 percent per month. It increased in all the depressions except that of 1921. In the 16 prosperity periods of the same years it increased at the average rate of .6 percent per month.

Greater differences are found if the measurements of the changes in the volume of bank credit are taken so as to compare changes of credit during the contracting phases of business cycles with those occurring during the expanding phases of the cycles. Between 1869 and 1938 there were 17 major cyclical declines in business activity. During nine of these periods of business contraction the volume of bank credit, as represented by the loans, discounts, and investments of all National Banks, increased as business activity fell from the peak of prosperity to the bottom of depression. In the eight remaining cases bank credit declined while business activity fell. The average change per month during all 17 periods of business decline was a credit increase of .10 percent.

In this same period of 70 years there were 16 cases of the expansion of business activity from the bottom of depression to the peak of prosperity. The volume of bank credit increased in all of these periods of business expansion, and the average rate of increase was .77 percent per month. During nearly all of the 71 years from 1868 through 1938 the long-term trend of bank credit has been a rising one, but the fluctuations above and below that trend have been relatively small. If one uses a moving centered average of the data of 17 call dates to represent the trend, the average of the plus deviations above the trend has been 2.7 percent and that of the minus deviations below the trend has been 2.2 percent.

This whole matter of the relationships between changes in business activity and those in the volume of bank credit is so important in the discussion of business cycles that still another diagram has been introduced covering the period of 72 years from 1867 through 1938. In Diagrab 16 on page 123 the solid line represents the volume of industrial production. It was computed from a quarterly index of per capita production prepared by the writer. The data from 1899 to date are based on the Federal Reserve (Thomas) index in which the average for the years 1923, 1924, and 1925 are equal to 100. The data have been multiplied throughout by the population figures so that they are no longer on a per capita basis.

That change will explain why the data in those three years of 1923, 1924, and 1925 are now represented by a line somewhat above the level of 100, for by that time the population had increased to above 100 millions. The quarterly data have been smoothed by a five place centered moving average. The solid line represents the long-term growth in the volume of industrial production, with the major depressions showing as downward curves while the recoveries appear as upward curves. It will be noted that the space between each two horizontal lines in the uppermost portion of the diagram is five units, while that in the next lower portion is 10 units, and in the two lower ones it is 50 units.

The dotted line represents the volume of bank credit of all National Banks in hundreds of millions of dollars. It is a five place centered moving average of the figures reported at call dates. The contours of the two lines show that there has not been any close correspondence between the upward and downward cyclical turns of industrial production and those of bank credit during this long

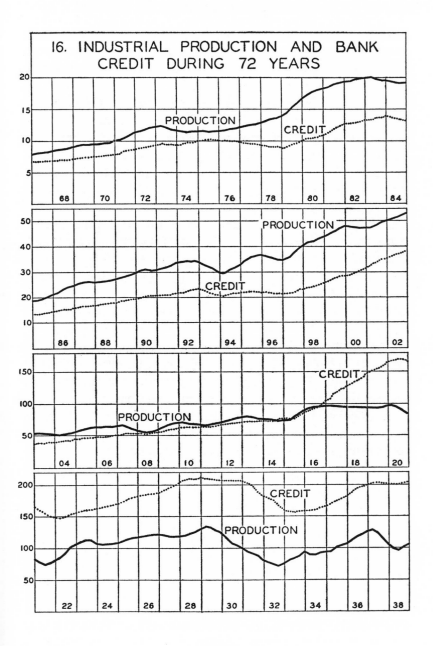

16. INDUSTRIAL PRODUCTION AND BANK CREDIT DURING 72 YEARS

period. It is true that the minor fluctuations have been smoothed out by the moving averages, but the major ones remain, and they show a remarkable degree of independence between the movements of the two lines.

In a number of instances the solid line representing industrial production turns downward at the beginnings of depressions, and upward at the starts of recoveries, before the corresponding movements of the dotted line representing bank credit. In other cases the dotted line of bank credit continues its upward trend in almost complete disregard of downward turns of industrial production. In the late 1870's and in 1921-22 bank credit declined while industrial production was increasing, and in the years from 1899 to 1914 there are instances in which bank credit increased while industrial production was declining.

The general conclusion of this chapter is that the records of American business and banking over a period of nearly three-quarters of a century do not support the theory that downward turns in business cycles can have usually been caused by decreases in the volume of bank credit, or upward turns in business by increases in bank credit. The evidence appears rather to indicate that in most of the cases the cyclical downturns of business have caused the decreases in bank credit, and that sometimes the upturns in business have resulted in increases in bank credit. During extended periods bank credit has continued to increase with almost complete disregard for business recessions.

Chapter XIII

CYCLES OF SECURITY ISSUES

EVIDENCE presented and discussed at some length in Chapter XII indicates that the growth of bank credit in this country over the past 70 years or so has not been characterized by well-defined cyclical fluctuations corresponding to the cycles of business activity as reflected by industrial production. It appears that bank credit has usually increased more rapidly in periods of business expansion than it has in times when production was being contracted, but the curves representing the growth of bank credit do not clearly exhibit the wave-like fluctuations that might well be expected to correspond to the recurring business cycles.

This absence of pronounced cyclical fluctuations on the part of bank credit raises an interesting and important question with respect to the well-defined fluctuations that have been shown to exist in the flow of new security issues. If bank credit does not regularly increase and decrease with the expanding and contracting phases of business cycles, why should the flow of new security issues do so? If the amount of outstanding short-term bank debt of business tends to show a long-term secular growth without much regard for the business cycles, why is it that we find well-defined cycles in the flow of new security issues, and why do the upturns and downturns of these cycles regularly precede the upturns and downturns of the business cycles?

The answer is not to be found in the fact that bank credit as reflected in the diagrams presented in the preceding chapter includes bank investments as well as loans and discounts. That possibility has been carefully checked and the results show that the flow of loans of national banks has shown over the years much the same sort of disregard for business cycles as has that of the loans and investments combined. It has long been a generally accepted assumption among economists that the volume of business debt was largely increased in the expansion phase of each new business cycle, but if that assumption is of doubtful validity in the case of short-term business debt, it calls for questioning in the case of long-term debt.

Unfortunately our records of new security issues are not well adapted for answering searching questions about the amounts and proportions in which the different sorts of new security issues have been sold to the public over long terms of years. However, an attempt has been made to compile the most helpful of the available material covering the period of the past 39 years, and the results are presented in Diagram 17 on page 127. In the upper portion of the diagram the area of the heavily cross-hatched surface represents in billions of dollars the volume of new issues of domestic corporate bonds. The lightly cross-hatched area represents the issues of common and preferred stocks.

The period covered is the 20 years from 1900 through 1919. The data are plotted by months and the data lines are 12 months moving centered totals of the original figures. The data from 1900 through 1905 are based on the tabulations drawn off from the listing statements of the New York Stock Exchange. They include the issues of the domestic, non-financial corporations, but only those which appear to have been sold to the public for cash. From 1906 through 1919 these series have been averaged with those of the tabulations of the New York Journal of Commerce. The annual totals as they appear in the diagram are closely similar to those of the Journal tabulations.

Recurring cycles are clearly shown in this diagram as they have been in the earlier diagrams discussed in previous chapters. It is evident that the wave-like contours of the recurring cycles were largely produced by major fluctuations in the flow of new issues of stocks, but changes in the volume of flow of new bond issues also contributed much to form the successive waves which correspond to the series of business cycles. In a few cases as in 1901 and 1902,

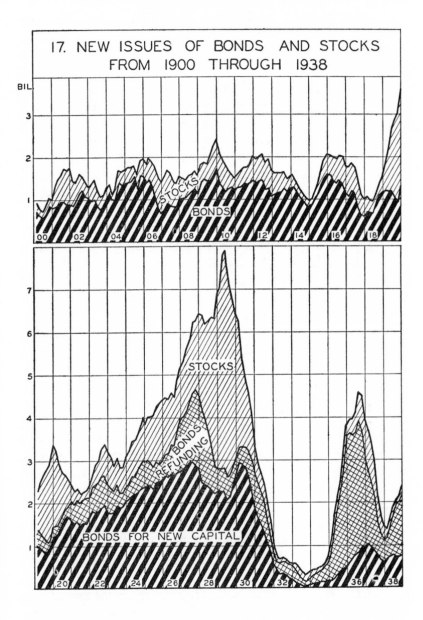

17. NEW ISSUES OF BONDS AND STOCKS FROM 1900 THROUGH 1938

just before the Rich Man's Panic of 1903-04, and again in the prosperity of 1912, and in 1919, the increases in new stock issues contributed major parts of the cyclical expansions of the issues.

The lower portion of the diagram covers in similar fashion the 20 year period from 1919 through 1938, and here an additional subdivision of the bond issues becomes possible. The data are those of the compilations of the Commercial and Financial Chronicle. They cover the domestic, corporate issues of these years, less those of the investment trusts. Again the lightly cross-hatched area represents the stock issues, and the area below that corresponds to the bond and note issues. These have been divided into two classes, of which the lower one, represented by heavy cross-hatching, consists of the issues sold to raise new capital, while the one in double cross-hatching between that and the stocks represents the refunding issues. There were a few refunding issues among the stocks, mostly those of preferred shares, but they are not sufficiently large in volume to be very important.

So far as this discussion is concerned the most important feature of this lower portion of the diagram is the fact that before the Great Depression the cyclical fluctuations in the volume of financing by bonds and notes were contributed almost entirely by the refunding issues. The line forming the upper limit of the doubly cross-hatched area representing bond and note financing for the raising of new capital shows almost no tendency toward cyclical fluctuations during the nine year period from 1919 through 1927. The small peak in 1920 is an apparent exception, but the records show that it was entirely accounted for by an unusually large issuance of notes in that period of high interest rates.

It is most regrettable that the records do not make it possible to carry back into earlier years the subdivisions of the data of new issues into the classifications of those sold for refunding purposes and those floated to raise new capital. The evidence that we have appears to indicate that the cyclical fluctuations in the flow of new security issues are mostly due to recurring wave-like changes in the flow of new stock issues and in those of bonds sold for the purpose of refunding old bond issues.

If this is indeed the case we must conclude that it has been the general rule in this country before the Great Depression that both the long-term funded debt of corporations, and their short-term bank debt, have tended to increase gradually and rather steadily over the years without much regard for business cycles, and that the wide cyclical swings in the volume of new security issues have been mainly contributed by changes in the flows of new stock issues and of those of bonds sold for refunding purposes. If this is true, as it appears that it may probably be, it means that the formation of new corporate debt has had less to do with business recoveries following depressions than has generally been assumed, while the refunding of bonds and the issuing of stocks have been of the first importance.

Much popular support has been accorded in this country in recent years to the theory that we should adopt the policy of having a compensatory national budget which would regularly have operating deficits in times of depressions by lifting expenditures above revenues, and then make good the deficits by spending less during periods of prosperity than the amounts brought in by the taxes. The chief argument adduced in support of the theory has been the allegation that recovery from depression could only come in any event through the creation of a large volume of new debt, and that it might well be in the public interest to have that new debt public in character rather than having it that of private corporations.

This argument is deprived of much of its support if it be true that business recoveries have in the past been largely financed in this country by the sale of new issues of stock, and in only small degree by increases in the funded debts of corporations, and by bank borrowings. Issues of new stock represent venturesome capital subscribed by investors because of their confidence in the prospects for future profits. Somewhat similar comments may be made about corporate expenditures taken from earned surpluses for the purposes of expansion and for improved equipment. Certainly the most convincing symptom of a healthy industrial economy is its ability to finance its need for new capital by selling common stock, and probably our past business recoveries have been largely financed by that method.

There are two further features of Diagram 17 which deserve comment. One of them is the clear evidence that most exceptionally large volumes of new stock issues were marketed during the great speculative era which came to a close with the stock market collapse in the autumn of 1929. It is noteworthy too, and somewhat astonishing, that toward the end of that period in 1927 and 1928 there was a huge volume of refunding old bond issues. Considered in retrospect it seems strange that the corporations which were then refunding their bond issues did not instead take advantage of the insatiable public demand for stocks by selling shares and retiring their funded obligations. Many of them did so, but the diagram shows that many others regarded the market activity as offering good opportunities for refunding their old bonds.

The other noteworthy feature of the diagram is the impressive evidence it affords of the extremely small volume of new stock issues marketed during the past eight years of the depression period. Our traditional American method of financing a business recovery by marketing new issues of stocks has not been in operation in these recent years. There was a slight revival of it in 1936 and 1937, but not on a sufficiently large scale to be effective. Probably the most potent contribution to recovery that could be made by the national administration, and by the Securities and Exchange Commission, would be the adoption of policies designed to bring about a revival of the public marketing of new issues of stocks.

There is abundant evidence indicating that the most important monetary change which characterizes the early stages of business recoveries is not a series of increases in the volumes of short-term and long-term credit in use, but instead vigorous expansions in the employment of the credit already available. There are two long series of measures of such changes in the use of credit which were developed a number of years ago by Carl Snyder who was then statistician of the Federal Reserve Bank of New York. They are described in his book published by The Macmillan Company in 1927, and entitled, "Business Cycles and Business Measurements."

One of them is his Clearings Index of Business which covers the period from 1875 to date, and which until a few months ago was still regularly computed and published each month by the New York Federal Reserve Bank. That index reflects the volume of checks cashed each month by banks in leading cities. Since most of our business transactions, or at least major parts of them in value, are carried to completion by means of checks rather than by payments in currency, the changes in the index reflect changes in the actual volume of buying and selling and paying for services that are going on from month to month.

During the period of 65 years covered by the index check transactions have increased sharply with each recovery from depression, and have declined rapidly following each downturn from prosperity. The swings are wide ones, ranging from numbers 20 percent or more above the computed normal level in some of the prosperity periods, to those 20 percent or more below the normal level in some of the depressions, and to levels far lower still in the recent depression years. The average of all the plus and minus deviations for the entire period since 1875 is a little more than 10 percent, and that average deviation includes of course the months of no deviations from normal.

Mention has already been made of the average deviations from trend of the series of bank credit measurements made from the data of the loans and investments of all National Banks as reported at the call dates. The average deviation of the fluctuations of that series from 1868 through 1938 amounted to 2.6 percent, and there is not a very close relationship between the plus deviations of that series and the data of business activity in prosperity periods, and between the minus deviations of bank credit and the data of business in depression periods. It should be noted in connection with the Clearings Index of Business that it has the defect of being strongly influenced by increases in the volume of check transactions which result from speculative activity in the stock markets.

In addition to this index Carl Snyder developed an index based on the velocity of circulation of the demand deposits of banks and termed it an Index of Business Activity from Variations in Rate of Deposit Turnover. That index also begins in 1875, and it affords measures of the differences between the rates at which existing bank credit was being used in periods of prosperity and its rates of turnover during times of depression. As in the previous case the swings are wide ones, and this index also is much influenced by changes in the activity of stock market speculation.

During the period from 1875 through 1925 the velocity index shows an average deviation from trend amounting to nearly seven percent. The fluctuations of the velocity index have been abnormally great since 1925. At the culmination of the great stock market speculation in October of 1929 the index for New York City rose to 228 and by April of 1939 it had fallen to only 31. The index for 101 reporting cities was 190 in October of 1929 and fell to 45 in April of 1939. The low figures of recent years result from the combination of subnormal business activity which demands only relatively small volumes of check transactions, and the greatly increased volumes of demand deposits largely brought about by federal deficit financing and by large gold imports.

There are two chief conclusions derived from the material considered in this chapter. The first is that the cyclical swings of security issues in this country have been mainly caused by changes in the volume of new financing done for the purpose of raising new capital by the sale of stock issues, and by changes in the volume of refinancing of old bond issues. It appears to be probable that the growth of financing by the creation of new debt in the form of new issues of bonds has not been largely cyclical in nature.

The evidence concerning new financing by bond issues does not cover a sufficient term of years to be conclusive. We do, however, have long-term records showing that there has been little relationship between business cycles and the fluctuations of short-term bank credit, and we have some evidence showing little relationship between business cycles and new financing through the creation of bonded indebtedness. It seems probable that the generally accepted assumptions which hold that business recoveries in this country have usually been accompanied by important accentuated increases in the volume of business debt are not valid.

The second main conclusion of the chapter is that in this country business recoveries have been accompanied by greatly increased utilization of existing credit rather than by important increases in the amounts of credit. Downturns of business cycles have usually been accompanied by sharp decreases in the use of existing credit rather than by contractions of the amounts of credit. In some of our most severe depressions there have been important contractions of both the long-term funded debt of corporations and of their short-term bank debts, but these debt contractions appear to have been those of exceptional instances rather than characteristic features of ordinary business cycles.

Chapter XIV

THE MONETARY MECHANISM OF CYCLES

Despite the adverse conclusion reached in Chapter XII about purely monetary theories of cycles, there appears to be much illuminating material to be gained from further study of the banking figures. Cyclical changes within the banks appear to have been for many decades the controlling factors in determining changes in short-term interest rates. Cyclical changes in the direction of movement of short-term interest rates seem to have resulted in changes in the courses of security prices. These changes from advancing trends to declining trends, and back again, for bond and stock prices have resulted in creating market conditions that were alternately favorable and unfavorable for the floating of new security issues.

We may well start on an examination of these matters by considering cyclical changes in the deposits and in the loans and investments of all National Banks. Diagram 18 on page 135 shows in its upper part the familiar black silhouette of three typical cycles of business activity during a 10 year period. The solid line in the lower portion shows typical cycles of the deposits of National Banks, and the dashed line represents the typical cycles of loans and investments in the same institutions.

The typical cycles of deposits and of loans and investments were made by finding the percentage deviations at call dates of the deposits and of the combined loans and investments from their 17 place centered moving averages. Figures for the months between call dates were then supplied by straight-line interpolation, and 12 months centered moving averages of these completed series were then computed. The data for the seven full cycles L, M, N, Q, R, S, and T were then combined, first by adding them with their downturns located at the same month, and then with their upturns located at the same month, and finally averages were found of these 14 series of numbers.

Before all this work was carried through, the typical lags and leads of the series were determined by finding the numbers of months between the downturns of bank deposits and of bank **credit** and those of business activity in the 15 cycles for which the data

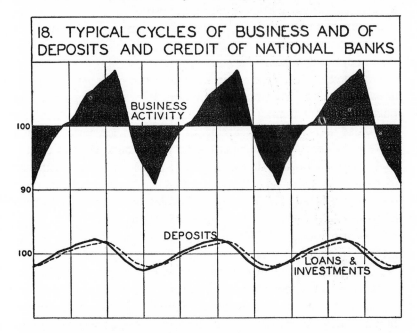

18. TYPICAL CYCLES OF BUSINESS AND OF DEPOSITS AND CREDIT OF NATIONAL BANKS

were available, and carrying through the same operations for the upturns. The typical lags and leads were determined by finding the averages of these results, and their medians, and the averages of median groups. If necessary a partly arbitrary decision was made on the basis of these several findings. The methods used are more fully explained in Chapter VIII.

The typical cycle of bank deposits is based on the data for net deposits as tabulated by Professor Young. Its downturn comes seven months before that of the business cycle, and its upturn four months before the upturn of business. The typical upswing is 24 months in length, and the typical downswing is 16 months. The average monthly deviation is only 1.44 percent. The cycle of the loans and investments is later than that of the deposits. Its downturn comes four months before that of business activity, but its upturn comes two months before that of business. The upswing is 25 months in duration, and the downswing lasts 15 months. The average monthly deviation is only 1.19 percent.

It must be remembered in studying Diagram 18 that the declines in deposits, and in loans and investments, which are shown in the typical cycles as regularly accompanying the contraction phases of the business cycles, were not in fact always or even usually actual dollar decreases. That has already been shown in Diagram 15 on page 119 where it may be seen that the loans and investments continued to increase during many of the depression periods. When there were increases in such periods they went on at less rapid rates than they did during the prosperities, and so when deposits, or loans and investments, are represented as deviations from their own trends, as they are in the typical cycles, they appear as a series of upward and downward wave-like oscillations.

This principle is well illustrated by the action of the bank investments. It has often been assumed that the banks were important factors in causing the downturns of bond prices in periods of prosperity, and in bringing about their upturns in periods of depression. The assumption is most plausible, for it might naturally be supposed that near the tops of prosperity periods, when bond prices were high, the banks would sell some of their bond holdings with the double purpose of taking profits on them and of securing funds to lend to commercial borrowers. If many banks sold bonds at about the same time, that might initiate the downturn in bond prices.

Similarly it would seem reasonable to believe that during depression periods, when the banks held ample loanable funds and bond prices were low, they might well purchase more bonds so as to employ their funds. If many banks made such additional investments at about the same time, that policy might well result in bringing about an upturn in bond prices. A study of bank investments over the 70 year period from 1869 through 1938 affords little support for such assumptions.

In that long period there were 17 downturns of business cycles, and bank investments were being reduced during 10 of them, as they should have been according to the theory, but in the seven remaining cases the banks were increasing their holdings. In the same period there were 17 upturns of business cycles, and during 10 of them the banks were adding to their bond investments, as they should have been according to theory, but in the seven remaining cases the banks were reducing their holdings. It seems clear that the sales and purchases of bonds by banks cannot have been responsible in most cycles for initiating the cyclical downturns and upturns of bond prices.

In Diagram 18 the pattern of movement of the bank loans and investments has a wave-like contour, but the fluctuations are very minor ones in terms of percentages. The waves are deviations from trends that were for the most part steeply rising ones, so that the apparent contractions were often either very slight or even actual increases. Diagram 18 may appear to contradict the evidence of Diagram 15 on page 119, but it does not in reality do so, for the fluctuations of bank deposits and of bank loans and investments, which appear as a series of upward and downward wave-like oscillations, are in reality conventionalized representations of deviations from trends.

While these wave-like changes of deposits, and of loans and investments, were going on in the banks important changes were continuously taking place in bank reserves. Under the provisions of the National Bank Act, and prior to the establishment of the Federal Reserve System, the National Banks that were located in reserve cities were required always to have reserves amounting to at least 25 percent of their deposits, while banks in other places had to keep their reserves equal to at least 15 percent of deposits. These reserves were mainly cash. They were made up of lawful money, consisting of specie and bank notes. However, the law permitted banks to count as reserves their own deposits with correspondent banks, so there was some duplication, and the actual cash reserves were always somewhat less than the nominal and required reserves.

The amounts of these duplications were of considerable size. In the autumn of 1899 the required reserves were 20.8 percent of the deposits of all National Banks, and the reserves shown by their reports amounted to 29.3 percent of their deposits, but the actual cash holdings of all the banks were only 15.4 percent of their deposits. Banks throughout the country regularly kept part of their cash reserves on deposit with New York banks, which paid interest on them. There were frequent and important shipments of these funds from New York to the interior banks when increased amounts of money were needed for trade or for harvesting and moving crops, and shipments back to New York when the cash needs of the interior banks decreased.

In addition to such recurring shifts of cash from the New York banks to the interior and back again there was another and most important continuous movement of cash as the business cycles went through their processes of expansion to prosperity, and of contraction to depression, and back to prosperity once more. As each period of prosperity developed, cash flowed out of the banks and into the possession and use of the public, where it was needed for the increased pay rolls and for hand-to-hand use as trade became more brisk and prices rose.

Contrariwise as each period of decline and depression developed, cash flowed back from the public and into the banks. The result of this continuous inflow and outflow of cash, to and from the banks, was that at some time in each prosperity period the reserves of the banks became relatively low, and in each depression period the reserves were well above requirements. When the reserves fell to near the legal limits in times of prosperity people became alarmed about the safety of the banking situation, and sometimes, when reserves still continued to fall, panics developed.

Diagram 19 on page 139 shows in its shaded areas the changes in the deposits of National Banks during three typical cycles. The lowest area in heavy cross-hatching shows the changes in the part of the deposits which were the cash reserves. During the seven business cycles which were included in the computations used in calculating the data for these typical cycles, the averages of the cash reserves amounted to 17.7 percent of the averages of the total

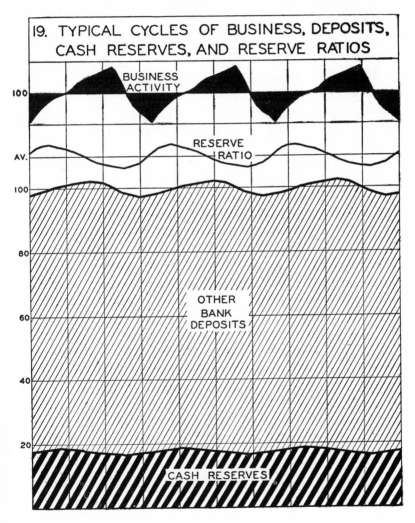

19. TYPICAL CYCLES OF BUSINESS, DEPOSITS, CASH RESERVES, AND RESERVE RATIOS

deposits. That proportion is so small as compared with all deposits that the fluctuations of the cash reserves appear to be of only minor size.

In reality the fluctuations in the cash reserves are much wider than those of total deposits if one considers them both in terms of their averages. The average monthly deviation of total deposits is 1.44 percent, but the average monthly deviation of cash reserves is 2.98 percent, or more than twice as great. However, the reserve ratios which were of controlling importance in shaping the policies of the banks were not the direct ratios which might be computed by dividing the actual portions of the deposits which consisted of lawful money by the total bank deposits. They were rather the reserve ratios as legally defined and as computed after taking into account as well the deposits which the banks had with correspondent banks.

Thus in Diagram 19 the cash reserves of all National Banks, as represented by the heavily cross-hatched area at the bottom of the diagram, amounted to 17.7 percent of the total deposits during the seven business cycles from which the typical cycles were computed. The legal reserves as actually computed by the Comptroller of the Currency during those same seven cycles were decidedly larger, and amounted on the average to 27.9 percent of the net deposits. It is these legally computed reserve ratios that are represented by the wavy line in Diagram 19 that is drawn in the space between the black silhouette representing the typical cycles of business activity, and the cross-hatched area representing the typical cycles of deposits in all National Banks.

The axis of the curve for the reserve ratio is marked in the diagram as being its average, and that average was actually equal to 27.9 percent of the net deposits of the banks during the seven business cycles from which the typical cycles were computed. The low point of the typical cycle of the reserve ratios was 3.2 percent below the average, and it was reached four months after the downturn of business activity. The low point of the reserve ratio was reached at the time when the reserves of the banks were least adequate, and when there was often real credit stringency. The high point of the cycle of reserve ratios was reached only 15 months later, and it came six months after the upturn of business. Then the reserves were most ample and there was no credit stringency.

In the typical cycles of the reserve ratios the high point is 3.6 percent above the average, but the actual range of the reserve ratios as they are recorded for the entire system in the old annual reports is much greater than the data of the typical cycles would suggest. In the period from 1881 through 1914 the lowest reserve ratio reported for the system was only 21.6 percent, while the highest one was 36.4 percent. The average for that whole period was 28.4 percent. The reserve ratios were of the utmost importance to the banks, for failure to maintain the reserves above the low limits established by law was penalized by prohibiting the banks from continuing to do business.

There is ample evidence indicating that during the years before the establishment of the Federal Reserve System in 1914 the fluctuations in the levels of short-term interest rates varied with the fluctuations in the reserve ratios of the banks. When business was slow, the part of the cash money of the nation that was not needed for pay rolls and retail trade flowed into the banks. It lifted their reserve ratios and created easy money conditions which resulted in low interest rates. When business became active, more money left the banks and went into use in pay rolls and trade. Then bank reserves fell and as that happened interest rates rose.

As a result of this unending process of the inflow of cash money into the banks, followed by its outflow from the banks, the levels of short-term interest rates fluctuated in close relationship to the percentages of the total cash money not in banks. Professor Allyn A. Young includes in his article in the Review of Economic Statistics for 1924 a table on Money in National Banks and Estimated Money in Circulation, Not in Banks at Dates of Call, 1901-14. The data have been carried backward through 1896 by the same methods that he used, and the data showing the percentages of money in circulation outside of the banks are represented for the

20 year period through 1915 by the dashed line in Diagram 20 on this page.

Professor Young's data for the percentages of money not in banks were given as of the call dates of the National Banks, and the figures for the intervening months were supplied by straight-line interpolation. Then a 12 months moving centered average of the figures was computed and the results are represented by the dashed line in Diagram 20. The scale for this line is at the right hand end of the diagram. In the autumn of 1907, just before the panic of that year, the proportion of the money not in banks is

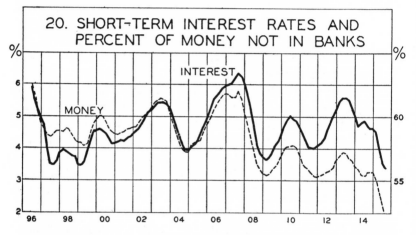

shown as being about 64 percent. The extremes are much smoothed out by the use of the moving average, and the original computations show that at one call date of that year the money not in banks was almost 65 percent of all the money in circulation.

By the middle of 1915, before the recovery from the depression of 1914 had made much progress, and when gold imports from Europe were getting well under way, the proportion of money not in banks had fallen to below 53 percent. The solid line in the diagram is a 12 months centered moving average of short-term interest as represented by rates on four to six months commercial paper. The scale is at the left. The cycles and the turning points of the two lines correspond almost perfectly. They indicate that before the establishment of the Federal Reserve System it was the general rule that short-term interest rates fluctuated inversely with the reserve ratios of the banks. When bank reserves were low, interest rates were high, and when reserves were high, interest was low.

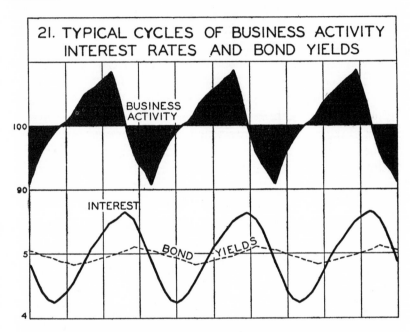

It has long been a commonplace of financial observation that long-term interest rates follow short-term rates, but that they do so slowly, with far less fluctuation, and with a good deal of lag in the timing of their turning points. Diagram 21 on this page shows how these movements worked out in the typical cycles which were again based as to their contours and amplitudes on the records of seven business cycles, but with their lags and leads based on the records of 15 cycles. As in the previous diagrams the black silhouette at the top represents the typical fluctuations of cycles of business activity.

In the lower part of the diagram the solid line represents the fluctuations of short-term interest rates which are those of commercial paper. The dashed line represents the long-term interest rates as represented by bond yields. The short-term rates move upward for 23 months and downward for 17 months. Their highest points are reached four months after the downturns of business activity, and their lowest points eight months after the upturns of business. The upward movements and the downward movements of the bond yields both last for 20 months.

The lowest points of the bond yields correspond with the highest points of bond prices, and they are reached shortly after business activity has crossed the normal line on the way upward to prosperity, and 13 months before the business downturns. These lowest points of the bond yields are six months later than the lowest points of the short-term interest rates. The highest points of the bond yields correspond with the lowest prices for bonds, and they are reached shortly after business activity crosses the normal level on the way downward. These highest points of the bond yields are three months later than the highest points of the short-term interest rates.

The chief conclusion of this chapter is in reality the chief conclusion of this book. It is that there has long operated in this country a monetary mechanism that has been responsible for bringing about most of the long succession of recurring business cycles that have followed one another throughout our national history. The operation of this monetary mechanism has at times been interrupted or much modified by wars and by developments originating in foreign countries, but during most of the decades of our history our own monetary and banking laws, regulations, and practices have been chiefly responsible for our recurring depressions.

A condensed outline of the controlling factors in our typical business cycles includes a succession of four sets of developments. Starting at the bottom of a business depression there has been an expansion of business activity, shortly preceded and accompanied by a sharp increase in the marketing of new securities, largely consisting of stock issues. Conditions have been favorable for the marketing of these securities, for security prices have turned upward, interest rates have been low, and bank reserves have been ample. The expansion of business has been largely financed by the use of the proceeds from the sales of the new securities, and industrial and other companies have also relied on their own earned surpluses to pay for the increases in their operations.

The second important development has been invisible to the public and the press, and one that has been little understood and not closely followed in financial circles. As business activity has developed, cash has flowed out of the banks and has been used in public circulation to meet the requirements of expanding pay rolls and those of increased retail trade. This has resulted in decreasing the reserve ratios of the banks, and concomitantly in lifting short-term interest rates.

A third development has come after short-term interest rates have risen rather slowly for some months and then have begun to stiffen at an accelerated pace, and that development has been a downturn in security prices with bond prices usually turning downward first and being followed by stock prices. These downturns in security prices have created unfavorable conditions for the further marketing of additional issues of new securities with the result that there has been a decrease of the inflow of new funds into productive enterprise.

Some months have usually elapsed before the decrease of the inflow of new funds into enterprise has resulted in a downturn of business activity, and meanwhile cash has continued to flow out of the banks, reserve ratios have continued to decline, and short-term interest rates have advanced to still higher levels.

The fourth characteristic development has been the downturn of business activity, promptly followed by a return flow of cash back into the banks, and by a rapid rise in the reserve ratios. Meanwhile short-term interest rates have turned downward and a little later on long-term rates have followed them. This means that bond prices have turned upward again, and at about the same time stock prices have turned upward also, thus creating once again favorable conditions for the marketing of new issues of securities, and so a new business cycle has been started on its way.

These characteristic developments of the recurring business cycles operated with a considerable degree of regularity before the establishment of the Federal Reserve System, and with less regularity through the war period and up to the beginning of the Great Depression. They appear to be inescapable as long as the supply of credit is controlled by the reserve requirements of banks. The lengths of business cycles have been mainly dependent on the rates of outflow of cash from the banks to public circulation, and on the rates of subsequent inflow back to the banks.

Diagrams and data of earlier chapters have shown that past business cycles have been of widely varying durations, but in a good many of them there have been characteristic developments so nearly evenly spaced as to indicate that some essential recurring process must have operated as a regulator of the time elements involved. A good example of this sort of regularity is supplied by data measuring in months the time elapsed in a succession of cycles between the point of lowest production of pig iron and the high of bond prices.

In Cycle L that span was 17 months, in M it was 15 months, in N 15 months, in O 14 months, in R 19 months, in S 13 months, in T 13 months, and in W it was 14 months. At first thought there would seem to be little likelihood of there being a nearly constant time relationship between the occurrence of the lowest monthly production of pig iron in a depression, and the subsequent highest record for bond prices. It seems probable that the relative regularity of the elapsed times in the cycles mentioned was in reality produced by the nearly constant rates at which cash flowed out from the banks into public circulation, and then back from the public and into the banks again.

CHAPTER XV

THE PAST TWENTY-FIVE YEARS

SINCE the outbreak of the World War in 1914 there have been six business cycles in this country, including the present one that is still incompleted as this is being written in the summer of 1939. All of them, or perhaps all except one, have differed in important respects from most of the prewar cycles. Cycle U began shortly after the outbreak of the war. There was an increase in the volume of new security issues which got under way just before the business upturn, and that increase followed upturns in bond and stock prices in normal fashion. Nevertheless it is clear that the business recovery of 1915-16 was not mainly financed by funds derived from the sales of new securities. It was instead chiefly financed by the huge purchases of the warring nations overseas.

Following the close of the war there was the short Cycle V which began after an exceptionally sharp increase in the volume of new security issues, and came to its end after the flow of new issues had largely decreased. Nevertheless it seems clear that the principal motivating force which brought Cycle V into being was the unexpected post-war demand from Europe for all sorts of goods which were urgently needed to make good the shortages that had developed there during the war years. The cycle came to an end in the post-war depression of 1921 which followed the sudden declines of commodity prices that took place in most countries throughout the world in the summer and autumn of 1920.

Cycle W, which lasted from the serious depression of 1921 to the brief one of 1924, is the one cycle of the past 25 years which appears to have been a fully normal cycle when considered in the light of business cycle theory. It began with a vigorous increase in the volume of new security issues, which got under way after bond prices had turned upward. The cycle was of nearly normal duration, for it lasted 36 months. It came to an end after interest rates had stiffened, bond and stock prices had turned downward, and the flow of new security issues had diminished.

After Cycle W there followed the long Cycle X which included the New Era period with its great speculation in real estate, and its still more spectacular speculation in stocks. It lasted for nearly eight years. It brought on the Great Depression, and it ended with the banking crisis in the early spring of 1933. It began in normal fashion, but the downturn of business in the autumn of 1929 was precipitated by the collapse of stock prices, and can hardly be attributed to the decline in the volume of new security issues which had begun in the summer of that year.

The quarter of a century that has elapsed since the outbreak of the World War has been a period of recurring inflations in this country. During the war and the two years immediately following it we had a price inflation which lifted the levels of wholesale prices until they were almost two and a half times as high by the summer of 1920 as they had been in 1914. Then in the New Era period which terminated in 1929 we had an inflation of real estate values and an enormous security credit inflation. There was drastic deflation from 1929 to 1933, but now we have new inflations of bond prices and of almost idle bank deposits.

In these past 25 years the old-time drastic regulation of credit expansion through the harsh restraints imposed by limited bank reserves has been displaced by the super-elastic reserve regulation of the Federal Reserve System. Under the provisions of the Federal Reserve Act the credit-expansion powers of the available reserves were greatly magnified, and during and after the war the reserves themselves were increased by gold imports. These changes resulted in an enormous increase in bank credit. In 1914 the deposits of all banks amounted to something more than 18 billion dollars, but by 1930 they had increased to nearly 60 billions. It was that increase which financed the New Era excesses.

During the years since 1929 the old normal economic mechanism of business cycles has been only partly in operation, and one of the reasons for that is that there has taken place a fundamental change in the nature of the long oscillations in the flow of new security issues which formerly accompanied the cycles. Diagram 22 on page 150 shows the changes in certain flows of new money into our business economy since the beginning of 1929. The black silhouette at the top shows, as in many of the former diagrams, the changes in business activity as represented by the volume of industrial production fluctuating above and below its computed normal level. The contour has been smoothed by a three months centered moving average.

Below the black silhouette in the upper portion of the diagram there is a line which shows the changes in the totals of new funds contributed monthly to the economy by domestic corporate security issues sold to obtain new capital, by the new security issues of states, municipalities and other governmental subdivisions, and by the expenditures of the Federal Government in excess of its revenues. The scale is in millions of dollars and the totals were running at about 650 millions a month early in 1929. They declined sharply by the end of that year, and then rose again early in 1930 as corporations increased their expenditures in response to the pleas made to them by President Hoover. This total line, and the lines in the lower portions of the diagram, have been smoothed by five place centered moving averages.

There was an irregular decline in the total inflow of new funds until the autumn of 1933, and it is to be noted that business activity had turned upward some months earlier. That upturn appears to have been financed mainly by the funds already in the possession of corporations. From late in 1933 to the autumn of 1936 there was a large increase in the inflow of funds and in business activity, and the downturn of the funds was followed by a serious decrease in business in 1937. Another advance in the inflow of funds took place in 1938, and that was shortly followed in turn by another business upturn.

In the three lower divisions of the diagram the lines represent

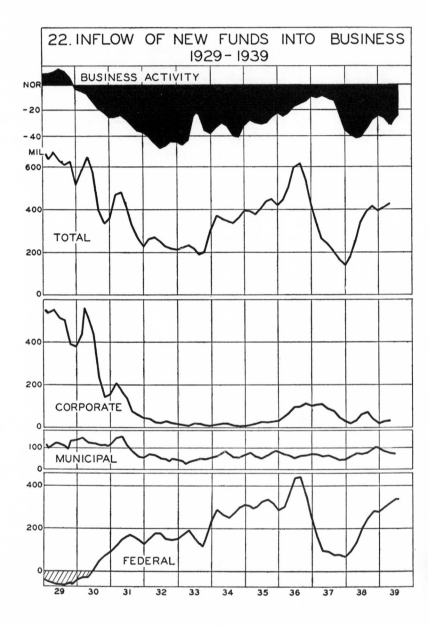

22. INFLOW OF NEW FUNDS INTO BUSINESS
1929 – 1939

BUSINESS ACTIVITY

NOR
- 20
- 40

MIL
600
TOTAL
400
200
0

400
200
CORPORATE
0

100
MUNICIPAL
0

400
200
FEDERAL
0

29 30 31 32 33 34 35 36 37 38 39

the changes in the three components of the total inflow. The highest one of the three shows the totals of the new security issues sold by domestic corporations to obtain new capital. The data up to the summer of 1934 are taken from the tabulations of the Commercial and Financial Chronicle, and do not include the issues of investment trusts. The data since the summer of 1934 are taken from the tabulations of the Securities and Exchange Commission supplemented by the Chronicle data for issues of new capital put out by railroads. In the four years from 1932 through 1935 the new corporate money was almost negligible in amount, and its totals since then have been small indeed as compared with those of predepression years.

In the second division from the bottom the line represents the totals of the issues sold for new capital by municipalities and other public subdivisions. They have been as high in recent months as they were before the depression, and they did not fall to very low levels even in 1932 and in 1933. New financing of this sort does not appear to be of much importance in the study of business cycles. The municipalities and other subdivisions contribute materially to the inflow of new funds into our business economy, but the flow is not often much influenced by business cycles.

The line at the bottom of the diagram represents the expenditures of the Federal Government in excess of its revenues. These spendings are the ones that are referred to by government economists as the income-producing expenditures of the public treasury, and commonly discussed by the public as the pump priming expenditures. In 1929 and in early 1930 the line drops below the base line of the diagram and makes a small area that is crosshatched. In those months the government was still taking in more through taxation then it was spending, and it was using the difference to reduce the debt. Its contribution to the flow of funds at that time was a negative one.

Federal income-producing expenditures increased rapidly but somewhat irregularly from the middle of 1930 to the autumn of 1936. The sudden increase in the summer of that year was caused by the payment of the bonus to the veterans. From the autumn of 1936 to the end of 1937 the income-producing expenditures of the government decreased and most of the decline took place in the first six months of that period. In the latter part of the period the sales of new issues by corporations were also declining and the combined result was a reduction in the total inflow of funds that carried them downward from well over 600 millions a month in the summer of 1936 to less than one-quarter as much by October of 1937.

It seems wholly probable that we have here the chief explanation of the exceptionally abrupt decline in business activity which took place in the autumn of 1937, and which continued with decreased violence in the early months of 1938. It was not merely an exceptionally sudden and severe business decline. It was also a great disillusionment, for it made the people realize that a self-sustaining recovery cannot be brought into being by lavish public spending. That decline brought a business cycle to its termination, but it did not come as the result of any normal interplay of the forces bringing about changes in interest rates, security prices, and the marketing of new issues of corporate securities.

In recent years business cycles have undergone structural changes in this country, and for the time at least some of the old sequences are suspended. Nevertheless, in one fundamentally important respect the business cycles of the past 25 years, and even those of the past 10 years, all resemble the cycles of earlier decades. In all of them the downturns of the cycles have taken place when there came decided decreases of the inflows of new funds into business enterprise. Shrinkages in the inflows of new funds into business have resulted in the downturns of the cycles, whether those shrinkages came because of the operation of normal economic forces, or because of governmental action in managed economics.

In the past the forces which have caused the contractions of the inflows of new funds into business have usually been internally generated, as they were in most of the prewar cycles, and probably in the case of Cycle W in 1923. Sometimes the forces causing the contractions have come from external sources, as appears to have happened when the approaching end of the World War brought about the downturn of Cycle U in 1918, and when the collapse of commodity prices brought about that of Cycle V in 1920, and when the crash of stock prices suddenly precipitated the downturn of Cycle X in 1929.

Another exceptional instance of an external cause being responsible for the downturn of a business cycle is furnished by the case of Cycle Y in 1937 which appears to have had its downturn caused by the sudden and drastic reduction in the flow of the income-producing expenditures of the Federal Government. Somewhat similar comments may be made about the upturns, for all of them appear to have been caused by increased business expenditures which can usually be traced to inflows of funds derived from sales of new securities. Sometimes the causes of upturns may originate in other sources, as in the upturn of 1933 which appears to have been financed by funds from corporation treasuries, and in that of 1938 when federal and municipal expenditures appear to have been the most important factors.

It is most regrettable that we do not have more ample information about the expansions and contractions of the inflows of new funds into industrial enterprises. Throughout most of this book the available data of new security issues have been discussed almost as though they constituted measures of the inflows of new funds into business enterprises. This course has been followed because no other source of information is available, but of course these data are sadly incomplete. We do not have separate records in earlier years of the commercial loans of banks, nor do we know anything of the security issues and private borrowings of thousands of small industries which do their financing in their own local communities. The data of security issues are indicators of the changes in the inflows of funds, but they are not inclusive measures of them.

In Diagram 22 the data of new issues are those of the securities sold to obtain new capital, and they do not include the refunding issues, although in nearly all the previous diagrams both classes are included together. There are two reasons why Diagram 22 has been constructed on this different basis. One is that the records are available for doing it, while in most of the earlier periods there were no data with which to show separately the issues for new capital and those for refunding. The other, and controlling, reason is that it is only during the past 10 years that the peace-time expenditures of government in excess of revenues have made important contributions to the flow of new funds into our national business economy.

One thing which Diagram 22 shows impressively is that the past 10 years of depression have been years of most restricted inflows of new funds into corporate enterprises. It would be wise for Americans to note that these past years when little new capital has been flowing into corporate enterprises have been depression years. They might then extend the observation and realize that through all the decades as far back as the data of new issues run, we have had depressions in this country whenever there were meager flows of new capital into business undertakings.

In recent years the timing mechanism of business cycles which has operated in the past has stopped functioning. Business cycles were formerly wave-like oscillations in the volume of trade and industry which tended to recur with considerable degrees of regularity. They did so because there was in operation a monetary mechanism which brought about alternate periods of high interest rates and low interest rates. These recurring wide oscillations of interest rates resulted in alternating rising markets and falling markets for securities, which created in turn favorable market conditions and unfavorable conditions for selling new securities and so obtaining additional capital for business undertakings.

The oscillations of the short-term interest rates were caused by alternating periods of easy credit conditions and stringent credit conditions within the banks, and those changes resulted from the expansions and contractions of the reserve ratios of the banks which were controlled by the amounts of cash money which the banks held. Cash flowed out of the banks when business was active, and that finally resulted in high interest rates. It flowed back when business was dull, and then interest rates fell. The root cause of business cycles was the control of credit expansion by bank reserves. The reason for the tendency toward regularity in the recurrence of cycles was the relative steadiness of the rates at which cash flowed out of the banks during expanding business and back into them when business contracted.

This intricate mechanism is now partly disrupted. The expansions and contractions of credit are no longer closely controlled in this country by bank reserves, for the present reserves of the banks are vastly in excess of their needs. Interest rates no longer rise and fall in close relationship to contractions and expansions of bank reserves. The outflows of cash from the banks, and the subsequent inflows back to the banks, have ceased to have much significance for business. In these respects the old-time monetary mechanism which formerly operated to bring about the turning points in business cycles, and to regulate the timing of their recurrences, has partly ceased to function.

Business cycles still follow one another in an unending procession. Their downturns still follow contractions in the volume of inflow of new funds into business, and their upturns occur when there are renewed expansions in those inflows. The causes of those changes in the flows of funds into productive enterprises used normally to be generated by the processes of business and banking. They may now have their origins in changes of policies controlling the expenditures of the Federal Government, and in changes in the laws, regulations, and attitudes through which the administration at Washington may seek to control business activity, and to institute managed economics.

CHAPTER XVI

A LONG BUSINESS INDICATOR

THROUGHOUT this book the thesis has been developed that there is a special significance in the fact that security prices and the volume of new capital issues have turned downward shortly before the downturns of most business cycles, and that they have turned upward before the business upturns. The argument has been that the downturns of the security prices have created market conditions that were unfavorable for the sale of more capital issues, and that the upturns of the prices have restored favorable market conditions. These changes of direction in the trends of security prices and in the volumes of new capital issues have resulted in cyclical fluctuations in the amounts of new money flowing into corporate enterprises.

There is one simple test which should throw considerable light on the degree of regularity with which such changes of direction in the trends of security prices and of the volumes of capital issues have in fact preceded the downturns and the upturns of the business cycles. That test can be carried through by computing the data of a single line representing in the earlier years of the long period under review a smoothed average of the courses of the security prices, and for the years since the early 1860's a line representing a smoothed average of the security prices and of the capital issues.

Such a line has been constructed for the entire period of 108 years covered by the diagrams of this book. From 1831 through 1862 it is a simple unweighted average of the 12 months moving centered averages of the bond and stock prices. Beginning with 1863, when the data of the capital issues became available, it is an average of the three series, but no longer an unweighted average. The data of new issues are small in volume in the 1860's and 1870's, and they were given a weight of only .04 in 1863, while the bond prices and stock prices were each given a weight of .48.

In each following year up to and including 1880 the weight given the new issues was increased by .02, and those of the bonds and stocks were decreased by .01 until the weights were .40 for the issues and .30 for the bonds and the same for the stocks. That weighting of .40 and .30 and .30 was continued through 1938. It should be noted that the two price components are 12 place moving centered averages, while that of the issues is a 12 place moving centered total. It follows from this construction that the line could not have been computed promptly enough to have served as a satisfactory instrument of business forecasting if it had been in use in earlier decades, but nevertheless it serves now as a test.

The use of the 12 place averages and the 12 place total as components makes the indicator line undesirably sluggish in its movements, but the extreme irregularity of the original data of the security issues makes the use of some such smoothing device unavoidable. The course of the indicator line through the 26 successive business cycles is shown in Diagram 23 on page 158, and in Diagram 24 on page 160. Both diagrams are of the three story variety with each section covering 18 years. The black silhouettes at the top of each section represent the monthly changes in business activity. The downturns of the cycles are marked by the light vertical dashed lines, and the upturns by the heavy ones. The cycles are designated by the letters at the tops of the sections between the arrows.

According to theory the indicator line should be moving downward as it crosses each light vertical dashed line, and it should be moving upward as it crosses each of the heavy ones. In nearly all the cases it behaves in that way, but in a few instances its changes of direction are made too sluggishly to render that possible. The first such instances come at the upturns from Cycle E to Cycle F in 1854, and from Cycle F to Cycle G in 1858. At both of those turning points short sections of dashed line have been added below the solid indicator line to show where composite lines made of

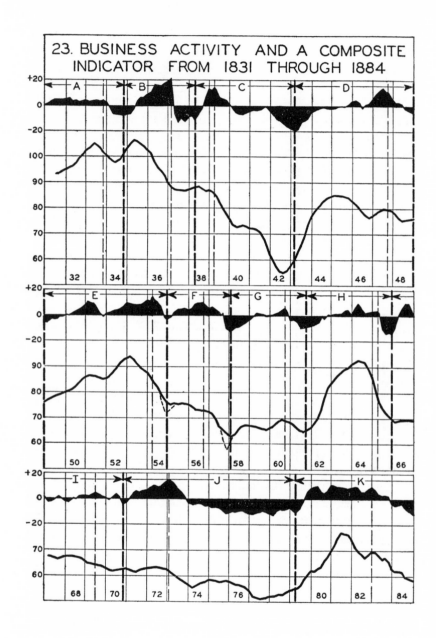

23. BUSINESS ACTIVITY AND A COMPOSITE
INDICATOR FROM 1831 THROUGH 1884

five-place centered moving averages of the price data would have run if they had been used instead of the more sluggish 12 place averages. Both of them show upturns preceding the business upturns.

The next case in which the upturn of the indicator line comes after the business upturn instead of preceding it is at the end of 1865 at the upturn from Cycle H to Cycle I. In that case business recovery seems to have been under way before the average of the bond and stock lines began to advance. The Civil War came to an end in April of that year, and the cessation of hostilities was at once followed by a short but sharp depression. Stock prices turned upward with the advent of peace, and continued to advance during most of the rest of the year, but bond prices continued to fall until March of 1866.

In 1882 there is a dip in the composite line due to a dip in the volume of issues and accompanied by one in business activity, but there was a recovery before the end of the year and the indicator line is moving downward again as it crosses the light vertical dashed line marking the downturn of the cycle. There is a genuine exception in 1888 when the composite line is moving downward when it crosses the heavy dashed line marking the end of Cycle L. Both the bond line and the stock line were moving upward, but the line of security issues was declining, and sustained business recovery did not get under way until it had turned upward.

There is another genuine exception in 1891 at the time of the Baring Crisis when business activity was briefly curtailed due to fears of a banking crisis in England, and then promptly resumed when it was realized that the crisis had been averted. During the World War in 1918 the volume of security issues was being restricted by governmental action and the line was moving upward from a very low level at the time of the downturn of Cycle U.

The indicator line crosses the light and heavy dashed lines 50 times in the long period covered by the two diagrams, and there are four instances in which it was not moving upward or downward as it should have been according to theory. One of them comes at

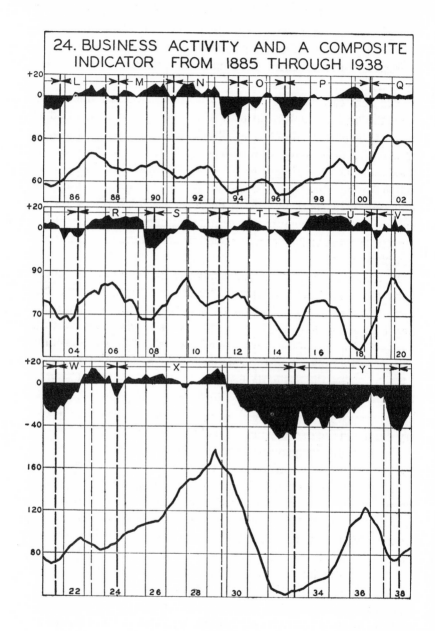

24. BUSINESS ACTIVITY AND A COMPOSITE
INDICATOR FROM 1885 THROUGH 1938

the end of the Civil War and another at the end of the World War when the business cycles were subject to most exceptional influences. Another came at the time of the recovery from the Baring Crisis in 1891, and one of them in 1888 when Cycle M started a recovery, suffered a relapse, and then resumed its recovery after the volume of security issues had begun to expand.

The record is a remarkably consistent one, and especially so in view of the fact that the indicator line is a very simple and almost crude statistical device for use in making such a test. It will be noted that although the line has a very good record with respect to its crossings of the dashed lines it makes a good many false turns between the dashed lines which would have been misleading to anyone who had been trying to use it as an actual instrument of business forecasting.

Most of the false intermediate turns result from irregularities in the series of security issues, and there does not seem to be any simple and easy way to avoid them. In a good many instances they may be traced to exceptionally large individual issues of securities such as those which were formerly floated at frequent but irregular intervals by the American Telephone and Telegraph Company, and by some others of the great corporations.

Despite all its shortcomings the indicator line reflects the high degree of regularity with which stock and bond prices have turned downward before the downturns of our business cycles and by doing so have created unfavorable market conditions for the further marketing of new securities, and the regularity with which they have turned upward before the upturns of the cycles and brought about favorable market conditions for floating new issues. For the past 75 years the line includes the data of the new issues as well as those of the bond and stock prices, and it continues to turn upward and downward with almost unbroken regularity shortly before the upturns and downturns of the business cycles.

CHAPTER XVII

SEQUENCES WITHIN CYCLES

ONE of the sayings of the late O. P. Van Sweringen embodied the key explanation of the business cycle, although neither he nor his associates recognized it as being the key. He used to say, "You can't finance on a falling market," and since he held control over some 260 corporations he spoke from an abundance of experience. He meant that most new financing must be done while security prices are rising, for when they are declining most investors are reluctant to make new commitments, since they believe that by waiting a little longer they will be able to make their contemplated purchases at lower prices.

That simple observation that rising security prices favor new financing, while falling prices hinder it, explains why it is that the flow of new funds into business enterprises has always been an undulating one, with the volume of the inflow of new funds moving in long wave-like fluctuations which have preceded by some months the fluctuations of industrial production that have largely constituted the business cycles. The new funds flowing into corporation treasuries from the proceeds of the sales of new securities have promptly been used for more construction, new equipment, stocks of materials, and increased pay rolls. When the flows of funds have decreased these expansions have terminated.

It has long been a commonplace of financial comment that business confidence increases, and business sentiment becomes more optimistic, when stock prices are advancing. A great deal of derision has been directed at business men because they seemed to permit their judgments to be shaped and their attitudes to be guided by merely transitory changes in the quoted prices of stocks and bonds. Probably the business men have been more nearly in the right than have their critics, for the rising security prices were in reality facilitating business improvement and increased employment, while falling security prices were the forerunners of business contraction and unemployment.

This book has supported the thesis that business cycles are caused by long undulating fluctuations of the inflows of new capital into business enterprises. The cause of these undulations has been the succession of bull markets and bear markets for security prices which have resulted in creating alternating periods of favorable and unfavorable conditions for marketing new capital issues of securities. The transitions from rising trends in the security markets to falling trends and back upward again have been brought about by alternating expansions and contractions of short-term interest rates, which have resulted in turn from decreases and increases in the reserve ratios of banks. Cyclical fluctuations in the reserve ratios have been mostly due to outflows of cash from banks to public circulation during business expansions, and return flows during contractions. The rates of these outflows and inflows have controlled the durations of the cycles.

This theory is not entirely new. Parts of it have been previously developed by supporters of monetary theories of business cycles, and particularly by Mr. R. G. Hawtrey, a distinguished British writer on banking and economics. Mr. Hawtrey has recognized and expounded the role of the reserve ratios of the banks in controlling the fluctuations of short-term interest rates, and that of the rates of outflow of currency from the banks to public circulation, and its subsequent return inflow, in accounting for the former relative regularity and periodicity in the alternating periods of prosperity and depression, of expansion and contraction.

The crucial difference between the theory propounded by Mr. Hawtrey and that supported in this book lies in the explanation of the rôle played by the changes in the levels of short-term interest rates in bringing about the turning points in the business cycles. Mr. Hawtrey argues that while ordinary changes in interest rates do not produce important differences of costs in the profit and loss accounts of the average business, they are highly important to the merchants who have large overturns of goods and make small margins of profits.

He claims that merchants place large orders for increased stocks of goods when interest rates fall to low levels in times of slow business, and that they curtail their orders when interest rates advance sufficiently to make them decidedly important as items in the costs of doing business. These increases and decreases in the volumes of orders of the merchants result in fluctuations of demand which reach back to the producers and so bring about fluctuations in production and employment in manufacturing industries. The theory is closely related to the consumer purchasing power theories of cycles in that it starts off by attributing the genesis of the cyclical fluctuations of business to changes in the demand for consumers goods.

The theory supported in this book traces the influence of the changes in interest rates directly to the security markets and through them to undulations in the inflow of funds into business enterprises and in primary degree into the industries turning out producers goods. This is not a theory of derived demand for durable goods fluctuating in response to changes in the demand for consumers goods. It is instead the theory that business cycles are mainly caused by changes in the volume of purchases of durable goods by business enterprises, resulting from changes in the volumes of new investments in the securities of these enterprises, and in some instances from other changes in the inflow of new funds into business channels, as for example those resulting from large foreign orders during the World War, and those from governmental income-producing expenditures during recent years.

Diagram 25 on page 166 has been constructed for the purpose of repeating in summary form an account of the successive sequences in a typical business cycle which have been discussed in preceding chapters. The diagram begins at the top with a black silhouette showing a typical cycle of business activity as represented by changing volumes of industrial production above and below the computed normal level. The typical cycle is 40 months in duration, or three and one-third years, with the expansion phase from the upturn in depression to the peak of prosperity lasting 27 months, and the phase of contraction from the downturn of prosperity to the bottom of depression lasting 13 months.

Shortly after the peak of prosperity the cash in banks is at a minimum, for during recovery and prosperity currency has been flowing out of the banks and into general public circulation for use in pay rolls and retail trade. As business contracts, and while depression lasts, the currency has been flowing back into the banks again because not so much of it has been needed for public circulation. When recovery has carried business activity back upward to about the theoretical normal level this inflow of cash to the banks has been completed, and those institutions hold a maximum amount of cash money.

The changes in the amounts of cash held by the banks, and in the volumes of the deposits in the banks, control the reserve ratios of those institutions, which the laws compel the banks to maintain above certain specified lower limits. Thus under normal conditions the expansions of bank credit are controlled by reserve ratios, and in practice it has been true that interest rates have varied in nearly direct relationship to the proportions of all currency in circulation not held by banks, and so inversely with the proportions of it held by the banks. The patterns of the changes in the reserve ratios are nearly the same as those of the interest rates and they are shown in Diagram 19 on page 139, while correspondences between interest rates and circulating money are shown in Diagram 20 on page 142.

Because of the interactions of the flows of cash from the banks into public circulation and back again, and of the falling and rising reserve ratios, short-term interest rates have regularly fallen as the proportion of cash in the banks has risen, and the interest rates have risen as the proportion of cash in the banks has fallen. When the banks have held relatively large proportions of the cash the credit conditions have been easy and interest rates have been low,

25. TYPICAL SEQUENCES IN A TYPICAL BUSINESS CYCLE

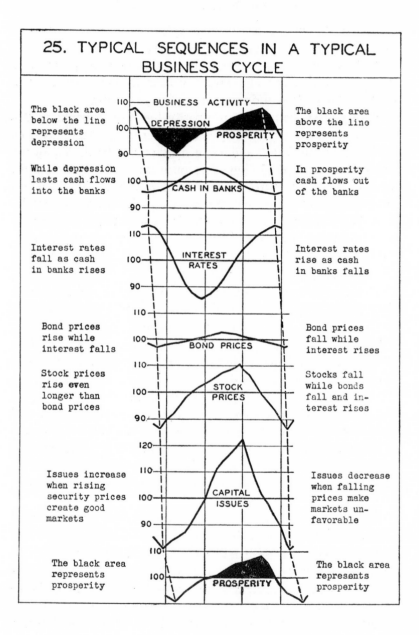

The black area below the line represents depression

While depression lasts cash flows into the banks

Interest rates fall as cash in banks rises

Bond prices rise while interest falls

Stock prices rise even longer than bond prices

Issues increase when rising security prices create good markets

The black area represents prosperity

The black area above the line represents prosperity

In prosperity cash flows out of the banks

Interest rates rise as cash in banks falls

Bond prices fall while interest rises

Stocks fall while bonds fall and interest rises

Issues decrease when falling prices make markets unfavorable

The black area represents prosperity

BUSINESS ACTIVITY
DEPRESSION
PROSPERITY

CASH IN BANKS

INTEREST RATES

BOND PRICES

STOCK PRICES

CAPITAL ISSUES

PROSPERITY

but when the banks have held relatively small proportions of the cash there has been credit stringency, and interest rates have been high.

Long-term interest rates, as represented by bond yields, have moved with short-term rates, but with much less amplitude of fluctuation, and always with a considerable lag in their timing. Since bond prices are high when their yields are low, and prices low when yields are high, it has followed that the highest prices for bonds have been recorded some months after the lowest short-term interest rates have been reached, and that the lowest bond prices have been quoted a little after the highest short-term interest rates.

Stock prices have moved with bond prices, but they have swung through much wider fluctuations, and they have made their cyclical upturns and downturns somewhat later. The bull markets for stocks have characteristically been longer than those of bonds, and their bear markets have been shorter. It is worth noting that in the typical cycle the major part of the bull market for stocks takes place during business depression, and most of the bear market is completed during business prosperity.

Capital issues show the widest amplitude of fluctuation of any of the financial series shown in the diagram. They have almost the same periods of expansion and contraction as the stock prices and they lag a little behind them in their timing, for their upturns and their downturns are characteristically a little later than those of the stocks. Capital issues increase in volume when rising security prices create favorable market conditions for selling new securities, and they decrease in volume when falling prices bring about unfavorable market conditions for new flotations.

By the time capital issues have reached their lowest volume depression has set in and is growing more serious, but nevertheless the processes are under way which are arranging conditions for a new recovery. Cash in banks is low and reserve ratios are high but the return flow of cash from the public to the banks has already begun. Interest rates are high, but they have begun to ease off, and they are on the way downward. Bond prices have stopped falling and have turned upward. Stock prices also have made their upturn and a new bull market is starting to get under way. Market conditions have once more become favorable for attracting the new funds of investors and another upswing in the volume of capital issues is about to take place.

By means of text and diagrams the chapters of this book have traced the records of some of the most important of American financial series through 26 business cycles from 1831 through 1938, and in part through 1939. Many of the data used have been unsatisfactory in quality, especially in the earlier years, and some of them were not available for use in the early decades of the period covered. Nevertheless the inquiry has shown that there has been a high degree of consistency and regularity in the patterns followed by the several financial series through the long sequence of business cycles.

It has been shown that bond prices and stock prices have almost invariably turned downward shortly before the downturns of business activity in the cycles, and that with somewhat reduced consistency they have turned upward just before the upturns of the cycles. These downturns and upturns of the security prices have regularly taken place after the cyclical upturns and downturns of short-term interest rates. The upturns and downturns in the cycles of security prices appear to have come as consequences of the cyclical turns in the short-term interest rates, and the interrelations of the movements of the series are of such character that it seems justifiable to consider the upturns and downturns of the security prices as being caused by the corresponding downturns and upturns of the interest rates.

The most important contribution of new statistical data made by the volume is that of the series of listings of new corporate securities on the New York Stock Exchange. This series provides an indicator of the timing of major changes in the volume of the inflow of new capital into business enterprises back into the 1860's. Our longest previously available series was that of the Journal of Commerce which begins in 1906. The new data enable us to study the cyclical changes in these volumes of capital flow over a period of some 75 years.

The records show that the flow of capital funds from new security issues has an unbroken record of having turned downward before the downturns of all of the 16 business cycles that have been completed in this country in the years covered by the statistical series of security issues. The record of upturns has two, perhaps three, exceptions. The flow of capital funds from new security issues was late in turning upward in 1888. The upturn of business which initiated Cycle M is listed in the tables of this volume as having taken place in July of 1888. That recovery suffered a relapse and business activity dipped below the normal level again in June of the following year. By that time the volume of new issues had begun to advance, so it appears that there was not in that case a genuine exception to the general rule.

In 1891 the records show a genuine exception. Cycle M came to its end in April of 1891 in the Baring Crisis which originated in England, and which was promptly cured without having resulted in the depression which was then almost universally feared and expected in all the commercial nations. Business activity had suddenly dropped to low levels in this country between the late autumn of 1890 and the early spring of 1891. When it was realized here that the English banking situation was once more in order, business activity made one of the most rapid recoveries on record and was back at prosperity levels by early summer. It is clear that in this instance recovery was not brought about by the inflow of new funds. Business had briefly and drastically curtailed its activities and then, when it found that its alarms were needless, it promptly resumed operations.

The other exception is the recovery of 1933 following the banking crisis. That recovery was preceded by upturns of bond and stock prices, but the initial upturn of business activity seems to have been financed by the use of corporation funds drawn from their own treasuries. In the entire long period up to 1933 there is no instance in which the flow of new funds from security issues shows an important decline without that development being followed by a downturn of business activity, nor is there any instance of the issues showing an important advance that was not promptly accompanied and followed by business recovery and prosperity.

Causation is extremely difficult to establish in the social sciences. Students in the physical sciences generally accept as a working theory the Hume principle of causality which regards a hypothesis as proven when it has been shown that the "cause" A is invariably associated with the "effect" B; that A is never present without B; that B is never found without A; and that there is no further invariable element C from which A and B may both proceed, not as a cause-effect with relation to one another, but as joint effects.

If we make a rigorous application of the Hume principle to the data that have been considered in this book it can hardly be claimed that it has been demonstrated that changes in the inflow of new funds into business enterprise have been the causes of the turning points in American business cycles. Nevertheless, there is a mass of persuasive evidence indicating that this is the case.

It is clearly impossible to make a definitive case for one invariable origin because the timing and the occurrences of the turning points of business cycles may be influenced by a variety of forces of varying potency. Not all of them originate in the routine developments of business and finance in the country being studied. Among the external developments there may be included such forces as those of wars, political struggles, foreign depressions, disorders of monetary systems, and troubles arising from unwise banking legislation.

The theory of the business cycle that has been set forth in these pages is a flexible theory in that it does not exclude non-cyclical forces which may not only influence the timing of the turning points, but may even initiate upturns and downturns. It explains the regularity of recurrence which has characterized some series of cycles, but allows for changes in the duration which might well result from imports and exports of gold and from changes in the use of currency by the general public. It is an explanation of cycles which involves a fundamentally monetary factor, and allows for international relationships and complications between cycles in different countries. It helps to explain the cumulative nature of the processes of expansion and contraction after the upturns and the downturns have taken place.

In the development of the theory of the turning points of business cycles discussed in this book it has been shown that for more than 100 years security prices have turned upward and downward with almost unbroken regularity shortly before the upturns and downturns of American business cycles. During 70 years the flow of new security issues has moved similarly. There has been introduced an explanation of the intricate monetary mechanism which has caused the long undulating movements in short-term interest rates which have resulted in the turning points in the cyclical movements of the security prices. The reasons for the former relative regularity in the periodicity of the recurring cycles have been set forth.

It has been shown that during most of the past 40 years for which the data are available the cyclical increases and decreases of the inflows of money into business enterprises from the sales of new security issues have been closely comparable in amount to the cyclical dollar increases and decreases in the pay rolls of the factory workers engaged in the industries producing durable goods, except during the war period. The cyclical changes in the volumes of the security issues have preceded the corresponding changes in the total pay rolls of those factory workers. The explanation is unavoidably long and complicated, and tediously statistical, but the writer believes that it accounts for the turning points in our business cycles. The cause of business cycles seems to be the changes in the flow of new money into business enterprises.

APPENDIX A

Col. 1. Percents by which business activity rose above or fell below the computed normal level each month from 1831 through 1939 according to the index of American Business Activity of the Cleveland Trust Company. See Appendix C.

Col. 2. Bond prices in dollars. See Appendix D.

Col. 3. Stock prices in dollars. See Appendix E.

Col. 4. Discount rates on four to six months commercial paper. See Appendix F.

Col. 5. New corporate bonds listed on the New York Stock Exchange and sold for money. Data are in millions of dollars. See Chapters III and VII.

Col. 6. New corporate stocks listed on the New York Stock Exchange and sold for money. Data are in millions of dollars. See Chapters III and VII.

Col. 7. New corporate financing by bonds and notes according to the compilations of the New York Journal of Commerce. Data are in millions of dollars. See Chapters V and VII.

Col. 8. New corporate financing by stocks according to the compilations of the New York Journal of Commerce. Data are in millions of dollars. See Chapters V and VII.

TABLE 9

Date	1 Business Activity	2 Bond Price	3 Stock Price	4 Coml. Paper
1831				
J	+ .9	99.7	86.4	5.50
F	+2.0	97.8	85.7	5.50
M	+3.3	98.4	87.2	5.50
A	+4.1	98.6	86.2	5.50
M	+5.2	99.1	86.5	5.50
J	+5.1	98.9	87.5	5.50
J	+5.4	102.4	87.1	6.00
A	+5.1	103.5	85.4	6.50
S	+5.4	103.7	84.2	7.00
O	+5.0	104.7	84.7	7.00
N	+5.8	104.3	83.0	7.00
D	+5.4	104.2	84.2	7.00
1832				
J	+5.5	105.0	84.9	7.00
F	+6.1	107.7	84.7	6.50
M	+5.1	107.8	85.4	6.00
A	+3.0	108.4	85.9	6.50
M	+3.4	108.8	84.9	7.00
J	+4.1	110.1	86.4	6.00
J	+3.1	107.8	86.6	6.00
A	+2.7	108.0	88.0	6.00
S	+4.0	109.4	89.4	6.00
O	+3.6	113.1	92.3	6.00
N	+5.9	112.7	94.9	6.00
D	+4.3	111.1	97.2	6.00
1833				
J	+5.1	110.3	98.8	6.00
F	+2.5	107.9	99.7	5.50
M	+2.2	108.1	100.9	5.50
A	+3.3	108.8	102.8	6.00
M	+3.6	109.9	103.3	6.00
J	+3.5	108.8	103.3	6.50
J	+3.3	108.4	102.1	8.00
A	+3.2	110.6	102.6	8.00
S	+3.7	109.9	100.2	8.00
O	+4.0	108.6	100.3	10.00
N	+3.0	106.6	96.7	11.00
D	+2.5	104.8	94.6	13.50
1834				
J	−1.7	99.8	91.4	19.00
F	−2.0	96.8	87.1	.....
M	−5.0	97.4	88.8	.....
A	−6.2	96.4	96.7	.....
M	−6.4	98.9	97.6	.....
J	−7.0	98.6	95.1	.....
J	−7.5	99.5	94.3	.....
A	−7.3	101.8	97.6	.....
S	−7.0	106.5	98.7	.....
O	−7.4	105.3	100.4	.....
N	−7.0	103.0	102.4	.....
D	−6.8	106.1	103.6	10.00

TABLE 9—(*Continued*)

Date	1 Business Activity	2 Bond Price	3 Stock Price	4 Coml. Paper
1835				
J	− 6.4	104.1	105.4	5.00
F	− 6.0	102.6	103.6	.....
M	− 5.0	102.6	109.2	.....
A	− 1.5	103.4	111.1	.....
M	+ 1.5	103.3	118.0	.....
J	+ 4.3	103.8	117.7	.....
J	+ 5.8	101.1	115.9	.....
A	+ 6.1	100.6	118.1	.....
S	+ 5.9	98.3	113.4	.....
O	+ 6.0	94.4	111.9	.....
N	+ 7.2	94.0	106.6	.....
D	+ 8.8	91.2	105.5	9.00
1836				
J	+ 9.9	89.1	105.3	10.00
F	+11.1	88.2	111.9	10.00
M	+14.4	89.3	112.0	12.00
A	+17.4	88.0	109.2	13.50
M	+17.3	86.9	108.2	16.50
J	+16.5	86.4	107.2	13.50
J	+16.5	83.7	106.0	16.50
A	+16.2	82.0	103.6	21.00
S	+17.1	82.1	101.6	24.00
O	+18.1	80.1	98.1	30.00
N	+18.4	79.9	95.6	27.00
D	+18.9	79.7	97.6	27.00
1837				
J	+17.1	83.1	102.5	16.33
F	+21.0	79.8	102.0	18.00
M	+19.5	80.9	96.6	21.67
A	− 6.6	78.4	87.1	27.67
M	−14.3	78.5	78.6	29.50
J	−13.3	82.8	77.5	11.00
J	−11.4	88.5	87.1	7.50
A	−10.0	94.0	87.5	7.50
S	−10.1	91.7	88.0	7.00
O	−12.7	88.5	88.7	6.50
N	−11.3	82.3	90.7	7.50
D	− 9.3	85.7	90.1	10.00
1838				
J	− 9.8	91.5	88.9	11.00
F	− 8.4	89.4	86.9	12.00
M	− 7.1	91.7	83.7	15.00
A	−11.8	80.8	82.0	15.00
M	−10.6	83.3	86.9	8.67
J	− 6.0	84.0	90.6	6.50
J	− 4.6	88.5	90.8	6.00
A	− 1.0	90.4	93.7	6.50
S	− 1.6	89.3	94.5	6.50
O	+ 7.0	88.5	91.8	6.50
N	+10.8	85.9	92.3	7.00
D	+13.7	81.6	91.2	7.67

TABLE 9—(*Continued*)

Date	1 Business Activity	2 Bond Price	3 Stock Price	4 Coml. Paper
1839				
J	+14.0	82.0	92.6	7.50
F	+12.9	81.3	93.6	7.50
M	+15.2	80.6	90.6	7.50
A	+12.5	78.3	91.0	7.50
M	+ 9.8	77.8	92.7	7.50
J	+ 6.2	77.3	91.6	9.00
J	+ 5.1	74.1	88.1	11.50
A	+ 5.1	72.8	85.9	13.50
S	+ 4.3	72.0	83.6	18.00
O	+ 3.5	71.3	79.0	25.50
N	+ 2.2	63.3	77.1	29.67
D	+ .5	61.6	79.4	14.00
1840				
J	− 1.2	60.8	81.9	9.00
F	− 2.9	68.0	80.5	10.50
M	− 5.8	67.0	78.4	10.50
A	− 6.0	68.0	79.0	9.50
M	− 6.9	62.5	80.2	7.00
J	− 6.9	62.9	81.2	7.00
J	− 6.3	63.3	81.7	6.50
A	− 7.0	63.0	81.4	6.25
S	− 6.2	63.5	82.5	6.50
O	− 5.3	64.0	85.4	6.50
N	− 4.4	64.7	84.5	6.50
D	− 3.5	64.9	83.3	6.50
1841				
J	− 2.6	66.3	81.0	6.50
F	− 2.9	66.3	80.7	6.50
M	− 3.7	60.8	75.4	6.50
A	− 3.6	58.4	76.6	6.50
M	− 3.4	61.2	79.7	6.00
J	− 2.9	64.7	79.7	6.00
J	− 1.7	61.0	80.5	6.00
A	− .8	60.6	79.2	6.00
S	− .9	61.5	77.6	6.50
O	− 1.7	59.0	75.8	6.75
N	− 2.8	56.5	75.1	7.50
D	− 4.6	51.5	71.5	10.50
1842				
J	− 6.5	48.0	64.5	10.50
F	− 7.7	42.6	63.7	10.50
M	− 8.1	42.6	61.5	10.50
A	−10.8	36.4	60.9	8.00
M	−11.3	42.0	64.4	8.00
J	−12.2	46.0	66.0	8.00
J	−14.3	49.8	63.9	8.00
A	−14.7	49.8	62.1	7.25
S	−14.2	49.9	62.9	7.00
O	−16.7	50.1	63.1	6.25
N	−16.7	50.2	61.9	6.25
D	−18.1	50.3	61.9	7.50

TABLE 9—(*Continued*)

Date	1 Business Activity	2 Bond Price	3 Stock Price	4 Coml. Paper
1843				
J	−18.6	49.9	61.0	6.00
F	−19.1	49.8	64.5	5.50
M	−18.4	49.8	64.5	5.50
A	−18.8	49.8	65.5	5.00
M	−17.0	62.5	72.0	4.75
J	−12.3	65.0	74.5	4.33
J	−11.4	67.3	74.0	4.00
A	−11.5	70.1	75.5	3.62
S	−10.7	72.9	76.0	3.75
O	− 9.3	70.7	76.0	3.75
N	− 8.4	74.8	78.0	3.75
D	− 4.9	79.3	84.5	3.75
1844				
J	− 4.1	72.8	82.5	4.00
F	− 2.9	75.2	84.5	4.00
M	− 2.0	69.7	86.0	4.50
A	− 1.5	72.4	89.0	5.00
M	− 1.0	78.1	92.0	5.00
J	− .7	72.0	92.5	5.00
J	− .5	75.2	91.0	5.00
A	− .6	75.2	93.0	5.00
S	− 1.1	76.8	94.0	5.25
O	− 1.5	82.4	95.0	5.00
N	− 1.8	77.7	92.3	5.25
D	− 1.8	74.3	91.0	5.00
1845				
J	− 1.6	75.3	89.0	5.50
F	− 1.7	76.4	93.0	5.75
M	− 1.0	77.4	93.5	5.75
A	− .5	78.5	92.5	5.75
M	− .1	79.6	93.0	5.75
J	− .2	79.2	92.0	5.75
J	− .3	79.0	91.5	5.87
A	− .1	78.6	90.5	6.00
S	+ .4	78.2	91.5	6.00
O	+ 1.5	77.8	93.0	5.75
N	+ 2.5	77.4	95.0	6.50
D	+ 3.6	77.0	96.5	8.00
1846				
J	+ 4.3	71.5	87.0	8.00
F	+ 4.5	71.9	90.0	8.50
M	+ 3.7	72.5	93.0	7.50
A	+ 2.8	71.4	84.0	10.50
M	+ 1.1	69.7	84.0	10.00
J	− 1.4	69.9	89.0	10.00
J	+ 1.0	69.0	86.0	9.66
A	+ 1.6	69.5	87.0	8.50
S	+ 1.6	69.9	85.0	7.50
O	+ 2.0	69.7	84.0	7.00
N	+ 3.0	69.5	84.0	6.50
D	+ 4.7	67.2	82.0	6.50

TABLE 9—(*Continued*)

Date	1 Business Activity	2 Bond Price	3 Stock Price	4 Coml. Paper
1847				
J	+ 6.9	68.0	82.0	10.00
F	+10.1	68.4	87.0	10.00
M	+ 9.8	67.5	86.0	9.00
A	+11.8	70.0	87.0	8.50
M	+12.5	73.2	89.0	8.00
J	+14.3	73.2	95.0	6.50
J	+12.0	71.8	96.0	6.50
A	+11.9	71.3	97.0	8.00
S	+11.9	72.1	95.0	9.00
O	+ 9.3	71.0	91.0	10.50
N	+ 6.8	69.0	86.0	13.50
D	+ 4.8	68.3	83.0	15.00
1848				
J	+ 3.4	67.4	82.0	18.00
F	+ 2.7	67.1	85.0	15.00
M	+ 3.1	70.0	86.0	13.50
A	+ 2.6	69.4	84.0	15.00
M	+ 1.9	69.7	82.0	13.50
J	+ 1.5	71.1	82.0	16.50
J	− 1.0	71.1	80.0	16.50
A	− 2.2	69.9	79.0	13.50
S	− 2.0	69.9	79.0	13.50
O	− 2.9	70.0	76.0	16.50
N	− 4.4	70.4	75.0	16.50
D	− 5.4	71.3	80.0	13.50
1849				
J	− 4.1	73.1	80.0	12.00
F	− 4.7	73.7	80.0	10.50
M	− 1.5	73.4	83.0	13.50
A	− 2.2	75.4	81.0	13.50
M	− 2.1	76.7	83.0	10.00
J	− 2.5	79.3	85.0	8.00
J	− .7	78.0	84.0	8.00
A	− 1.3	77.7	81.0	8.00
S	− .7	75.7	81.0	9.00
O	− .7	76.7	80.0	9.50
N	− .5	77.9	80.0	9.00
D	+ .1	77.1	80.0	10.00
1850				
J	+ .2	77.3	80.0	9.75
F	− .6	77.9	79.0	8.50
M	+ .6	80.1	82.0	8.50
A	+ 1.8	81.7	81.0	8.75
M	+ 2.1	83.3	84.0	8.00
J	+ 2.5	82.1	86.0	7.75
J	+ 3.4	81.0	83.0	6.75
A	+ 3.7	81.0	84.0	7.50
S	+ 4.8	81.6	85.0	8.25
O	+ 5.6	80.8	90.0	7.50
N	+ 6.8	82.0	91.0	7.50
D	+ 8.2	82.5	95.0	7.50

TABLE 9—(*Continued*)

Date	1 Business Activity	2 Bond Price	3 Stock Price	4 Coml. Paper
1851				
J	+10.9	79.0	94.0	6.75
F	+ 9.6	81.5	95.0	7.75
M	+ 9.7	81.4	94.0	7.75
A	+ 9.0	78.6	96.0	8.00
M	+ 7.8	81.1	95.0	7.00
J	+ 7.4	78.7	96.0	8.00
J	+ 4.3	76.6	93.0	10.00
A	+ .7	76.4	87.0	11.00
S	+ .7	76.1	88.0	13.50
O	− .9	76.3	89.0	15.50
N	+ .9	78.2	91.0	10.50
D	+ 1.3	79.3	92.0	10.50
1852				
J	+ .3	79.8	89.0	8.75
F	+ 1.3	79.3	89.0	8.00
M	+ 2.2	79.7	94.0	6.50
A	+ 2.8	81.9	96.0	6.00
M	+ 3.5	82.0	98.0	6.00
J	+ 3.3	81.7	98.0	5.75
J	+ 4.4	83.1	99.0	5.75
A	+ 4.7	84.4	101.0	5.75
S	+ 5.6	83.0	102.0	6.50
O	+ 6.5	81.5	103.0	6.00
N	+ 7.4	82.9	106.0	6.00
D	+ 9.5	83.2	110.0	6.00
1853				
J	+ 9.0	84.1	105.0	7.00
F	+ 8.9	83.5	104.0	9.50
M	+ 8.6	82.0	103.0	11.00
A	+ 8.2	80.6	102.0	10.25
M	+ 8.1	81.0	105.0	8.00
J	+ 7.5	83.0	104.0	8.50
J	+ 8.4	82.6	103.0	9.00
A	+ 8.0	79.5	98.0	9.50
S	+ 8.5	78.4	96.0	11.00
O	+ 9.0	78.7	95.0	13.50
N	+ 9.7	73.7	89.0	15.00
D	+12.1	79.7	96.0	10.33
1854				
J	+12.2	78.7	94.0	8.50
F	+10.9	77.3	94.0	8.00
M	+14.6	78.5	98.0	9.00
A	+11.5	78.5	96.0	11.00
M	+10.0	76.8	93.0	11.00
J	+10.0	76.7	93.0	10.00
J	+ 9.2	74.9	85.0	9.50
A	+ 5.9	71.4	79.0	9.50
S	+ 1.8	68.5	74.0	11.00
O	− 2.2	74.5	77.0	11.00
N	− 2.2	74.1	74.0	11.00
D	− 3.8	72.8	67.0	15.00

TABLE 9—(*Continued*)

Date	1 Business Activity	2 Bond Price	3 Stock Price	4 Coml. Paper
1855				
J	− 3.0	72.6	67.0	12.50
F	− 2.0	73.6	74.0	10.00
M	− .1	76.8	76.0	8.00
A	+ 1.6	76.3	76.0	9.00
M	+ 2.5	80.5	76.0	7.25
J	+ 3.9	79.4	77.0	6.50
J	+ 4.1	76.1	80.0	6.50
A	+ 3.6	77.6	79.0	7.50
S	+ 3.9	78.8	78.0	7.50
O	+ 5.2	78.4	75.0	8.25
N	+ 2.7	78.1	66.0	11.00
D	+ 3.9	77.4	68.0	13.50
1856				
J	+ 4.6	75.3	68.0	11.00
F	+ 5.5	76.0	68.0	9.50
M	+ 6.7	76.4	72.0	10.00
A	+ 9.3	78.3	73.0	8.50
M	+10.1	78.5	72.0	7.50
J	+ 9.6	73.8	70.0	7.50
J	+ 9.7	74.9	71.0	7.50
A	+ 9.4	74.7	71.0	7.50
S	+ 9.2	76.1	68.0	8.50
O	+ 8.0	75.3	68.0	9.50
N	+ 5.9	76.1	68.0	9.50
D	+ 5.2	75.3	71.0	10.50
1857				
J	+ 5.9	76.9	71.0	9.50
F	+ 6.8	77.5	69.5	8.75
M	+ 5.8	77.6	69.3	9.50
A	+ 4.5	77.4	67.7	8.50
M	+ 4.4	76.7	66.3	7.50
J	+ 1.7	75.1	62.2	7.50
J	− .3	75.1	61.0	9.50
A	+ .5	74.3	57.9	9.50
S	− 2.7	67.7	49.2	24.00
O	−10.1	63.2	41.6	28.00
N	−12.0	67.9	47.5	19.00
D	−10.7	70.5	49.3	12.00
1858				
J	−13.0	72.7	50.4	8.17
F	−11.7	76.7	55.0	5.83
M	− 6.6	79.5	55.8	5.33
A	− 9.3	80.0	52.8	4.83
M	− 8.0	81.0	53.1	4.50
J	− 9.4	81.7	50.7	4.50
J	−10.0	82.2	50.9	4.50
A	− 7.5	82.3	50.1	4.00
S	− 6.7	83.2	49.3	4.00
O	− 5.7	85.4	50.7	4.50
N	− 5.5	86.5	50.1	4.67
D	− 3.7	86.8	49.0	5.00

TABLE 9—(*Continued*)

Date	1 Business Activity	2 Bond Price	3 Stock Price	4 Coml. Paper
1859				
J	− 1.8	86.7	48.8	5.17
F	− .7	86.9	48.0	5.83
M	+ .3	86.9	47.9	5.67
A	+ 1.6	87.2	46.5	5.50
M	+ 1.4	85.6	44.8	6.33
J	+ .5	83.4	44.8	7.33
J	+ .8	83.5	45.0	6.83
A	+ .3	84.1	45.1	7.08
S	+ .5	85.8	46.8	7.08
O	− .8	85.3	45.7	7.42
N	− .6	84.8	46.2	7.17
D	− .3	85.1	45.3	7.67
1860				
J	− .7	85.4	44.2	8.50
F	− .1	86.0	44.4	7.17
M	+ .4	86.8	46.3	5.67
A	+ 1.0	87.9	48.4	4.75
M	+ 1.6	89.5	49.1	4.50
J	+ 2.2	91.1	49.4	5.00
J	+ 3.3	91.9	50.6	5.67
A	+ 4.6	92.2	53.5	6.00
S	+ 4.7	92.1	54.8	5.67
O	+ 2.6	91.5	52.6	5.67
N	− .4	87.3	46.8	9.00
D	− 3.8	83.5	43.4	14.00
1861				
J	− 3.6	86.8	47.7	11.50
F	− 3.5	87.7	47.3	8.50
M	− 2.3	88.6	48.2	7.00
A	− 5.5	87.8	44.4	5.50
M	− 7.6	83.5	41.0	5.50
J	− 9.8	84.1	41.0	5.50
J	− 9.8	86.5	42.4	5.50
A	− 9.7	86.3	41.5	5.50
S	− 9.6	85.0	41.3	5.50
O	− 8.4	84.3	42.8	5.50
N	− 8.4	84.9	43.1	5.50
D	− 8.3	85.1	41.7	5.50
1862				
J	− 7.3	89.7	43.7	7.50
F	− 7.3	93.2	45.1	8.00
M	− 6.1	92.2	46.6	8.00
A	− 5.0	93.0	45.9	8.00
M	− 2.7	97.9	47.8	4.00
J	− .5	100.5	49.9	3.50
J	− .7	99.6	48.5	4.50
A	− 1.7	101.7	49.9	4.50
S	− .7	105.1	53.2	4.25
O	+ .3	109.3	58.4	4.50
N	+ .1	111.7	58.7	4.50
D	.0	110.8	59.5	4.50

TABLE 9—(*Continued*)

Date	1 Business Activity	2 Bond Price	3 Stock Price	4 Coml. Paper	5 Bonds Listed
1863					
J	− .3	120.6	66.8	4.50	....
F	+ 1.3	124.7	68.8	4.50	....
M	+ .9	122.8	67.2	4.50	....
A	+ .7	117.3	68.0	4.50	....
M	+ 1.2	117.2	74.1	4.50	....
J	+ 1.6	115.8	71.3	4.50	....
J	+ 2.3	114.7	72.5	4.75	2.0
A	+ 3.9	113.9	77.3	5.25	....
S	+ 4.4	114.0	77.0	5.50	....
O	+ 4.0	114.8	78.8	5.50	....
N	+ 3.1	112.3	78.7	6.00	.1
D	+ 1.0	110.1	77.7	6.00	....
1864					
J	+ 3.1	108.5	80.3	6.00	....
F	+ 6.8	109.3	83.8	6.00	....
M	+ 8.3	113.4	89.3	5.50	.6
A	+ 9.8	118.0	90.6	5.50	.2
M	+ 9.6	118.5	86.2	5.50	....
J	+ 5.9	121.1	87.5	5.50	....
J	+ 4.1	129.2	86.2	6.00	1.5
A	+ 2.3	129.0	86.1	6.00	....
S	+ 2.8	120.5	80.7	6.00	....
O	+ 2.6	111.6	75.1	6.25	....
N	+ 2.8	113.0	78.9	6.50	....
D	+ 3.4	109.9	77.9	8.00	2.1
1865					
J	+ 3.0	106.1	73.7	7.50	....
F	+ 4.0	103.2	71.5	7.75	....
M	+ 4.0	98.1	64.5	8.00	....
A	+ 2.5	9 6	63.3	7.50	....
M	− 5.1	97.1	64.4	6.75	....
J	− 9.8	93.3	62.9	6.75	....
J	−13.0	95.2	65.3	6.50	....
A	−13.5	94.9	63.9	7.00	2.2
S	−14.0	94.3	66.3	6.75	....
O	−13.0	93.2	67.7	8.00	2.7
N	−14.0	91.9	68.1	9.50	....
D	−13.8	91.3	66.9	8.00	....
1866					
J	−10.8	90.5	63.4	7.95	.6
F	− 8.3	89.9	61.2	7.75	1.8
M	− 5.2	89.0	61.1	7.70	.9
A	+ .4	89.8	61.8	7.40	1.3
M	+ 5.2	91.6	62.9	6.55	....
J	+ 6.9	92.2	63.4	6.20	8.3
J	+ 8.1	93.6	64.1	6.40	6.9
A	+ 9.2	94.4	66.3	6.10	....
S	+ 8.6	95.0	66.0	5.45	....
O	+ 9.5	95.4	67.7	5.70	1.4
N	+ 4.2	96.0	66.3	6.85	....
D	+ 1.6	94.5	64.6	7.00	....

TABLE 9—(*Continued*)

Date	1 Business Activity	2 Bond Price	3 Stock Price	4 Coml. Paper	5 Bonds Listed
1867					
J	0	94.2	61.7	7.50	7.0
F	− 3.0	93.9	60.8	7.40	....
M	− 2.8	93.7	59.8	7.50	.8
A	− 2.4	93.1	58.2	7.75	....
M	− 1.2	92.9	58.6	7.00	....
J	− .4	92.9	60.2	8.30	....
J	+ .3	94.6	62.2	7.50	....
A	+ 1.9	94.8	62.0	7.30	4.0
S	+ 2.1	94.6	61.4	8.15	1.7
O	− .2	93.4	60.9	10.00	....
N	− 1.5	92.6	60.4	10.10	1.3
D	− 2.0	92.2	60.9	10.00	....
1868					
J	− 3.2	93.7	62.8	7.20	7.1
F	− 2.7	94.8	63.9	7.00	....
M	− 2.2	95.1	62.8	7.90	3.3
A	− .5	94.6	62.1	8.10	7.3
M	+ .1	95.3	63.9	7.20	.6
J	− .2	95.6	64.6	6.40	....
J	+ .4	95.7	64.2	7.90	19.4
A	+ 2.0	95.5	63.2	6.70	10.0
S	+ 2.5	94.5	63.5	6.95	....
O	+ 2.0	93.6	63.6	7.80	....
N	+ 1.6	92.5	61.5	10.15	4.1
D	+ 2.0	91.7	62.4	9.00	....
1869					
J	+ 1.1	91.6	64.2	8.35	2.5
F	+ 1.9	91.5	64.3	7.80	....
M	+ 2.3	91.0	63.4	9.50	....
A	+ 2.8	90.7	63.8	10.05	1.0
M	+ 4.2	92.1	66.2	7.60	5.6
J	+ 4.9	92.3	66.4	9.60	6.5
J	+ 4.1	91.5	65.8	10.00	3.3
A	+ 2.6	91.6	66.2	9.65	2.7
S	+ 1.6	90.9	61.7	10.50	2.0
O	+ .9	89.7	60.3	10.35	13.0
N	+ .6	89.3	59.6	11.70	....
D	+ .2	88.8	58.1	10.10	....
1870					
J	− .3	89.9	58.7	8.95	15.0
F	− 1.0	92.7	60.1	7.50	....
M	− .5	94.0	59.4	7.50	....
A	+ 1.0	93.7	59.9	7.15	2.5
M	+ 2.5	94.5	61.4	6.05	3.7
J	+ 3.5	95.2	61.4	5.10	2.0
J	+ 2.5	95.5	59.2	6.25	4.1
A	+ 1.0	94.5	57.7	6.95	1.4
S	− 1.6	94.2	57.9	7.00	....
O	− 4.8	94.0	57.3	7.05	17.6
N	− 4.0	93.8	56.9	7.15	1.1
D	− 3.0	93.3	55.8	7.35	10.4

TABLE 9—(*Continued*)

Date	1 Business Activity	2 Bond Price	3 Stock Price	4 Coml. Paper	5 Bonds Listed
1871					
J	− 2.6	94.2	55.7	8.00	8.8
F	+ .4	94.8	56.4	6.45	18.5
M	+ 2.4	95.0	57.9	6.20	....
A	+ 4.2	95.2	59.6	6.70	3.2
M	+ 6.2	96.0	61.1	5.40	2.0
J	+ 6.1	96.1	60.6	4.85	....
J	+ 6.4	96.2	59.6	4.70	3.9
A	+ 5.6	96.7	60.1	5.20	3.5
S	+ 5.8	97.1	60.7	6.35	1.6
O	+ 6.0	95.2	57.7	9.40	5.0
N	+ 6.1	94.6	58.4	9.00	....
D	+ 6.3	95.4	59.6	9.80	30.0
1872					
J	+ 7.7	98.3	60.7	9.30	11.5
F	+ 8.6	98.8	61.0	8.20	4.4
M	+10.7	97.8	62.9	8.65	3.5
A	+10.5	97.9	64.8	8.50	....
M	+10.4	98.0	64.8	7.25	21.3
J	+ 9.1	98.6	64.1	6.00	8.0
J	+ 8.9	100.0	63.7	6.40	....
A	+ 9.5	99.0	62.7	7.55	4.6
S	+11.4	98.1	61.9	10.00	....
O	+12.0	97.4	62.1	11.10	14.0
N	+13.9	96.8	61.9	12.35	1.4
D	+13.6	96.7	63.4	10.90	1.5
1873					
J	+14.6	97.7	63.4	9.40	2.5
F	+14.3	98.0	64.1	9.15	....
M	+13.8	97.7	63.4	10.10	....
A	+12.1	97.3	62.3	10.75	7.0
M	+10.4	97.6	62.6	8.20	1.0
J	+ 7.7	98.1	61.9	6.80	2.0
J	+ 5.8	98.7	61.7	6.50	6.8
A	+ 5.0	98.6	61.7	7.20	....
S	+ 2.8	96.8	57.0	12.50	....
O	+ 1.0	91.8	52.0	17.00	.5
N	− 2.0	91.5	50.1	13.85	2.0
D	− 3.7	94.1	54.8	10.15	....
1874					
J	− 2.7	97.3	57.6	7.40	....
F	− 3.8	98.9	59.1	6.00	....
M	− 4.9	98.9	58.3	6.15	....
A	− 3.9	99.1	56.8	6.30	....
M	− 4.0	98.2	55.4	5.60	....
J	− 3.1	98.9	55.1	5.65	10.0
J	− 3.4	98.9	55.1	5.90	....
A	− 3.9	98.9	55.2	5.45	....
S	− 4.4	99.4	56.0	6.25	5.0
O	− 5.7	100.3	56.0	5.80	16.8
N	− 6.1	101.8	56.2	5.60	4.6
D	− 5.5	102.0	56.2	6.00	1.0

TABLE 9—(*Continued*)

Date	1 Business Activity	2 Bond Price	3 Stock Price	4 Coml. Paper	5 Bonds Listed
1875					
J	− 7.4	103.1	55.8	5.75	9.6
F	− 6.8	103.8	55.5	5.20	....
M	− 7.2	103.9	56.1	5.90	....
A	− 6.6	105.3	56.9	5.45	16.0
M	− 7.0	106.0	54.7	4.55	8.6
J	− 7.5	105.6	53.6	4.55	7.5
J	− 8.3	106.6	53.8	4.30	....
A	− 9.2	106.8	53.9	5.00	3.1
S	−11.0	107.5	53.5	5.95	....
O	−11.8	106.9	52.7	6.35	....
N	−12.6	107.7	53.5	6.45	....
D	−11.5	108.9	53.5	6.65	....
1876					
J	− 9.8	110.1	54.2	6.45	7.8
F	− 9.7	111.4	55.1	5.85	....
M	−10.6	112.2	54.8	5.40	....
A	−10.4	111.5	52.8	5.50	14.8
M	−10.1	111.0	50.8	5.10	....
J	− 9.9	111.7	50.5	4.75	2.4
J	− 9.3	113.1	49.9	3.80	....
A	− 9.5	113.7	47.7	3.60	.9
S	− 9.8	112.2	45.0	4.75	6.5
O	−10.9	112.0	44.7	5.65	6.3
N	−11.2	112.4	43.9	5.50	10.2
D	−11.5	112.5	43.6	5.85	....
1877					
J	−12.0	113.1	43.0	5.55	4.7
F	−12.2	112.3	40.4	4.50	2.1
M	−11.4	110.7	38.4	4.45	1.0
A	−10.7	110.4	35.6	4.45	....
M	−10.0	111.3	35.6	4.00	12.3
J	−10.2	112.5	33.2	4.05	....
J	− 9.1	113.6	34.4	4.25	....
A	− 8.8	112.9	36.7	5.70	1.4
S	− 9.6	112.5	39.0	6.40	15.2
O	−10.4	111.8	40.1	7.25	.3
N	−11.1	112.0	39.3	6.30	....
D	−11.8	112.8	39.2	5.60	5.1
1878					
J	−11.9	112.8	38.9	5.85	14.0
F	−12.7	112.9	38.3	5.35	....
M	−12.5	112.8	38.9	5.15	3.3
A	− 9.7	112.8	40.0	5.35	10.0
M	− 7.6	113.4	40.1	4.45	13.8
J	− 8.1	115.0	41.0	3.80	5.0
J	− 8.3	115.0	41.8	3.60	14.5
A	− 8.6	114.3	41.3	3.80	....
S	− 8.8	114.5	42.3	4.60	12.6
O	− 8.2	115.0	41.8	5.45	15.8
N	− 7.4	115.9	41.6	5.15	....
D	− 7.0	116.5	41.3	5.05	....

TABLE 9—(*Continued*)

Date	1 Business Activity	2 Bond Price	3 Stock Price	4 Coml. Paper	5 Bonds Listed	6 Stocks Listed
1879						
J	− 9.3	118.8	42.7	4.30	5.2	....
F	−10.0	121.7	44.2	3.80	....	....
M	−11.0	119.3	43.6	5.05	7.6	....
A	−10.4	118.9	44.8	5.45	12.0	....
M	− 8.6	121.4	47.1	4.45	4.6	....
J	− 7.1	122.0	47.6	4.25	17.1	....
J	− 4.3	122.8	48.3	3.90	38.8	....
A	− .8	122.4	48.8	5.55	.3	....
S	+ 3.1	119.9	50.4	5.80	4.4	....
O	+ 5.8	119.6	55.9	5.90	7.0	....
N	+ 6.9	120.0	58.9	6.25	14.1	....
D	+ 8.5	120.6	58.7	5.95	6.6	....
1880						
J	+ 8.2	121.5	60.6	5.40	32.2	....
F	+ 9.4	122.8	61.8	5.25	2.5	....
M	+10.8	122.9	62.7	5.50	15.7	....
A	+10.2	122.1	61.5	5.50	19.8	......
M	+ 8.0	122.0	56.7	5.20	23.2	....
J	+ 5.9	122.8	56.9	4.55	38.4	....
J	+ 4.8	124.5	59.4	4.45	32.0	....
A	+ 4.5	125.5	61.8	5.05	.6	....
S	+ 4.4	125.9	61.7	5.25	4.5	....
O	+ 6.1	126.9	63.3	5.10	17.1	....
N	+ 8.7	129.4	66.6	5.50	6.0	....
D	+11.3	131.3	69.5	6.00	27.4	....
1881						
J	+11.7	132.5	73.0	5.25	42.9	....
F	+10.6	130.6	72.7	5.38	12.0	....
M	+ 9.7	129.0	73.6	5.55	15.2	....
A	+ 9.4	129.2	73.5	5.19	28.2	....
M	+ 9.3	132.4	76.6	4.00	44.4	....
J	+ 9.5	134.1	77.5	3.50	27.0	....
J	+ 9.5	133.5	74.9	4.00	58.9	....
A	+ 8.9	132.3	73.2	4.95	43.7	....
S	+ 8.1	129.7	73.8	5.69	25.1	....
O	+ 8.5	128.2	72.6	6.25	21.2	....
N	+ 9.2	128.8	73.0	6.25	38.1	....
D	+ 9.2	127.8	70.9	6.25	36.7	....
1882						
J	+ 9.5	127.9	69.4	5.60	32.0	....
F	+ 9.8	127.0	67.9	5.62	4.2	....
M	+10.6	126.0	67.8	5.62	23.1	....
A	+ 9.3	127.3	67.8	5.06	14.6	3.0
M	+ 7.3	127.8	66.9	4.85	9.2	....
J	+ 5.2	127.6	66.6	5.19	7.9	....
J	+ 4.1	127.9	70.3	4.62	27.6	....
A	+ 5.4	126.8	72.4	5.65	31.3	.8
S	+ 7.0	126.1	73.1	6.75	13.8	....
O	+ 8.3	126.4	71.2	6.65	23.7	....
N	+ 9.1	125.4	68.2	6.50	15.8	....
D	+ 9.2	125.5	68.4	5.88	18.4	....

TABLE 9—(*Continued*)

Date	1 Business Activity	2 Bond Price	3 Stock Price	4 Coml. Paper	5 Bonds Listed	6 Stocks Listed
1883						
J	+ 8.2	126.2	67.6	5.50	13.1	....
F	+ 6.7	125.3	66.0	5.38	21.0	....
M	+ 5.0	124.7	66.7	6.38	52.8	....
A	+ 3.6	125.2	68.2	5.81	18.5	....
M	+ 3.3	125.0	67.0	5.35	37.0	3.5
J	+ 2.7	125.0	67.8	4.75	25.4	....
J	+ 2.7	124.8	66.4	4.80	8.7	....
A	+ 2.9	123.7	63.5	5.69	5.5	....
S	+ 3.4	123.5	64.3	6.00	13.9	....
O	+ 2.4	123.7	62.6	6.00	13.3	....
N	− .7	124.7	63.5	5.69	5.7	....
D	− 3.6	125.2	62.0	5.50	42.4	....
1884						
J	− 5.0	126.1	59.9	4.95	15.1	....
F	− 4.6	127.4	61.5	4.75	7.0	....
M	− 4.1	128.6	61.2	4.62	12.0	....
A	− 4.3	129.4	58.7	4.72	13.3	....
M	− 4.1	126.9	53.7	5.06	3.6	....
J	− 3.2	123.9	50.1	5.75	8.3	....
J	− 4.8	123.7	51.5	5.95	14.7	....
A	− 7.4	125.6	54.9	5.50	7.8	....
S	− 9.1	125.4	52.9	5.50	26.4	....
O	− 9.6	125.6	51.2	5.50	11.2	5.0
N	−10.1	125.4	50.1	5.19	1.7	10.4
D	−11.1	126.6	50.1	5.00	2.9	1.2
1885						
J	−12.3	127.8	48.6	4.69	13.7	....
F	−12.6	128.7	49.9	4.50	2.7	....
M	−12.3	129.3	50.0	4.45	14.2	1.2
A	−11.3	129.4	50.0	3.94	2.3	....
M	−13.1	129.5	49.6	3.69	3.0	3.6
J	−10.4	130.7	49.2	3.55	5.4	.7
J	− 9.9	131.1	51.2	3.50	9.8	....
A	−11.8	130.9	53.9	3.69	5.1	....
S	−11.8	131.1	53.4	3.75	....	....
O	− 9.6	132.0	56.4	4.00	6.9	7.5
N	− 7.2	132.4	60.0	4.44	8.4	....
D	− 3.6	132.5	59.6	4.50	9.6	3.0
1886						
J	− 5.3	134.6	59.3	4.31	21.8	5.8
F	− 5.3	136.8	60.2	3.91	2.6	....
M	− 1.8	136.8	59.2	3.88	8.4	....
A	− 2.0	136.3	58.3	4.25	8.4	3.0
M	− 1.2	136.4	57.2	4.06	1.9	2.2
J	+ 3.1	137.1	59.6	3.85	16.4	3.6
J	+ 4.0	138.1	60.6	3.94	25.8	....
A	+ 2.3	137.5	61.1	5.25	13.7	....
S	+ 2.6	135.7	62.6	5.81	6.5	.5
O	+ 2.8	135.7	64.4	6.06	18.2	....
N	+ 3.5	135.7	65.8	5.90	4.5	8.0
D	+ 5.2	134.8	64.2	6.00	11.5	5.2

TABLE 9—(*Continued*)

Date	1 Business Activity	2 Bond Price	3 Stock Price	4 Coml. Paper	5 Bonds Listed	6 Stocks Listed
1887						
J	+ 4.1	135.7	63.1	5.50	44.6	.5
F	+ 7.4	134.8	62.6	4.81	40.0	....
M	+10.5	134.2	64.1	5.35	18.6	8.0
A	+ 9.7	133.8	65.6	5.38	19.6	2.2
M	+ 4.4	134.0	66.6	5.20	25.3	5.5
J	+ 3.5	133.6	64.8	5.12	24.5	8.3
J	− .2	132.7	63.1	6.19	75.2	1.7
A	+ 5.0	131.3	61.5	6.35	7.1	.6
S	+ 8.0	128.6	60.8	6.94	19.5	4.0
O	+ 7.0	127.8	58.8	6.38	14.4	9.5
N	+ 7.2	128.9	59.8	5.80	12.8	....
D	+ 3.8	129.4	59.6	6.00	17.9	2.4
1888						
J	+ .1	131.4	59.6	5.55	24.3	....
F	− .4	132.3	59.2	4.81	24.3	.6
M	− 1.2	131.6	57.1	5.22	23.1	7.6
A	− 2.2	131.6	57.2	5.41	4.8	....
M	+ .4	132.1	58.1	4.82	24.6	....
J	− 1.0	132.8	56.1	4.25	20.8	....
J	− 1.2	134.4	57.7	4.10	23.4	.9
A	+ 2.2	134.4	58.8	4.38	20.0	....
S	+ 2.6	133.0	60.4	5.28	11.0	1.2
O	+ 6.3	132.5	60.1	5.08	17.1	.6
N	+ 4.0	132.8	58.6	4.75	3.7	....
D	+ 5.9	133.0	57.8	4.97	6.1	....
1889						
J	+ 6.0	134.3	58.2	4.65	26.6	5.3
F	+ 4.9	135.4	59.1	4.25	3.4	....
M	+ 3.7	134.7	58.0	4.50	12.6	7.1
A	+ 1.4	134.6	57.8	4.25	14.6	.4
M	+ 1.1	135.8	59.4	3.84	33.1	.3
J	− .2	137.2	60.3	3.88	13.8	2.7
J	+ 2.2	136.5	59.1	4.40	12.3	1.0
A	+ 2.6	135.8	59.9	5.16	5.9	....
S	+ 1.6	135.1	61.3	5.28	11.4	....
O	+ 5.9	133.2	60.3	6.00	23.1	3.1
N	+ 6.0	131.7	59.6	6.00	12.3	1.0
D	+ 6.3	131.1	59.2	6.09	36.1	3.5
1890						
J	+ 9.2	131.5	59.5	5.15	21.0	12.2
F	+ 8.5	131.3	58.9	5.03	9.6	5.4
M	+10.0	130.5	58.5	5.50	12.7	1.9
A	+11.2	129.9	59.6	5.10	21.3	.1
M	+12.8	130.0	62.3	5.06	18.8	4.0
J	+10.9	129.4	61.7	5.00	26.2	3.0
J	+10.3	128.9	61.3	5.05	41.9	4.0
A	+ 8.2	127.8	59.9	5.59	22.6	.4
S	+11.0	126.7	58.9	5.75	16.6	6.5
O	+12.3	125.7	56.3	5.90	30.2	.9
N	+ 8.7	123.9	52.2	7.50	24.8	5.6
D	+ 4.1	122.3	50.8	7.30	16.1	.7

TABLE 9—(*Continued*)

Date	1 Business Activity	2 Bond Price	3 Stock Price	4 Coml. Paper	5 Bonds Listed	6 Stocks Listed
1891						
J	+ 2.4	125.0	53.1	5.69	12.6	9.7
F	− 1.2	124.8	53.8	5.00	22.4	1.6
M	− 6.5	123.0	52.8	5.25	2.4	7.1
A	− 6.2	122.5	54.6	5.08	18.9	2.7
M	− 3.0	121.3	54.5	5.38	23.4	3.0
J	+ 4.5	119.5	53.2	5.50	13.3	4.8
J	+ 8.8	119.8	52.4	5.60	18.7	15.4
A	+ 8.8	119.6	54.2	5.75	5.7	.6
S	+12.8	119.3	58.7	5.80	11.9	6.8
O	+12.6	120.9	58.7	5.53	21.3	.5
N	+ 9.9	121.5	57.7	5.06	7.1	1.5
D	+11.5	122.6	59.6	4.82	5.8	10.1
1892						
J	+12.5	123.7	60.0	4.16	26.0	.3
F	+13.9	124.3	60.2	3.69	16.7	2.5
M	+10.0	124.0	60.9	3.98	15.2	4.0
A	+ 7.9	124.4	60.7	3.47	14.2	6.6
M	+ 5.9	124.9	60.7	3.16	16.3	8.9
J	+ 5.9	125.5	60.4	2.96	21.8	3.4
J	+ 2.4	125.7	60.6	3.47	24.7	7.3
A	+ 2.3	125.2	61.4	4.00	12.9	....
S	+ 3.5	123.9	59.8	4.75	40.4	3.0
O	+ 4.9	123.7	61.0	5.16	3.7	9.9
N	+ 6.7	123.2	60.7	5.12	18.2	20.1
D	+ 8.4	122.4	60.0	5.62	11.7	7.8
1893						
J	+ 6.0	123.0	60.8	5.09	14.4	17.3
F	+ 6.8	123.6	59.6	4.97	17.8	3.0
M	+ 6.8	122.6	57.4	6.80	5.8	6.9
A	+10.0	122.1	57.4	5.75	29.0	12.2
M	+ 9.8	120.7	52.3	6.65	28.9	14.5
J	+ 3.8	118.6	50.0	8.75	21.1	11.6
J	− 5.9	115.0	45.2	9.75	3.9	9.9
A	−16.3	112.0	44.3	9.70	5.7	.5
S	−19.8	115.3	47.3	8.28	4.6	....
O	−19.1	116.5	48.6	5.91	3.1	4.1
N	−16.5	119.0	49.3	4.38	7.4	....
D	−15.6	120.7	47.8	3.66	5.0	2.5
1894						
J	−15.2	120.4	46.4	3.50	6.9	....
F	−15.0	121.8	47.1	3.25	2.5	....
M	−12.5	122.7	48.4	3.00	16.5	....
A	−14.1	124.1	49.1	3.09	8.8	1.0
M	−18.6	123.8	47.3	2.92	13.7	11.5
J	−19.9	123.8	46.6	2.91	10.1	5.4
J	−15.3	123.2	45.7	3.00	15.9	1.9
A	− 7.7	123.6	47.5	3.08	6.7	....
S	− 6.0	124.4	48.5	3.28	6.2	....
O	− 5.2	125.4	46.6	2.75	6.8	1.2
N	− 4.4	126.0	46.6	2.81	7.7	....
D	− 3.7	125.8	46.1	2.88	4.3	3.0

TABLE 9—(*Continued*)

Date	1 Business Activity	2 Bond Price	3 Stock Price	4 Coml. Paper	5 Bonds Listed	6 Stocks Listed
1895						
J	− 3.9	125.2	45.2	3.10	5.0	1.6
F	− 7.7	123.9	44.7	3.62	7.6	....
M	− 8.5	123.0	44.7	3.91	17.9	....
A	− 9.1	123.0	46.6	3.97	3.7	14.3
M	− 7.7	124.5	49.1	2.78	11.7	17.1
J	− 5.3	126.5	50.2	2.63	10.3	16.3
J	− 1.9	127.4	50.5	2.95	13.5	11.3
A	+ .4	128.7	51.0	3.53	13.2	....
S	+ 2.5	128.2	51.4	4.03	39.4	.5
O	+ 5.6	127.6	50.8	4.78	18.1	....
N	+ 5.3	126.8	49.0	4.12	5.0	7.3
D	+ 4.6	124.7	46.2	4.75	18.4	.4
1896						
J	− .1	122.8	45.3	6.00	8.9	....
F	− 1.5	123.7	47.2	5.81	7.4	.3
M	− 4.9	123.8	46.4	5.22	1.7	....
A	− 3.9	123.5	46.9	5.28	3.5	....
M	− 6.0	123.5	46.6	4.53	19.5	....
J	− 6.8	123.9	45.8	4.25	9.8	9.3
J	− 9.1	121.0	42.7	5.05	13.9	....
A	−14.8	115.2	40.5	7.81	3.6	5.0
S	−17.9	117.1	42.5	8.35	1.0	1.2
O	−17.3	118.2	43.4	8.56	12.0	....
N	−14.6	120.7	46.4	5.34	6.5	....
D	−12.0	121.8	44.8	3.72	16.7	2.5
1897						
J	−10.9	123.3	44.4	3.32	8.6	.3
F	− 9.5	124.0	43.9	3.00	4.7	2.5
M	− 9.8	125.2	44.2	3.35	9.3	.3
A	−10.0	124.7	42.8	3.53	4.1	.4
M	−11.6	125.0	43.0	3.53	13.5	....
J	−10.4	125.9	45.0	3.12	20.7	2.0
J	−10.6	127.2	46.8	3.44	60.1	.5
A	− 7.4	126.3	50.1	3.72	2.7	....
S	− 2.3	125.8	52.4	4.10	18.1	1.3
O	− 1.1	125.5	50.7	4.19	12.8	7.0
N	+ .1	125.9	48.8	3.38	10.5	....
D	+ 1.3	127.2	50.1	3.42	10.8	.8
1898						
J	+ 1.1	127.6	51.0	3.25	18.1	.6
F	+ 2.5	127.3	50.8	3.13	15.0	1.8
M	+ 1.1	124.3	48.4	4.65	20.2	....
A	0	121.0	47.7	5.75	19.7	.5
M	− .6	122.2	50.8	4.52	9.8	5.6
J	+ .6	124.3	52.8	3.22	10.4	9.8
J	− 1.7	125.9	53.1	3.66	5.6	32.1
A	− .3	126.5	55.0	3.68	11.7	.9
S	0	125.6	54.9	4.12	11.8	3.6
O	− 1.1	126.3	53.9	3.41	10.2	4.6
N	+ .1	127.4	55.6	3.30	21.9	1.1
D	+ 1.0	128.4	59.0	3.03	22.1	1.3

TABLE 9—(*Continued*)

Date	1 Business Activity	2 Bond Price	3 Stock Price	4 Coml. Paper	5 Bonds Listed	6 Stocks Listed
1899						
J	+ 1.1	129.8	63.1	2.90	23.7	1.3
F	+ .4	129.5	65.5	3.12	43.4	4.4
M	+ 2.6	128.9	66.3	3.91	28.4	19.5
A	+ 1.6	130.0	67.2	3.69	12.4	....
M	+ 2.3	131.4	64.3	3.60	10.9	....
J	+ 3.6	131.8	63.0	3.31	1.6	.5
J	+ 3.7	131.0	65.1	3.66	50.6	4.3
A	+ 6.0	130.1	66.7	4.35	26.0	3.3
S	+ 7.6	128.5	65.9	4.94	23.4	12.0
O	+ 8.6	126.9	65.6	5.20	17.1	6.0
N	+ 8.6	126.0	66.9	5.44	6.9	.8
D	+ 9.6	124.5	62.4	5.88	6.6	.2
1900						
J	+10.5	125.5	62.8	4.92	14.7	3.2
F	+10.9	126.2	63.8	4.41	10.8	20.0
M	+10.1	126.3	64.4	4.88	1.7	11.4
A	+ 9.2	126.3	65.1	4.25	24.5	.5
M	+ 8.0	125.7	62.1	3.50	48.9	2.6
J	+ 6.5	125.3	60.3	3.69	9.9	....
J	+ 1.2	125.3	60.3	4.05	30.0	1.0
A	− 1.3	125.1	61.0	4.19	3.8	4.0
S	− 4.0	124.8	59.7	4.34	9.3	3.4
O	− 4.6	124.5	61.9	5.05	3.4	4.9
N	− 4.7	125.2	66.7	4.41	3.0	.6
D	− 2.7	126.0	70.6	4.75	25.8	6.2
1901						
J	+ .3	126.3	72.1	4.03	18.8	1.1
F	+ 1.6	126.8	73.9	3.69	37.0	17.1
M	+ 2.9	126.5	76.6	3.75	46.8	2.1
A	+ 5.0	125.9	83.1	3.98	7.6	....
M	+ 4.4	124.6	78.8	3.97	45.9	11.0
J	+ 3.5	125.3	86.7	3.94	10.9	64.1
J	+ 4.4	124.6	80.9	4.30	35.9	20.7
A	+ 4.2	124.0	81.9	4.50	12.2	47.4
S	+ 1.1	123.5	81.7	4.94	9.0	2.3
O	+ 3.6	123.5	80.6	4.65	5.4	4.3
N	+ 3.3	123.9	82.6	4.72	31.6	....
D	+ 2.6	123.9	81.1	4.95	23.1	16.2
1902						
J	+ 2.3	124.0	82.2	4.44	13.4	54.4
F	+ 2.0	124.1	82.9	4.00	48.3	16.8
M	+ 2.4	123.8	83.1	4.34	19.6	1.5
A	+ 4.3	123.9	85.9	4.48	14.9	27.0
M	+ 4.5	123.3	85.6	4.53	40.7	.6
J	+ 2.7	122.6	85.1	4.44	14.7	.4
J	+ 3.6	122.3	87.4	4.62	24.3	....
A	+ 2.6	121.4	89.3	4.84	46.0	2.3
S	+ 4.3	120.8	89.5	5.65	8.9	1.5
O	+ 3.3	119.3	86.5	5.94	30.5	1.4
N	+ 2.9	118.7	83.3	5.75	55.2	17.7
D	+ 4.5	117.9	81.5	6.00	7.8	.3

TABLE 9—(*Continued*)

Date	1 Business Activity	2 Bond Price	3 Stock Price	4 Coml. Paper	5 Bonds Listed	6 Stocks Listed	7 J. of C. Bonds	8 J. of C. Stocks
1903								
J	+ 4.3	117.9	85.0	5.12	50.4	23.6	....	....
F	+ 3.8	117.4	84.5	4.84	19.6	18.6	....	....
M	+ 4.8	115.6	81.3	5.53	4.7	13.3	....	....
A	+ 5.9	114.5	77.9	5.19	28.3	....	....	....
M	+ 5.5	115.1	76.3	4.75	14.4	2.3	....	....
J	+ 4.6	114.2	72.1	5.10	2.3	36.9	....	....
J	+ 4.1	112.8	68.8	5.47	22.4	....	....	....
A	+ 2.3	111.2	66.5	5.94	5.4	22.7	....	....
S	+ .9	111.0	64.9	6.00	57.5	.6	....	....
O	− 3.7	112.1	62.9	5.84	18.1	....	....	....
N	− 7.5	112.7	63.1	5.97	15.3	....	....	....
D	−11.0	112.1	65.9	5.85	28.5	.4	....	....
1904								
J	− 7.1	112.2	66.7	4.91	8.4	.5	....	....
F	− 3.6	111.8	64.6	4.78	52.6	.7	....	....
M	− 4.1	110.9	64.6	4.68	4.2	7.0	....	....
A	− 2.3	111.3	66.0	4.06	40.4	3.0	....	....
M	− 4.3	111.5	64.6	3.93	53.1	5.0	....	....
J	− 6.7	112.2	64.8	3.56	29.9	5.7	....	....
J	− 4.7	113.2	67.5	3.53	32.1	10.5	....	....
A	− 8.0	113.1	69.8	3.88	5.6	2.1	....	....
S	− 5.1	112.8	72.8	4.31	7.1	3.6	....	....
O	− 5.0	112.4	77.2	4.41	18.1	....	....	....
N	− .6	112.3	81.3	4.12	11.7	40.0	....	....
D	+ .6	112.3	82.2	4.28	56.9	11.4	....	....
1905								
J	+ 3.4	113.0	83.3	3.95	104.6	....	....	....
F	+ 4.0	113.6	87.0	3.84	15.9	12.0	....	....
M	+ 6.9	113.0	89.4	3.93	15.0	7.1	....	....
A	+ 8.2	113.0	88.5	3.97	49.1	2.0	....	....
M	+ 8.7	112.7	84.1	3.98	54.4	7.9	....	....
J	+ 8.5	113.0	85.1	3.75	33.1	15.0	....	....
J	+ 8.0	113.3	87.9	4.13	50.4	2.9	....	....
A	+ 8.2	112.7	91.3	4.20	5.0	....	....	....
S	+ 9.7	112.4	91.4	4.72	10.2	4.7	....	....
O	+ 9.4	112.2	92.6	4.95	57.1	....	....	....
N	+10.9	111.3	92.1	5.66	11.0	7.3	....	....
D	+11.8	111.1	94.5	5.81	2.5	23.3	....	....
1906								
J	+12.6	111.3	97.0	5.05	62.1	28.2	98.9	23.2
F	+12.0	110.8	96.3	5.03	6.0	4.2	241.3	36.1
M	+10.4	109.7	93.9	5.28	132.0	3.5	41.4	54.8
A	+ 8.9	109.1	92.6	5.44	27.3	1.0	66.1	34.3
M	+10.2	108.8	90.1	5.33	65.3	24.1	77.6	50.0
J	+ 9.1	109.1	91.3	5.25	22.6	12.8	96.4	7.1
J	+ 8.8	108.6	89.0	5.48	17.3	11.1	24.8	62.6
A	+ 9.4	107.8	95.6	6.00	29.9	4.1	34.2	32.8
S	+ 8.3	106.7	98.5	6.56	.2	35.2	13.5	32.5
O	+10.5	106.7	97.8	6.30	11.6	12.8	20.5	17.2
N	+10.7	106.8	97.1	6.25	16.0	6.0	20.3	33.3
D	+11.8	106.5	96.7	6.25	23.3	52.8	47.2	287.8

TABLE 9—(*Continued*)

Date	1 Business Activity	2 Bond Price	3 Stock Price	4 Coml. Paper	5 Bonds Listed	6 Stocks Listed	7 J. of C. Bonds	8 J. of C. Stocks
1907								
J	+11.5	106.0	93.1	6.15	36.4	48.9	171.9	19.8
F	+ 9.4	105.5	90.3	5.94	3.4	15.0	125.4	13.1
M	+ 9.0	103.7	81.4	6.19	3.2	13.0	36.0	34.0
A	+11.0	103.7	81.7	5.92	1.4	10.0	117.9	89.5
M	+11.6	103.2	79.0	5.44	14.7	11.1	48.8	3.2
J	+11.1	102.0	76.4	5.44	49.4	33.7	100.3	39.8
J	+11.2	102.0	79.3	5.75	32.4	28.1	80.0	19.0
A	+10.0	100.3	73.4	6.25	15.8	28.1	19.2	43.8
S	+ 8.3	98.9	72.4	6.81	27.6	17.8	39.6	24.4
O	+ 7.8	96.9	64.6	7.06	13.3	7.7	60.7	33.2
N	− 7.5	93.1	60.9	7.50	15.9	6.9	52.2	11.7
D	−17.2	95.6	64.0	8.00	8.9	27.8	107.8	102.7
1908								
J	−18.0	98.9	66.1	6.28	38.6	6.9	118.8	39.7
F	−17.4	99.3	63.8	5.06	....	6.9	66.0	13.3
M	−16.9	98.3	66.4	5.63	18.1	7.3	44.5	33.1
A	−16.7	99.1	69.9	4.38	12.6	6.9	182.2	57.5
M	−18.1	99.9	73.7	3.94	69.8	3.9	134.8	29.7
J	−17.2	99.8	73.8	3.65	48.4	24.1	113.6	2.9
J	−15.6	100.4	76.5	3.75	43.5	9.1	51.4	30.3
A	−12.8	101.0	79.8	3.59	32.4	5.8	43.1	59.1
S	−11.0	101.6	78.9	3.92	.8	18.7	47.3	6.0
O	−10.0	101.6	79.9	4.06	19.4	3.9	79.4	13.4
N	− 8.0	102.1	85.3	4.03	26.7	11.3	155.9	47.3
D	− 6.6	102.6	87.1	3.85	47.6	27.0	45.0	8.9
1909								
J	− 3.2	103.3	86.9	3.72	66.5	5.0	124.3	20.4
F	− 3.2	104.0	84.3	3.53	27.4	3.3	117.7	24.8
M	− 3.4	103.7	85.5	3.50	17.3	14.9	62.6	12.6
A	− 3.5	103.6	89.3	3.50	33.8	....	162.3	28.2
M	− 1.5	103.7	92.2	3.44	9.5	4.2	142.4	25.6
J	− .6	103.3	93.9	3.25	173.0	.1	114.5	25.1
J	+ 1.8	103.4	95.3	3.38	86.2	3.4	78.1	43.4
A	+ 4.2	102.9	97.5	4.02	28.2	9.0	58.1	24.9
S	+ 6.9	102.1	97.6	4.22	16.6	9.7	26.4	124.4
O	+ 9.0	101.8	98.0	5.03	61.7	8.2	107.6	54.8
N	+ 9.2	101.4	97.5	5.08	9.7	....	57.2	16.2
D	+ 9.4	101.3	98.7	5.09	45.5	85.8	74.6	210.3
1910								
J	+ 8.6	101.3	96.0	4.75	26.9	37.2	85.8	70.3
F	+ 7.2	101.2	92.3	4.44	17.9	44.9	61.6	35.2
M	+ 7.7	100.7	94.7	4.50	32.8	10.1	301.0	77.4
A	+ 5.5	99.7	92.5	4.75	61.4	2.7	72.6	20.1
M	+ 2.0	99.3	90.8	4.75	63.0	33.0	186.0	7.3
J	+ 1.7	98.9	86.5	4.81	17.0	20.7	85.2	45.9
J	− 1.3	98.4	82.1	5.38	33.7	3.8	37.0	23.2
A	− 1.7	98.3	84.0	5.43	12.9	....	39.8	23.7
S	− 2.2	99.2	84.7	5.53	9.0	.5	44.8	17.7
O	− 2.5	99.8	88.6	5.56	2.0	6.7	45.5	10.6
N	− 4.1	99.1	88.4	5.50	4.1	....	82.1	28.9
D	− 5.9	99.2	85.9	4.66	56.0	15.4	71.7	44.9

TABLE 9—(*Continued*)

Date	1 Business Activity	2 Bond Price	3 Stock Price	4 Coml. Paper	5 Bonds Listed	6 Stocks Listed	7 J. of C. Bonds	8 J. of C. Stocks
1911								
J	− 5.6	99.4	87.3	3.98	71.4	3.1	178.0	47.2
F	− 5.2	99.4	88.9	4.09	38.6	....	175.8	40.2
M	− 4.3	99.0	87.9	3.88	30.6	1.3	189.4	27.0
A	− 6.7	99.1	87.5	3.66	29.0	4.9	155.9	23.2
M	− 7.0	99.5	89.4	3.63	51.4	....	132.4	22.1
J	− 6.8	99.2	91.2	3.69	6.0	51.9	173.0	65.4
J	− 7.8	99.1	90.8	3.78	31.5	....	89.3	40.6
A	− 6.3	98.6	86.4	4.19	28.4	22.9	37.6	13.9
S	− 5.3	98.2	81.8	4.53	2.3	10.1	29.2	8.3
O	− 5.1	98.4	82.2	4.35	30.5	13.4	60.2	8.2
N	− 4.8	98.9	85.6	3.91	16.2	1.5	105.4	12.8
D	− 4.7	98.7	85.8	4.63	44.4	4.6	66.4	43.1
1912								
J	− 2.5	98.9	85.3	3.90	49.5	12.5	220.6	120.3
F	+ .9	99.1	84.4	3.75	45.9	....	133.9	105.8
M	+ 1.4	98.7	86.8	4.19	61.6	12.4	149.9	20.4
A	+ 3.4	98.5	89.7	4.15	1.0	23.2	194.9	73.2
M	+ 3.5	98.3	89.2	4.19	111.1	17.4	148.1	40.7
J	+ 2.9	98.0	89.4	4.00	35.8	4.4	149.4	149.8
J	+ 4.5	97.8	89.7	4.53	....	24.8	17.8	16.8
A	+ 5.7	97.0	91.7	5.00	19.1	.2	60.0	83.7
S	+ 5.6	96.5	92.2	5.56	25.1	9.1	56.0	5.8
O	+ 8.0	96.6	91.9	5.92	27.9	10.3	83.1	120.7
N	+ 8.1	96.6	90.7	5.72	12.3	2.2	111.0	29.1
D	+ 8.3	96.3	87.6	6.00	2.9	9.0	25.5	137.0
1913								
J	+ 9.2	96.6	86.0	4.66	14.1	18.7	103.0	46.9
F	+ 8.8	96.2	83.1	4.91	11.0	.2	180.3	163.0
M	+ 4.9	94.7	81.4	5.75	130.0	1.6	60.5	57.9
A	+ 7.0	93.6	81.3	5.53	9.6	....	175.4	18.3
M	+ 6.4	92.5	79.1	5.34	19.1	13.6	93.4	48.3
J	+ 5.7	91.5	75.1	5.88	9.7	6.0	150.0	30.4
J	+ 5.1	91.6	76.2	6.06	28.9	3.7	79.9	19.4
A	+ 3.3	92.2	78.3	6.00	24.5	13.6	53.3	18.2
S	+ 3.6	93.1	79.0	5.78	30.0	....	68.6	10.2
O	+ 3.8	92.3	76.5	5.69	41.4	3.8	97.5	11.2
N	− .5	91.1	74.5	5.56	18.2	27.6	73.9	13.1
D	− 3.0	90.9	74.5	5.68	34.9	14.9	58.3	14.8
1914								
J	− 1.3	92.6	76.7	4.53	37.2	.5	89.4	40.8
F	− .9	94.0	77.8	3.84	41.5	4.4	158.2	17.9
M	+ .9	93.5	76.4	3.88	48.1	1.6	94.4	38.8
A	− .8	93.5	74.5	3.73	15.3	.1	262.5	29.8
M	− 3.6	93.5	74.9	3.88	25.3	8.5	125.8	36.8
J	− 3.4	93.8	74.2	3.84	21.9	....	134.6	53.2
J	− 2.7	92.8	70.2	4.40	36.5	2.9	71.9	22.9
A	− 5.9	89.0	66.7	6.34	2.9	6.6	20.0	10.1
S	− 7.4	87.8	63.2	6.70	.8	.4	24.4	3.2
O	−10.3	86.7	59.7	6.44	4.5	6.0	83.8	7.6
N	−13.5	87.3	61.8	5.50	2.6	2.8	25.7	2.1
D	−13.6	88.5	67.3	4.35	.1	1.0	80.6	2.0

TABLE 9—(*Continued*)

Date	1 Business Activity	2 Bond Price	3 Stock Price	4 Coml. Paper	5 Bonds Listed	6 Stocks Listed	7 J. of C. Bonds	8 J. of C. Stocks
1915								
J	−11.8	89.7	67.7	3.84	16.9	2.2	120.9	6.8
F	− 9.3	89.8	66.8	3.75	10.0	....	248.5	15.7
M	− 8.1	89.1	68.5	3.38	2.0	2.1	51.8	5.5
A	− 5.9	90.0	73.7	3.66	12.3	6.6	133.1	20.5
M	− 4.7	89.7	72.1	3.72	61.0	2.1	89.8	8.5
J	− 1.4	89.0	72.9	3.65	79.0	1.8	9.8	57.3
J	+ .1	87.7	74.2	3.25	40.5	....	34.7	30.4
A	+ 1.4	87.1	77.2	3.53	56.6	1.8	65.7	2.8
S	+ 5.0	86.8	80.2	3.25	30.7	.4	64.7	7.1
O	+ 7.3	88.7	84.6	3.22	41.6	3.0	37.0	84.4
N	+10.1	91.4	87.5	2.98	6.6	7.5	103.9	126.0
D	+13.4	91.7	87.7	3.13	104.7	15.9	93.9	16.7
1916								
J	+12.3	92.0	85.6	3.13	15.2	13.8	146.6	46.2
F	+13.5	92.3	84.5	3.13	32.6	9.4	185.7	117.9
M	+14.3	92.0	84.1	3.13	57.4	15.0	217.7	56.9
A	+12.7	91.6	83.2	3.13	84.3	8.1	141.0	80.6
M	+14.2	91.4	85.0	3.13	25.7	....	134.5	57.4
J	+14.0	91.2	85.8	3.63	27.2	5.0	114.5	35.6
J	+11.4	91.0	84.6	3.97	28.2	4.1	91.4	44.9
A	+13.2	90.6	85.3	3.73	4.2	.4	43.4	102.9
S	+14.4	90.8	88.8	3.38	....	27.2	65.2	30.4
O	+15.5	92.0	91.5	3.38	2.3	6.2	39.6	71.4
N	+15.8	92.8	93.7	3.50	17.0	12.4	165.1	84.8
D	+13.9	92.7	89.9	3.91	84.5	7.3	60.2	52.6
1917								
J	+14.3	94.1	87.0	3.55	81.4	8.4	147.0	35.6
F	+12.7	92.6	82.0	4.09	4.0	65.4	133.5	80.4
M	+14.1	91.7	84.6	4.13	23.3	17.5	267.1	45.0
A	+13.1	89.5	83.4	4.28	22.3	14.5	56.1	74.0
M	+14.2	87.1	80.6	4.83	3.7	16.1	27.6	20.7
J	+13.4	86.1	82.2	5.00	31.2	26.4	35.4	24.2
J	+12.4	85.3	79.9	4.68	6.3	9.1	112.2	23.1
A	+12.5	84.7	77.6	4.81	.5	21.0	115.6	70.3
S	+ 9.1	83.0	73.8	5.19	65.6	2.8	52.2	28.6
O	+10.8	82.2	69.8	5.38	23.2	5.7	37.7	11.5
N	+10.6	79.8	64.0	5.47	1.1	10.3	63.1	27.4
D	+ 5.9	78.4	61.8	5.50	....	31.9	27.7	13.8
1918								
J	+ 1.5	79.0	65.1	5.58	1.4	6.3	113.7	51.0
F	+ 2.6	79.8	67.0	5.69	....	7.0	43.9	26.0
M	+ 7.1	78.7	65.6	5.88	.8	1.2	54.8	20.1
A	+ 7.5	77.8	65.1	5.90	....	7.3	8.1	15.8
M	+ 9.3	78.9	67.0	5.88	5.2	....	55.9	46.4
J	+ 6.9	78.0	67.2	5.88	6.8	7.2	239.8	14.0
J	+ 9.3	77.1	67.6	5.88	27.9	3.1	156.0	9.6
A	+10.6	77.0	68.3	5.94	50.7	.4	74.1	15.4
S	+ 8.5	76.2	68.0	6.00	15.0	7.3	38.8	20.9
O	+ 8.5	78.1	70.8	6.00	.4	.5	51.2	25.1
N	+ 6.0	83.1	72.6	5.97	8.3	5.4	63.5	26.5
D	+ 6.1	82.7	71.1	5.86	65.4	....	147.6	27.0

TABLE 9—(*Continued*)

Date	1 Business Activity	2 Bond Price	3 Stock Price	4 Coml. Paper	5 Bonds Listed	6 Stocks Listed	7 J. of C. Bonds	8 J. of C. Stocks
1919								
J	− .2	81.2	70.2	5.19	21.9	3.4	227.6	14.9
F	− 4.1	80.4	70.4	5.19	35.5	39.0	137.3	50.3
M	− 8.0	79.4	72.6	5.38	11.2	1.5	108.6	44.5
A	− 4.9	78.7	75.0	5.38	2.2	7.9	21.7	46.0
M	− 6.0	79.4	80.1	5.38	20.5	24.2	101.6	108.3
J	− .2	79.5	82.4	5.53	8.0	45.4	186.4	135.7
J	+ 4.3	78.4	85.0	5.42	75.2	38.8	170.9	200.0
A	+ 6.5	75.8	79.3	5.38	1.1	65.5	85.1	135.1
S	+ 3.8	75.2	80.6	5.38	23.1	39.3	111.8	267.8
O	+ 2.4	77.2	84.6	5.38	4.4	69.6	100.4	290.3
N	+ 1.0	75.3	82.1	5.50	2.0	91.5	54.6	199.1
D	+ 1.9	74.4	79.7	5.88	....	66.2	118.6	104.6
1920								
J	+12.3	74.7	78.1	6.00	61.2	55.0	130.7	207.7
F	+12.1	72.2	71.6	6.41	40.0	166.5	125.8	76.7
M	+ 9.4	72.2	76.8	6.68	5.5	15.9	157.9	117.9
A	+ 3.3	69.6	76.2	6.81	51.6	45.5	263.0	208.7
M	+ 5.4	66.7	71.4	7.16	63.8	43.3	172.3	72.8
J	+ 6.3	67.3	70.2	7.72	49.8	90.5	107.2	159.2
J	+ 3.8	67.7	70.1	7.84	11.1	128.0	153.9	87.0
A	+ 3.5	69.8	67.3	8.00	51.4	45.6	131.6	36.5
S	− .2	72.4	69.7	8.00	33.0	28.9	75.1	69.9
O	− 4.0	74.7	69.7	8.00	25.1	31.7	302.0	36.8
N	−12.3	73.5	66.2	7.94	52.3	15.6	147.2	29.5
D	−17.1	71.2	60.3	7.88	5.0	37.6	182.8	54.4
1921								
J	−23.0	73.8	62.3	7.83	52.7	11.3	221.5	35.9
F	−24.4	73.5	61.9	7.75	97.8	3.6	282.7	16.0
M	−26.8	72.6	60.4	7.63	79.7	3.9	112.4	26.3
A	−27.0	72.2	60.6	7.55	31.0	8.9	363.5	27.2
M	−24.9	72.0	62.5	6.88	147.5	16.3	162.9	14.7
J	−26.2	70.3	57.6	6.63	33.4	7.4	145.0	34.1
J	−26.4	72.2	57.2	6.28	18.0	27.7	85.0	85.5
A	−24.4	73.4	56.6	6.00	53.9	....	115.1	23.8
S	−23.4	74.6	58.0	5.90	42.8	47.9	186.2	19.6
O	−20.2	74.9	58.8	5.65	58.9	16.1	77.0	26.1
N	−20.4	78.2	61.9	5.13	6.4	47.4	214.0	41.9
D	−21.7	80.6	64.1	5.13	45.6	14.7	214.8	103.5
1922								
J	−18.6	82.2	63.4	4.88	99.0	18.1	184.3	25.4
F	−15.4	82.2	64.9	4.88	41.4	8.0	161.7	41.0
M	−11.2	83.0	67.3	4.78	127.9	27.8	191.7	92.0
A	−14.7	84.6	71.4	4.60	165.4	17.9	392.5	52.7
M	−10.5	85.1	74.1	4.25	119.5	29.3	269.4	131.3
J	− 6.3	85.2	73.4	4.05	86.1	15.9	185.7	143.6
J	− 6.6	86.9	74.0	3.94	63.7	4.8	210.9	22.1
A	− 7.9	87.8	76.7	3.91	27.3	30.5	71.0	151.6
S	− 3.7	88.1	78.8	4.25	34.6	41.3	223.7	52.6
O	+ 1.5	85.9	80.5	4.38	56.2	26.7	150.7	19.9
N	+ 5.6	84.5	76.6	4.63	54.4	28.4	120.9	96.0
D	+ 8.7	84.8	76.2	4.63	16.5	38.0	115.4	317.8

TABLE 9—(*Continued*)

Date	1 Business Activity	2 Bond Price	3 Stock Price	4 Coml. Paper	5 Bonds Listed	6 Stocks Listed	7 J. of C. Bonds	8 J. of C. Stocks
1923								
J	+ 7.3	84.8	76.6	4.63	62.2	13.5	466.5	166.3
F	+ 8.2	84.3	80.0	4.69	153.8	26.7	156.6	81.0
M	+11.1	82.0	81.1	5.00	66.7	88.2	147.3	166.6
A	+14.1	81.6	78.3	5.13	17.5	115.1	189.2	85.2
M	+13.8	82.9	74.7	5.13	25.6	6.2	178.9	169.3
J	+13.6	82.7	71.9	4.88	80.3	32.2	221.3	105.4
J	+11.2	82.6	69.4	4.94	59.9	55.3	158.8	78.5
A	+ 9.8	83.1	69.8	5.03	5.0	13.6	59.0	78.4
S	+ 6.4	82.4	70.3	5.16	29.7	17.2	167.8	37.7
O	+ 5.1	82.1	69.1	5.13	26.4	10.4	180.7	65.7
N	+ 3.8	82.7	71.3	5.09	12.8	26.7	241.4	133.5
D	+ 2.5	82.5	73.7	4.98	20.0	32.7	35.0	231.3
1924								
J	+ 5.4	83.3	75.4	4.88	....	....	236.6	22.3
F	+ 7.2	83.0	75.7	4.78	....	....	227.2	27.7
M	+ 4.9	82.9	74.2	4.59	....	....	177.5	109.8
A	− .6	83.6	72.5	4.63	....	....	264.6	1.4
M	− 7.1	84.5	72.3	4.23	....	....	158.9	22.3
J	−11.5	85.8	73.6	3.91	....	....	203.6	86.5
J	−12.7	87.1	77.1	3.53	....	....	236.0	39.8
A	− 7.7	86.6	79.7	3.23	....	....	202.5	69.7
S	− 2.8	86.9	78.9	3.13	....	....	235.0	44.3
O	− 2.0	87.6	77.9	3.13	....	....	293.1	90.9
N	− .1	87.7	82.3	3.28	....	....	135.9	61.6
D	+ 3.8	87.3	86.6	3.56	....	....	215.3	94.7
1925								
J	+ 7.6	87.7	89.4	3.63	....	....	395.1	78.2
F	+ 6.4	88.2	90.2	3.65	....	....	311.0	72.6
M	+ 5.1	88.8	87.8	3.94	....	....	216.0	108.3
A	+ 3.9	89.3	86.9	3.95	....	....	232.4	123.2
M	+ 3.6	90.7	89.7	3.88	....	....	177.7	69.8
J	+ 3.4	90.8	91.2	3.88	....	....	156.9	51.1
J	+ 4.2	89.9	93.8	3.93	....	....	206.1	115.0
A	+ 3.9	88.9	95.0	4.00	....	....	124.6	66.5
S	+ 1.7	89.7	97.2	4.25	....	....	170.7	63.4
O	+ 4.4	89.4	100.4	4.44	....	....	158.8	119.3
N	+ 7.2	89.7	103.6	4.38	....	....	185.3	66.1
D	+ 9.0	90.5	105.3	4.38	....	....	273.1	100.9
1926								
J	+ 5.7	90.9	105.9	4.31	....	....	375.5	171.4
F	+ 4.5	92.0	105.9	4.19	....	....	217.7	134.0
M	+ 5.2	91.9	99.6	4.28	....	....	173.1	128.0
A	+ 6.0	93.1	96.6	4.19	....	....	368.5	69.8
M	+ 4.8	93.9	96.9	4.00	....	....	217.9	35.8
J	+ 6.5	93.9	101.1	3.88	....	....	231.3	47.0
J	+ 6.3	93.4	104.0	3.97	....	....	240.4	28.7
A	+ 8.0	93.1	107.0	4.25	....	....	122.8	31.7
S	+ 8.7	93.2	108.5	4.43	....	....	240.1	37.1
O	+ 8.5	93.3	105.7	4.50	....	....	215.4	29.4
N	+ 7.3	94.2	107.2	4.44	....	....	215.9	55.7
D	+ 4.1	94.6	109.6	4.38	....	....	241.3	60.8

TABLE 9—(*Continued*)

Date	1 Business Activity	2 Bond Price	3 Stock Price	4 Coml. Paper	7 J. of C. Bonds	8 J. of C. Stocks
1927						
J	+ 3.9	95.2	108.8	4.13	262.4	123.0
F	+ 4.6	95.2	111.1	3.88	310.7	273.1
M	+ 6.3	96.1	112.4	4.00	286.3	138.8
A	+ 4.2	97.4	114.4	4.09	403.1	53.0
M	+ 4.9	97.5	117.6	4.13	539.4	105.5
J	+ 2.7	96.8	118.9	4.13	467.9	80.7
J	+ 1.6	96.7	120.7	4.06	262.8	77.3
A	+ 1.3	97.7	125.7	3.90	246.1	41.4
S	− .8	98.5	131.5	3.91	296.4	83.7
O	− 2.9	99.6	130.5	4.00	535.6	115.5
N	− 4.1	100.8	133.5	3.94	445.9	106.0
D	− 3.4	101.4	137.1	3.95	517.4	198.3
1928						
J	+ 1.1	101.3	137.1	3.88	379.4	240.1
F	+ 1.9	100.7	134.9	4.00	400.3	197.7
M	+ 1.6	100.7	140.7	4.15	398.7	228.5
A	+ 1.4	100.2	148.8	4.40	543.6	275.6
M	+ 1.2	99.2	155.1	4.55	257.7	418.0
J	+ 1.0	97.0	148.2	4.70	379.5	276.1
J	+ 1.7	95.6	147.1	5.13	69.0	428.4
A	+ 2.4	94.3	151.3	5.39	107.9	145.3
S	+ 4.9	95.4	159.7	5.59	218.7	137.6
O	+ 6.6	95.6	162.3	5.50	216.1	416.5
N	+ 8.2	96.5	174.5	5.38	249.5	425.5
D	+ 8.8	94.9	174.8	5.43	173.0	660.5
1929						
J	+10.2	94.2	187.1	5.50	233.7	375.0
F	+ 9.1	93.2	188.4	5.56	308.8	599.5
M	+ 8.9	92.2	191.0	5.69	351.8	522.7
A	+11.4	92.6	188.5	5.90	141.4	328.9
M	+12.0	92.2	189.7	6.00	150.9	369.2
J	+14.5	91.2	192.6	6.00	149.7	530.7
J	+13.4	90.8	209.4	6.00	366 7	338.4
A	+10.4	91.0	220.3	6.09	62.5	503.3
S	+10.2	90.3	227.5	6.13	162.3	436.7
O	+ 7.1	91.5	203.7	6.13	240.6	571.8
N	− .4	92.6	152.6	5.41	55.6	181.2
D	− 6.9	94.1	155.3	5.00	193.3	50.6
1930						
J	− 4.4	94.1	156.3	4.85	610.1	161.7
F	− 3.7	93.8	165.5	4.63	226.1	16.2
M	− 7.5	95.6	172.4	4.19	496.0	266.6
A	− 6.9	95.2	181.0	3.88	390.1	251.7
M	− 8.9	95.5	170.5	3.72	403.7	120.6
J	−12.6	96.0	152.8	3.50	455.1	116.6
J	−17.2	96.9	149.3	3.13	368.0	201.0
A	−20.1	98.2	147.6	3.00	132.1	259.6
S	−20.2	99.5	148.8	3.00	258.0	61.3
O	−22.1	98.8	127.6	3.00	151.2	19.0
N	−24.0	97.1	116.7	2.97	132.7	1.9
D	−25.9	94.5	109.4	2.88	103.7	16.9

TABLE 9—(*Continued*)

Date	1 Business Activity	2 Bond Price	3 Stock Price	4 Coml. Paper	7 J. of C. Bonds	8 J. of C. Stocks
1931						
J	−27.0	98.1	111.3	2.81	525.5	55.2
F	−24.3	98.1	119.8	2.50	84.3	26.9
M	−23.7	98.2	121.6	2.53	373.4	57.9
A	−23.0	97.1	111.6	2.40	351.1	21.5
M	−23.9	97.9	98.3	2.16	159.1	46.0
J	−27.6	97.1	95.1	2.13	231.3	....
J	−28.6	97.2	99.1	1.95	143.2	....
A	−32.2	94.4	95.3	1.88	34.7	9.0
S	−34.0	89.6	85.4	1.88	59.7	6.0
O	−36.7	82.4	69.2	3.38	13.7	....
N	−36.9	80.8	71.7	4.00	40.0	....
D	−36.1	72.0	58.4	4.00	23.1	....
1932						
J	−37.9	75.2	57.5	4.00	47.2	....
F	−40.6	75.2	56.5	3.88	47.7	....
M	−42.4	76.8	57.8	3.53	77.7	....
A	−46.0	71.8	45.7	3.38	72.7	....
M	−48.7	66.7	39.8	3.00	1.0	....
J	−49.6	65.1	34.3	2.78	40.9	....
J	−50.6	69.8	35.2	2.56	109.3	1.0
A	−48.9	77.7	52.1	2.38	99.1	1.9
S	−43.9	80.2	58.4	2.13	8.3	.4
O	−43.1	79.7	51.4	1.98	70.1	3.2
N	−44.9	77.9	47.9	1.63	35.2	3.8
D	−44.2	76.3	47.1	1.63	11.0	2.0
1933						
J	−45.1	80.1	49.1	1.38	61.9	3.3
F	−46.8	78.7	44.9	1.38	....	.2
M	−50.4	74.6	43.3	3.03	....	4.6
A	−44.5	71.7	46.5	2.66	26.4	3.1
M	−34.5	77.3	61.5	2.10	.5	1.0
J	−23.8	82.1	72.8	1.94	....	.8
J	−16.4	85.4	79.8	1.75	36.0	17.2
A	−24.0	86.2	74.4	1.75	....	.5
S	−30.0	82.2	75.5	1.53	30.0	9.6
O	−36.8	81.8	69.5	1.50	....	1.4
N	−40.2	76.0	69.8	1.50	....	10.6
D	−37.8	78.3	70.4	1.50	14.2	8.3
1934						
J	−35.4	84.8	74.6	1.50	28.0	2.7
F	−33.1	89.3	80.9	1.50	....	.4
M	−30.7	90.9	77.2	1.26	40.0	1.7
A	−29.1	92.2	79.6	1.25	17.7	3.0
M	−29.3	93.6	71.8	1.19	33.2	1.2
J	−31.1	95.5	73.1	1.00	159.5	19.5
J	−37.7	96.5	71.4	1.00	235.1	1.3
A	−40.3	95.5	67.5	1.00	25.9	2.2
S	−42.0	94.8	67.4	1.00	16.4	.1
O	−39.6	96.2	67.6	1.00	52.0	1.9
N	−38.9	97.2	68.3	1.00	11.8	1.4
D	−30.2	98.5	69.6	1.00	40.5	.1

TABLE 9—(*Continued*)

Date	1 Business Activity	2 Bond Price	3 Stock Price	4 Coml. Paper	7 J. of C. Bonds	8 J. of C. Stocks
1935						
J	−27.0	99.5	70.1	1.00	41.5	.8
F	−27.1	101.7	68.0	1.00	2.5	1.0
M	−28.8	102.2	64.6	1.00	133.5	. . . .
A	−30.6	102.5	67.5	1.00	271.9	5.2
M	−31.4	102.8	73.1	1.00	134.9	26.1
J	−30.0	104.0	75.5	1.00	356.8	1.7
J	−30.9	105.4	78.8	1.00	419.5	31.5
A	−29.4	104.2	83.0	.86	120.3	11.0
S	−27.1	104.5	85.0	.75	248.1	4.3
O	−24.1	106.6	85.2	.75	245.7	36.6
N	−23.4	108.1	93.3	.75	254.2	5.0
D	−19.5	109.1	95.3	.75	215.6	37.1
1936						
J	−22.9	111.3	100.1	.75	253.7	4.5
F	−25.4	113.0	106.1	.75	121.6	18.8
M	−26.3	114.1	108.7	.75	301.1	30.7
A	−20.1	114.1	109.0	.75	713.2	70.3
M	−20.2	114.7	101.0	.75	164.0	28.5
J	−17.9	115.0	105.6	.75	485.3	62.3
J	−15.0	116.2	109.2	.75	420.9	63.0
A	−15.1	116.9	113.0	.75	200.1	46.0
S	−14.4	118.0	114.1	.75	155.8	34.5
O	−13.8	118.0	118.7	.75	291.5	63.9
N	−10.8	119.1	124.2	.75	195.5	22.0
D	− 5.5	121.1	122.8	.75	405.4	57.4
1937						
J	−11.1	121.1	126.0	.75	141.4	117.1
F	− 9.7	116.5	129.5	.75	163.6	45.8
M	− 8.3	113.0	129.9	.82	179.9	53.8
A	− 8.4	109.7	124.5	1.00	49.0	39.8
M	− 8.5	112.7	116.3	1.00	100.2	16.7
J	−11.8	114.4	113.6	1.00	205.1	82.5
J	−11.9	115.5	117.8	1.00	58.2	82.6
A	− 9.7	115.8	120.5	1.00	31.7	14.2
S	−14.6	114.4	106.4	1.00	12.3	21.8
O	−21.6	114.7	91.4	1.00	133.9	20.9
N	−32.5	115.8	82.9	1.00	26.3	1.5
D	−35.6	116.9	82.2	1.00	19.4	7.6
1938						
J	−38.7	118.4	81.6	1.00	41.0	7.9
F	−39.7	117.2	80.7	1.00	69.7	.3
M	−39.8	116.5	77.9	1.00	57.9	3.1
A	−41.4	113.7	70.7	1.00	60.0	. . . .
M	−42.2	116.5	73.9	1.00	26.0	16.3
J	−41.5	115.1	73.1	1.00	241.3	2.2
J	−37.1	116.5	88.0	1.00	130.4	1.8
A	−33.4	118.0	89.5	1.00	227.2	3.7
S	−32.0	116.9	86.0	.90	80.2	5.1
O	−27.6	119.1	91.1	.78	342.3	13.8
N	−22.4	121.1	94.7	.75	33.5	32.8
D	−21.8	121.9	92.0	.75	167.8	25.5

TABLE 9—(*Continued*)

Date	1 Business Activity	2 Bond Price	3 Stock Price	4 Coml. Paper	7 J. of C. Bonds	8 J. of C. Stocks
1939						
J	−24.2	124.7	91.8	.75	.....	15.5
F	−25.8	125.1	90.1	.75	87.0	42.3
M	−26.7	125.5	91.7	.75	47.8	11.2
A	−31.2	124.2	81.9	.75	185.3	28.6
M	−31.4	126.4	83.1	.75	10.9	13.9
J	−27.0	128.1	86.0	.75	201.8	23.3
J	−24.9	129.4	86.1	.75	157.7	54.2

APPENDIX B

TABLE 10. PHYSICAL VOLUME OF MANUFACTURING PRODUCTION
OF DURABLE AND NONDURABLE GOODS, 1899–1918.

The Board of Governors of the Federal Reserve System published in the Federal Reserve Bulletin for January, 1939, two indexes for the period 1919–1938 based on a break-down of the Board's index of manufacturing production according to the durability of the product. The durable-manufactures index includes iron and steel, coke, nonferrous metals, lumber, cement, glass, automobiles, locomotives, and shipbuilding. Nondurable manufactures include textiles, leather, food, tobacco, paper and printing, petroleum refining, and rubber. These indexes were also published in the Survey of Current Business for March, 1939.

These indexes are constructed on the basis that the averages for 1923, 1924, and 1925 are equal to 100. In that base period the production of nondurable goods comprised somewhat over half, and the production of durable goods somewhat less than half, of all manufacturing output. If the data of the Federal Reserve table of durable manufactures are multiplied throughout by .463, and if those of the Federal Reserve table of nondurable manufactures are multiplied throughout by .537, the sums of the figures of the two tables will be the figures of the Federal Reserve index of manufacturing production based on the average of 1923, 1924, and 1925 being equal to 100.

The Federal Reserve index of manufacturing production has been carried backward in annual figures through 1899 by Dr. Woodlief Thomas and that index was published in the Federal Reserve Bulletin of January, 1931. The data of Table 10 show by months the amounts of the Thomas index as divided between durable and nondurable goods. The tables have been constructed as a part of this work. The data are continuous with those of the Federal Reserve index after the Federal Reserve figures for durable goods have been multiplied by .463 and those for nondurable goods have been multiplied by .537 as explained in the preceding paragraph. For further material about these data see Chapters IX and X. The data are seasonally adjusted.

TABLE 10

Durable

Year	Jan.	Feb.	Mar.	Apr.	May	June	July	Aug.	Sep.	Oct.	Nov.	Dec.
1899	16.8	16.1	16.1	16.9	17.8	18.4	19.1	19.2	19.2	19.7	20.1	20.4
1900	20.2	19.9	19.2	19.3	20.2	20.1	18.4	16.7	15.6	14.4	14.5	15.8
1901	16.8	19.4	19.5	19.9	20.9	21.6	21.6	21.2	20.9	21.3	21.3	19.6
1902	21.6	21.0	21.3	22.4	23.4	22.9	22.5	22.9	22.4	22.1	22.1	22.8
1903	21.7	22.4	23.2	23.9	25.2	25.9	24.5	23.7	24.0	20.9	15.6	12.3
1904	15.3	19.5	21.1	23.0	22.7	20.7	18.8	19.5	22.1	22.7	23.6	24.5
1905	23.7	23.8	25.5	26.2	26.0	25.0	23.8	24.5	26.0	27.1	27.5	27.9
1906	28.4	29.1	29.7	29.3	28.7	28.4	28.1	27.1	27.9	29.9	30.6	30.2
1907	30.6	31.4	30.4	31.0	31.5	31.8	31.2	30.9	30.6	31.0	25.5	17.4
1908	16.8	17.8	18.5	18.1	18.7	18.6	20.1	21.8	23.1	24.2	25.1	26.2
1909	26.0	26.8	26.7	25.8	26.7	27.8	28.7	30.3	32.2	33.5	33.7	33.7
1910	33.1	32.7	32.6	32.0	31.1	30.9	30.1	30.1	30.0	29.9	29.8	29.8
1911	28.3	28.2	28.5	27.8	27.7	27.3	27.1	28.5	29.6	29.7	29.1	28.7
1912	29.4	31.4	32.1	32.6	34.0	34.2	33.7	35.0	34.5	34.9	35.6	36.0
1913	36.7	36.2	36.0	36.4	36.1	38.0	34.1	32.7	33.3	32.9	30.6	30.6
1914	29.6	31.6	31.1	31.9	30.7	31.0	30.2	28.3	27.5	25.0	23.1	22.1
1915	22.9	24.9	28.9	30.3	32.2	34.2	35.3	36.1	37.9	38.7	38.6	43.9
1916	41.5	42.4	41.9	42.6	43.0	43.4	41.4	41.6	43.1	45.1	44.4	45.7
1917	46.6	43.4	43.4	44.9	45.3	45.0	43.4	41.8	40.8	43.5	43.5	41.6
1918	36.0	36.9	39.0	40.8	42.3	42.0	43.0	41.6	41.4	39.5	39.5	41.8

Nondurable

Year	Jan.	Feb.	Mar.	Apr.	May	June	July	Aug.	Sep.	Oct.	Nov.	Dec.
1899	17.5	18.2	18.7	19.4	20.0	20.4	21.0	21.5	21.5	21.6	21.3	20.9
1900	21.1	20.6	20.3	20.5	20.3	20.4	20.5	20.4	20.8	21.5	22.0	22.5
1901	22.2	22.5	22.8	22.9	23.2	23.0	22.7	22.7	22.7	22.4	22.5	22.6
1902	23.1	23.5	23.8	23.9	24.3	24.5	24.9	25.3	25.5	25.4	25.9	25.9
1903	25.5	25.6	25.6	25.7	25.8	26.0	26.2	26.2	25.8	25.6	25.3	25.1
1904	25.1	25.1	24.9	25.1	25.0	25.0	25.2	25.4	26.0	26.8	27.2	27.7
1905	28.8	28.9	29.1	29.2	29.5	29.3	29.6	29.7	30.0	30.2	30.9	31.0
1906	30.8	30.6	30.4	30.0	29.6	29.4	29.5	30.5	30.5	31.1	30.9	31.0
1907	31.3	31.3	31.3	31.2	30.9	30.2	29.2	28.6	28.6	28.1	27.9	27.5
1908	26.4	26.1	26.3	26.5	27.4	28.5	29.8	29.8	29.9	30.0	30.3	30.4
1909	31.1	31.4	31.3	31.7	31.8	31.9	31.9	32.0	32.2	32.4	32.6	32.6
1910	33.0	31.9	31.4	30.7	30.8	30.3	31.2	31.7	31.6	31.7	31.7	31.7
1911	30.7	31.1	31.3	32.0	31.5	32.0	31.2	30.7	30.7	30.7	30.9	31.6
1912	32.7	33.4	34.5	34.7	34.8	35.0	35.6	36.1	36.6	36.7	37.4	37.1
1913	37.4	36.5	36.3	36.1	36.4	36.2	35.5	36.1	37.0	37.8	38.2	37.3
1914	37.3	36.7	37.3	36.7	38.2	37.9	37.1	35.1	34.8	35.0	34.8	34.6
1915	35.0	35.5	35.7	36.5	37.1	37.3	38.1	39.2	40.4	41.8	42.9	43.5
1916	44.0	43.5	43.1	43.4	42.7	42.5	42.6	42.7	43.3	43.3	43.2	43.2
1917	42.9	42.3	43.3	43.4	42.4	42.0	41.7	41.7	42.7	44.2	44.4	44.4
1918	44.7	44.1	44.2	44.5	45.0	45.4	45.3	44.5	44.4	43.5	43.1	41.9

APPENDIX C

INDEX OF BUSINESS ACTIVITY

The Index of American Business Activity of the Cleveland Trust Company was originated in 1931. It runs by months from 1790 to date. The bank has published long diagrams showing the monthly changes in business activity and in wholesale prices over this period and these diagrams carry the data of the index. They have been distributed to persons who have requested copies of them, and each year they have been brought up to date and republished. The data of the index are also available in Section D of Basic Statistics published by the Standard Statistics Company. The bank has published and distributed 13 editions of the long diagrams of business activity since 1790 and this total circulation has been 193,500. The following paragraphs give a description of the index which is printed along the lower part of each of these long diagrams.

The index is composed of one set of 10 series of annual data from 1790 to 1855, and of another set of 10 series of annual data from 1855 to 1901. The fluctuations above and below normal were computed for each series separately, and the 10 were then combined in one. Normal values for each series were means between one set of lines running from one prosperity peak to the next, and another similar set of lines running from each depression bottom to the next. The annual figures from 1901 to 1919 are those of the Thomas index of manufacturing production with mineral production added, and from 1919 to date the monthly figures of the Federal Reserve (Thomas) index of industrial production have been used. All the data were reduced to a per capita basis.

The computations of the fluctuations of each of the 10 series constituting the index from 1855 to 1901 were carried through to include 1930, and the coefficient of correlation between each of them and the production series running from 1901 through 1930 was computed. Their deviations were then multiplied through by constants so as to equate their amplitudes of cyclical fluctuation. Each of the 10 series was then given a weight based on its degree of correlation with the production series, and with these weightings they were combined into a single index. The 10 series with those weights are pig iron consumption 15, railroad freight ton miles 15, cotton consumption 14, canal freight (New York and Sault

Ste. Marie) 12, coal production 12, construction of miles of new railroads 12, blast furnace activity 10, rail production 6, locomotive production 2, and ship construction 2. The 10 series combined give results closely similar to those of the production series for the overlap period from 1901 through 1930. The heights of prosperities, and the depths of depressions, are closely alike in the two series. The coefficient of correlation for the period is .95. Their average deviations for the period are equal.

In a similar way the computations of the fluctuations of each of the 10 series constituting the index from 1790 to 1855 were carried through to include 1882, and the coefficient of correlation between each of them and the first 28 years of the index running from 1855 to 1901 was computed. Their deviations were then multiplied through by constants so as to equate their amplitudes of cyclical fluctuation. Each of the 10 series was then given a weight based on its degree of correlation with the first 28 years of the index from 1855 to 1901, and with these weightings they were combined into a single index. The 10 series with these weights are commodity prices 20, imports 18, imports retained for consumption 16, government receipts 14, ship construction 12, government expenditures 6, coal production 6, exports 5, iron exports 2, and tons of registered shipping in service 1. The 10 series combined give results closely similar to those of the other index for the overlap period from 1855 through 1882. The heights of prosperities, and the depths of depressions, are closely alike in the two series. The coefficient of correlation for the period is .90. Their average deviations for the period are equal.

When the annual data were determined the monthly data were fitted to them. These monthly data were based on the figures of the business index of the American Telephone and Telegraph Company and on data for blast furnace activity from 1877 to 1919. Monthly data for bank clearings and for stock prices were used from 1861 to 1877, and those for security and commodity prices from 1815 to 1861. From 1790 to 1815 the monthly data are based on commodity prices.

APPENDIX D

BOND PRICES

From the beginning of 1831 to the end of 1856 the bond prices shown in Column 2 of Table 9 are an original series compiled for this book. Month by month prices were found for state bonds of New York, Ohio, and Kentucky, and yields to maturity were found for each bond in each month. Simple unweighted averages were computed for each month and these average yields were capitalized at 4.14 percent. This rate of capitalization is too low for these bonds, which almost throughout had coupons of six percent in the cases of the Ohio and Kentucky issues, and of five percent for the New York bonds.

Capitalization at the rate of 4.14 percent was decided upon in order to have the combined series match in price level with the Macaulay series, which was used beginning in 1857. The resulting prices obtained by this capitalization are lower than the actual average prices of the state bonds, but closely similar to the prices of the better rail and canal bonds of the period. The original sources from which the prices were compiled were the files of Nile's Register, Hunt's Merchants' Magazine, the Bankers' Magazine, the Shipping and Commercial List (New York), and in a few instances the daily sales slips of the New York Stock Exchange.

Beginning in 1857 the series is based on the carefully compiled yield data for high grade rail bonds compiled by Dr. Frederick R. Macaulay, and presented in Table 10 of his book on "The Movements of Interest Rates, Bond Yields, and Stock Prices in the United States Since 1856," published by the National Bureau of Economic Research in 1938. The unadjusted bond yields in Dr. Macaulay's table were multiplied by a progressively changing multiplier that was obtained by finding the percents that the average of the actual yields of the bonds were each January of the unadjusted yields. In January of 1857 the multiplier was .84 and this was progressively increased until it was 1.00 in December of 1908, after which the unadjusted yields were used unchanged to the end of 1933.

The new series of bond yields so obtained were capitalized at changing coupon rates that were obtained by finding the average coupon rates of the bonds used by Dr. Macaulay in compiling his index. The average annual coupon rate was used from 1857 through 1888 and then through 1933 a 10 place centered average of the annual coupon rates was used. The purpose of all this was to create a series of bond prices that would reproduce as nearly as possible the typical average dollar prices at which the bonds were actually bought and sold. The attempt was to make the price series reflect changes over the months and years as they actually appeared to business men who were watching the quotations as they were currently published in the public prints. The results are relatively satisfactory despite the method of capitalizing without assumed maturities.

From the beginning of 1934 to date the figures are those of Moody's AAA bond yields multiplied by 1.13 in order to equate them to the Macaulay yield series in 1934 and capitalized at 4.24 percent. That is the rate used in capitalizing the Macaulay yield series from June of 1925 to the end of 1933.

Appendix E

STOCK PRICES

Stock prices given in Column 3 of Table 9 from 1831 through 1845 are simple averages of two series, one consisting of rail stocks, and the other of bank and insurance stocks. During the first three years the average of the quoted prices of stocks of four canal companies were used in place of rail stocks, since no monthly data for rails could be found for those three years. Beginning in 1834 the rail stocks are those of Tables 69 and 70 in "Fluctuations in American Business," by Smith and Cole, published by the Harvard University Press in 1935. The data in Table 69 were multiplied by .78 so as to put them on the same base with those of Table 70. The series of bank and insurance stocks was taken from Table 62 of the volume by Smith and Cole.

The combined series appearing in Column 3 of Table 9 probably represents closely the prevailing levels of typical stock prices during those years. Hunt's Merchants' Magazine for 1845 carries a table on page 284 giving the prices of 15 railroad stocks and 23 New York City bank stocks in December of 1844. The average price of the 38 stocks in that month was 90.4, and in that month the average price of the stocks in Column 3 of Table 9 in this book is 91.0.

From the beginning of 1846 to the end of 1856 the data are the average prices of 26 rail stocks taken from Table 70 of the volume by Smith and Cole. A table in Hunt's Merchants' Magazine for February, 1857, shows that in December of 1854 the average of the actual quoted prices of 19 rail stocks was nearly the same as that of the index numbers of the Smith and Cole computations used as stock prices in Table 9 of this book.

From the beginning of 1857 to the end of 1870 the data of Table 9 are made by multiplying by a constantly changing multiplier the data for railroad stock prices computed by Frederick R. Macaulay and appearing in his book, "The Movements of Interest Rates, Bond Yields and Stock Prices in the United States since 1856," published in 1938 by the National Bureau of Economic Research. The multiplier for January, 1857, is 3.35; for February it is 3.34; and it is decreased by .01 each month until it is 1.41 in December, 1870. The Bankers' Magazine for 1870–71 carries a table on page 714 of Vol. 25 which gives the average of the highest and lowest monthly stock prices of 15 rail stocks in 1870 as being 59.2. The corresponding average of the stock prices for 1870 in Table 9 of this book is 58.6.

From the beginning of 1871 to the end of 1930 the data of Column 3 of Table 9 are made by multiplying by a changing multiplier the data of the All Stocks index appearing in the volume entitled, "Common-Stock Indexes, 1871–1937," published by the Cowles Commission for Research in Economics in 1938. The multiplier is 1.59 in 1871, and 1.58 in 1872, and it decreases by .01 each year until it is 1.00 in 1930. During the period from 1918 through 1930 the data of the Cowles index are those of the index of 419 stocks of the Standard Statistics Company, and the figures of that index from 1930 into 1939 are used in Column 3 of Table 9 of this book without modification.

The figures of the Cowles index multiplied by the constantly decreasing multiplier described above are found to be closely similar throughout to the average prices of actively traded stocks as computed annually by the Commercial and Financial Chronicle and published in the first or second number of each year. The attempt has been to create a continuous series of stock prices from 1831 to 1939 that would be closely representative of the averages of the dollar values of actively traded stocks as they would have been noted by business men who studied the stock quotations in the current publications during the years of the long period under review.

APPENDIX F

SHORT-TERM INTEREST RATES

The data for short-term interest rates given in Column 4 of Table 9 are discount rates on four to six months commercial paper. The data for the years from 1831 through 1860 are taken from "The Tariff Question," by Erastus B. Bigelow (Boston 1862). These figures are stated to be those of commercial paper in Boston and New York, but it is probable that they are Boston rates. The source of the figures for the years 1861 through 1865 is "Seventy-three Years' History of the Boston Stock Market," by Joseph G. Martin (Boston 1871). The data from 1866 through 1913 are those compiled by Professor W. L. Crum and published in the Review of Economic Statistics, January, 1923, and those from 1914 to date are compilations of the Standard Statistics Company.

The best source of information about early records of short-term interest rates is "The Movements of Interest Rates, Bond Yields and Stock Prices in the United States Since 1856," by Frederick R. Macaulay, published in 1938 by the National Bureau of Economic Research. Tables 24 and 25 and Appendix E of that volume should be consulted by students seeking information about sources of data.

INDEX

Aftalion, Albert, 91, 93
American business activity, see Business
  activity
American Telephone and Telegraph Co.,
  161, 205
*Analysis of Bank Statistics for the
  United States* (Young), 117
Austria, 28

Bank credit
  comparison with business, 117–124
  typical cycles of, 134–136
  New Era increase in, 148
Bank of the United States, 10, 17
Bankers' Magazine, 206, 208
Banking Act of 1935, 50
Bankrupt Act, 10
Baring Brothers, 32
Baring Crisis, 32, 36, 82, 83, 84, 159, 161,
  169
Bigelow, Erastus B., 5, 210
Bond prices
  typical cycles of, 63–70
  data, 173
  description of, 206
Bonds, state, 4
Bonus to veterans, 152
Boston Stock Market, History of
  (Martin), 210
Brookings Institution, 28
Business activity index, American
  typical cycles of, 63–70
  data, 173
  description of, 204
*Business Cycles, The Problem and Its
  Setting* (Mitchell), 66
*Business Cycles and Business Measure-
  ments* (Snyder), 131

California, 15
Cambridge University, 105
*Can America Spend Its Way Into Re-
  covery?* (Keynes-Laski), 106

Canada, 45
Capital funds, inflow into business, 149–
  155
Capital issues
  listings, 23–24, 53
  available series, 24
  Journal of Commerce, 39
  Commercial and Financial Chronicle,
    42
  Standard Statistics, 45
  Securities and Exchange Commission,
    49
  Moody, 62
  typical cycles of, 63–70
  data, 173
Capital Issues Committee, 42
Catchings, Waddill, 93
Census, 75, 76, 96, 99
Check transactions, 110
Civil War, see War
Clearings index of business, 131
Cleveland Trust Co., 4, 173, 204
Coefficient of correlation, 120, 121,
  205
Commercial and Financial Chronicle, 24,
  25, 42, 46, 49, 54, 55, 56, 58, 59, 60,
  61, 62, 128, 151, 209
Commercial paper, see Interest rates
Common - Stock Indexes, 1871 – 1937
  (Cowles), 209
Composite indicator of business, compu-
  tation of, 156–157
Comptroller of the Currency, 117, 140
Consumers goods, 96–100
Correlation, coefficient of, 120, 121, 205
Cowles Commission for Research in Eco-
  nomics, 23, 209
Credit, see Bank credit
Crum, W. L., 17, 66, 210

Debts, 9, 126, 129
  real estate, 18, 19
Department of Commerce, 97